1991

Biotechnology
and the
Assault on Parenthood

DONALD DE MARCO

Biotechnology
and the
Assault on Parenthood

IGNATIUS PRESS   SAN FRANCISCO

Cover design by Riz Boncan Marsella
Front cover photograph by Comstock, Inc.
Back cover photograph by Comstock, Inc. / Michael Stuckey

© 1991 Ignatius Press, San Francisco
All rights reserved
ISBN 0–89870–354–9
Library of Congress catalogue number 90–84688
Printed in the United States of America

To Germain Kopaczynski, O.F.M. Conv.
and
James E. McCurry, O.F.M. Conv.:

Franciscan embodiments
of gentle charity
and granite faith

Christmas Day 1990
Kitchener, Ontario

Contents

Foreword

July 25, 1978 was a memorable day in history. It was, first of all, the birthday of Louise Brown, the "miracle baby" of modern technology. Louise was the first child conceived in vitro to be born. Louise did not come into being in and through a personal act of love in which her mother and father gave themselves unconditionally to one another and, in so doing, received the gift of life. Rather, she came to be in a laboratory petri dish, the "product" of materials: sperm and ovum, "provided" by her parents. It was, secondly, the tenth anniversary of Pope Paul VI's prophetic encyclical, *Humanae vitae,* in which he affirmed that there is an "inseparable connection, willed by God and unable to be broken by man on his own initiative, between the procreative and the unitive meanings of the marital act".

In his encyclical, Paul VI was concerned primarily with the meaning of marriage as a specific kind of human reality, one inwardly capable of being integrated into God's covenant of grace, and contraception. Reaffirming the age-old wisdom of the Church, he branded contraception as an intrinsically disordered human act, precisely because contraception, as the deliberate choice to repudiate the procreative meaning of human sexuality in freely chosen acts of sexual union, severs the bond that God wills should exist between this meaning of human sexuality and its unitive meaning. Yet the teaching in *Humanae vitae* is directly relevant to the laboratory generation of human life. When new human persons come into being outside the marital embrace—whether through acts of fornication or adultery or through the use of biomedical technologies—a terrible tragedy occurs. The children so conceived are, of course, precious human persons, loved by God and called to a life of holiness. Yet the *means* used to give them life are gravely immoral and an affront to their dignity as persons.

It is, in short, of profound importance to human existence that children come to be in and through the marital act—the act in which husbands and wives become "one flesh". For children are not pets, objects of human desires, or products inferior in nature to their producers and subject to quality controls. They are, rather, persons equal in dignity to their parents and beings who are, as Augustine said long ago, "to be lovingly received, nurtured humanely, and educated religiously", i.e., in the love and service of God. And they can be so received, so nurtured, and so educated properly when they come to be in and through the act in which husband and wife, who have irrevocably given themselves to one another, become truly one flesh.

To articulate the truths summarized in the previous paragraph is, however, not an easy task, particularly today, in a contraceptive society enamored with technology. Fortunately, Donald DeMarco is both a committed believer and a first-rate philosopher. He has an uncanny ability to deflate rhetorically swollen arguments, to unmask the lust for power concealed beneath a veneer of praise for freedom and equality. Alive to the bodily, incarnate significance of our existence as human, *bodily* persons, he is keenly sensitive to the neognostic, neomanichean contempt of the flesh that permeates our culture and paves the way for sex without babies and babies without sex. With a poet's insight into reality, he knows how to open eyes to the beauty of marriage as the deeply personal and bodily union of man and woman who open themselves to the gift of life in and through the act in which they make themselves "one flesh".

The slogan of those who advocate contraception, abortion, and the making of babies in the laboratory is that "no unwanted child ought ever to be born". The banal slogan epitomizes the ideology that separates sex from babies and babies from sex. It is a slogan that turns children into "products", valuable because they are desired, and turns their generation into a "making". "No child—no human person—ought ever to be unwanted" is the truth at the heart of the Church's teaching on marriage and on the generation of human life. This truth recognizes that children are not products inferior to their producers but persons equal in dignity to their parents. They are gifts from God, not the end products of human artifice. DeMarco's book is invaluable for showing the banality of the slogan that is at the heart of contemporary biotechnology, and for showing the truth that is at the core of the Church's respect for human life as the life of persons who ought, like the Eternal Word who became flesh to be with them and for them, to be "begotten" in love, not "made" in the laboratory.

William E. May

Acknowledgments

I would like to express my sincere thanks to all those who assisted me in the researching and rethinking that this book demanded. I thank St. Jerome's College for granting me a sabbatical to do the researching and my esteemed colleagues in its philosophy department—Floyd Centore and Gerry Campbell—for their indefatigable patience in helping me to do the rethinking.

A very special thanks goes to Dr. Joseph Stanton for supplying me on a continuing basis with numerous texts of vital importance, and for allowing me to rummage through his extensive files at the Value of Life Committee office. Also, for supplying additional important documents, I would like to thank Mary Nowak, David Rooney, Richard Doerflinger, David McLaughlin, Rev. Paul Marx, O.S.B., Anneliese Steden, Nona Aguilar, Catherine Bolger, and Kathleen Winarski. For their valuable encouragement and help in many ways, I thank Fathers Liptak, Lescoe, and Lawler of Holy Apostles College in Cromwell, Connecticut, and the good Friars at St. Hyacinth College in Granby, Massachusetts, Prof. Charles Rice at the Notre Dame Law School, Gary Crum and Bob Marshall at the Castello Institute in Stafford, Virginia, the personnel at the Pope John Center in Braintree, Massachusetts, the Human Life Center in Steubenville, Ohio, and the Kennedy Bioethics Center in Washington, D.C.

Personal thanks are also in order to John Crosby, Janet Smith, David Warren, Shari O'Brien, and Fathers Kenneth Baker, S.J., John Miller, C.S.C., Alphonse de Valk, C.S.B., and John Hardon, S.J.

Finally, I wish to thank more librarians than I can possibly mention for their gracious and indispensable assistance, particularly those at Yale, Wesleyan, Notre Dame, Smith,

Hampshire, Amherst, Holy Apostles, the Universities of Alberta, Waterloo, and Indiana, Wilfred Laurier University, St. Jerome's, St. Michael's, and Redemption Colleges, various hospital medical libraries, and most especially, the librarians at the Kolbe Library at St. Hyacinth's College and Seminary.

Chapter One

The Meaning and Normalcy
of Marriage and Parenthood

"The friendship between man and wife", wrote Aristotle, "seems to be inherent in us by nature." For "man is an animal more inclined by nature to connubial than political society."[1] As we well know, Aristotle taught that man is a political and gregarious animal.[2] But, as a careful student of human nature and a meticulous philosopher who knew how to place things in their proper order, he clearly recognized that marriage, with its personal satisfactions, its intimacy, and its security, is naturally superior to the more tenuous and impersonal relationships that are characteristic of social intercourse. Moreover, the shared life of husband and wife in marriage offers an unparalleled opportunity for nourishing and maintaining the deepest of personal friendships. For much the same reasons, Aquinas could claim that marriage is indeed the very best of all friendships.

Nonetheless, the very naturalness that undergirds marriage is not something that every sociologist is able or willing to recognize. In particular, the authors of *The Imperial Animal*— two sociologists with the amusingly appropriate names of Lionel Tiger and Robin Fox—argue that marriage is purely a human invention that people may one day choose to eliminate. The fact that marriage is not found among chimpanzees, they reason, offers some strong and convincing evidence of marriage's lack of naturalness.[3]

Critics who fail to see the naturalness of marriage are handicapped by too narrow a notion of nature. They think nature

---

[1] *Nicomachean Ethics,* VIII, 12, 1162a, 16-19.
[2] *Politics,* i, 2.
[3] New York: Holt, Rinehart and Winston, 1971.

1

refers only to events or activities that take place without any reference to reason or freedom. Aquinas dealt with this problem by pointing out that marriage is certainly not natural if, by nature, one refers to things that result of necessity from the principles of nature, such as the natural upward movement of fire. But, Aquinas added, something is said to be natural if nature inclines to it, even though it does not bring it into fruition without the intervention of reason and free will.[4] It is in this second sense that marriage is natural. Just as in the case of art, nature can provide marriage with the substance and the aptitude, though not necessarily the finished product.

Marriage is natural because it provides a relationship that can meet the partners' fundamental human needs for love, understanding, friendship, and mutual support. And it can meet these natural needs in a union that is free, personal, and enduring. At the same time, marriage demands the ceaseless application of virtue and intelligence in order to meet the unpredictable challenges that life and society present. The inspiration and fulfillment of marriage are natural, though the cultivation and perfection of marriage are an acquired art.

The sheer naturalness of marriage is nowhere better demonstrated than by the natural blessings of health, vitality, and longevity it lavishes on its husband and wife beneficiaries. The data gained from a wide variety of studies indicates that married people have (1) lower mortality rates, (2) lower suicide rates, (3) lower rates of victimization through homicide, (4) lower rates of fatal automobile accidents, and (5) decreased morbidity due to coronary diseases and cancer of the digestive organs, among others.[5]

Associated with each 1 percent increase in the divorce rate is a .54 percent increase in the suicide rate.[6] Some researchers

---

[4] *Summa Theologica*, Q. 41, 1 Supl.

[5] Richard B. Stuart, *Helping Couples Change: A Social Learning Approach to Marital Therapy* (New York: The Guilford Press, 1981), p. 8.

[6] S. Stack, "The Effects of Marital Dissolution on Suicide", *Journal of Marriage and the Family*, 1980, pp. 42, 83–92.

have emphasized the loneliness that follows divorce as its major negative impact.[7] Others have stressed the loss of future orientation suffered by divorcés as being their major cross to bear.[8] Still others believe that in the loss of marital ties, divorced persons also lose their best defense against unrestrained self-indulgence, which is an important contributing factor in suicidal behavior.[9]

To illustrate, the suicide rate per 100,000 married men is 18. But for men who never married, the rate is 33.2 and for men who are divorced or separated, it leaps to 69.4. Divorced or separated women are more than 3 times likely to take their own lives than are married women.[10] Among the victims of homicide, 8.6 and 3 per 100,000 are married men and women, respectively. But the rate escalates to 39.2 and 10.6 if the respective parties are divorced or separated.[11]

People whose marriages have broken up are more than 3 times as likely to die because of an automobile accident as their married counterparts.[12] The figure increases by 371 percent for men and 328 percent for women who are divorced or separated. For those who are widowed, the increase is even higher, being 411 percent and 442 percent for widowers and widows, respectively.

The rate of admission to psychiatric outpatient clinics (per 100,000) for married men is 276 and for married women, 423.2. But among the never married the figures are 806.3 and 743, respectively, and for those divorced, it soars to 1,365.6

[7] J. J. Lynch, *The Broken Heart: The Medical Consequences of Loneliness* (New York: Basic Books, 1977).

[8] George Gilder, *Naked Nomads: Unmarried Men in America* (New York: Quadrangle Books, 1974).

[9] Emile Durkheim, *Suicide* (New York: The Free Press, 1966).

[10] National Center for Health Statistics, *Suicide in the U.S., 1950–1964*, Bethesda, Md.: Vital and Health Statistics, series 20, no. 5, 1967.

[11] National Center for Health Statistics, *Homicide in the U.S., 1959–1961*, Bethesda, Md.: Vital and Health Statistics, series 20, no. 6, 1967.

[12] Stuart, p. 12.

and 1,621.7.[13] Researchers have observed similar trends that indicate significantly higher rates of neuroses, psychoses, and other personality disorders among the never married, divorced, separated, and widowed as compared with people who are married.[14]

The dissolution of a marriage as well as the inability to find a marital partner is particularly devastating for men. The single man is more disposed to criminal behavior, violence, and the use of drugs and alcohol than is his married counterpart. According to a celebrated study by Jessie Bernard, single men are 3 times as prone to nervous breakdowns as are single women or married men. And reports from mental institutions show that single men are 22 times more likely than married men to be committed for mental disease.[15]

Divorced men suffer economically as well as emotionally and physically. Sociologist George Gilder finds that the economic setbacks among divorced men are so great that divorce is a stronger correlate of poverty than is race.[16] Thus, the social sciences are offering a daily refutation of Benjamin Disraeli's curious remark, "Every woman should marry—and no man."

In reviewing the high suicide rates of single men throughout Europe in the nineteenth century, Emile Durkheim offered the comment that "the bond attaching the [single] man to life relaxes because that attaching him to society is in itself slack." What could be a clearer indication of the superior naturalness of marriage? The bond of matrimony is more secure and durable than the "slack" attachments that exist between the individual and society precisely because it is more natural. And it is

[13] R. W. Redick and C. Johnson, *Marital Status, Living Arrangements and Family Characteristics of Admissions to State and County Mental Hospitals and Out-patient Psychiatric Clinics, U.S., 1970,* (Rockville, Md.: National Institute of Mental Health, Statistical Note 100, 1974).

[14] B. L. Bloom, *Changing Patterns in Psychiatric Care* (New York: Human Sciences Press, 1975).

[15] George Gilder, "The Princess's Problem", *National Review*, Feb. 28, 1986, p. 30.

[16] Gilder, 1974.

precisely when people are firmly committed to life that they find the motivation required to work harder, remain healthier, and live longer than those whose ties with life are comparatively loose and uncertain.

As the pertinent data categorically shows, people who marry and sustain their marriage stand a decidedly better chance of enjoying continued health and well-being than do those who do not marry or whose marriages are terminated either by death, divorce, or separation. Marriage counsellors find in such data a powerful argument for encouraging clients of theirs whose marriages may be shaky to work hard at strengthening their matrimonial ties. The alternative of separation or divorce, on a statistical basis, too often signals the start of a gradual process of deterioration. Efforts to improve troubled marriages—despite the current high divorce rate and the clamor for even easier access to divorce—make sense, statistics indicate, because marriage is the most bounteous source of benefits available to the overall health and happiness of husbands and wives. In fact, one prominent national survey concludes that "Marriage and family life are the most satisfying parts of most people's lives and being married is one of the most important determinants of being satisfied with life."[17] Samuel Johnson implied much the same thing when he remarked, "To be happy at home is the end of all human endeavor."

No one will deny that marriage has its share of restrictions and inconveniences. But these are mere trifles when compared with the essential benefits that marriage confers. The great German poet Goethe saw things in the right perspective when he wrote:

> Marriage is the beginning and summit of civilization. It tames the brute, and even the most civilized one has no better opportunity to prove that he is civilized. Marriage must be indissoluble; for it brings so much happiness that any unhappiness

[17] "Measuring the Quality of Life in America", *Institute of Social Research Newsletter*, 1974, 2, p. 4.

here or there is completely outweighed by that. . . . It may at times be inconvenient, this I can well believe—and this should be so. Aren't we also married to our consciences which we often would gladly get rid of, because it is much more inconvenient than any husband or wife could ever be?[18]

The naturalness of marriage is established in a spontaneous and unmediated attachment to life that is shared in a special way by husband and wife. But this naturalness is confirmed and reinforced through a reciprocal and communitarian bond between the partners that confers rich and diverse complementary benefits. It is fashionable to deny fundamental natural differences between the sexes. Nonetheless, much of this denial stems from an exaggerated fear that the recognition of difference will inexorably lead to the promotion of inequality. The natural differences between the sexes, however, should be affirmed since they provide the real possibility for an exchange of complementary gifts.

Modern neurophysiology corroborates this view of the complementarity of the sexes in its research on the structure and functioning of the male brain and the female brain. According to contemporary research, the two hemispheres of the brain develop and work differently in males and females. For most right-handed males, the right side of the brain controls spatial tasks, whereas the left side relates to language skills. But the situation is radically different for right-handed females, whose spatial and language functions are not concentrated in one or another hemisphere of the brain but distributed equally between both. Therefore, the lateralization of spatial and linguistic functions is naturally different in the sexes, being specialized and relatively concentrated in one or another cerebral hemisphere in the male, and less specialized and more uniformly distributed in the female.[19]

Researchers have studied the effects of unilateral brain le-

---

[18] *Die Wahlverwandtschaften,* pt. I, chap. 9.

[19] See Frederick Naftolin and Eleanore Butz, eds., "Sexual Dimorphism", *Science,* vol. 211, no. 4488, Mar. 20, 1981.

sions in males and in females and have found that such injuries tend to leave the former more impaired than the latter. They found that right-handed males suffering left-hemisphere damage were significantly more impaired than right-handed females in elementary language production and comprehension, in verbal intelligence, and in verbal memory. They also found that males, but not females, experienced impaired nonverbal intelligence as a result of right-hemisphere lesions.[20]

Moreover, even the slightest brain damage—occurring during or after birth—can have a more debilitating effect on males. This higher vulnerability of the male's left hemisphere, which controls language, is evidenced by the fact that males are four or five times more likely to suffer from language disorders and disabilities than females: boys are more likely to stutter (five to one), to be autistic (four to one), to suffer aphasia (five to one), and to have dyslexia (four to one).[21]

Because of the natural differences in the lateralization of functions in the two halves of the brain, the verbal and spatial functions are more likely to be unified or brought together in women, and more likely to be isolated or kept apart in men. Thus, the woman is more integrated, the man more abstracted. Men, in general, are superior at seeing invariance independent of context. They have a particular aptitude for maps, mazes, and math; at rotating objects in their minds and perceiving three-dimensional objects in two-dimensional representations. They are less dependent on situational variables for the solution of a problem. They are adept at abstracting from time and space to view things in their essential nature. Hence, they are better inclined toward philosophy. They are more narrowly focused and less distractable. Women, by contrast, are usually sensitive to context, adept at spotting information that is incidental to the task at hand. They tend to be superior in

[20] M. J. McGlone, "Sex Differences in Functional Brain Symmetry", *Cortex*, Mar. 1978, vol. 14, no. 1, pp. 122–28.

[21] See Dr. Jerry Levy, "Men, Women, and the Brain", *Quest/80*, vol. 4, no. 8, Oct. 1980.

certain verbal skills such as language fluency, grammar, and reading. They have better fine motor coordination and are more alert to details. They have a natural advantage in reading the emotional content of faces. Finally, they are particularly sensitive to odor and exceptionally sensitive to the presence and variation of sound.[22]

The important point that emerges through research on male brains and female brains is that each sex is comparatively strong in areas where the other is comparatively weak. Thus, there is evidence of a neurophysiological complementarity between the sexes. Nonetheless, the notion of complementarity remains ambiguous until man and woman regard each other as gifts. The mere presence of correlative strengths and weaknesses can just as easily occasion expressions of mutual exploitation. One feminist, for example, complains that the real problem between the sexes derives from the fact that "men and women are vitally different, not in those ways which provide for an interesting variety, but in ways which make of sexuality a veritable war zone."[23]

If the corresponding strengths and weaknesses between the sexes are to provide the basis for a positive alliance in which strength offsets weakness and weakness attracts strength, then love must be present. Love, because of its proclivity to give rather than to take, is necessary in order to fulfill the complementary nature of the sexes and to prevent differences from being misinterpreted as opportunities for exploitation or domination. The "opposite" sex is not an "opponent" but an opportunity for expressions of love that confer reciprocal benefits. Love is a kind of grace that perfects the sexes in their complementarity. It is the decisive proof that the sexes are indeed complementary gifts and not mutual antagonists or natural enemies. The acts of giving and receiving love show

[22] Jo Durden-Smith and Diane De Simone, "Is There a Superior Sex?" *Reader's Digest,* Dec. 1982, pp. 169–76.

[23] Ingrid Bengis, *Combat in the Erogenous Zone* (New York: Knopf, 1972), p. 82.

that sexual differences are mutually beneficial; the refusal to love makes sexual differences appear mutually disadvantageous, preventing unity and discouraging the formation of friendship.

In Achim von Arnim's novella *The Mad Invalid* (*Der tolle Invalide auf dem Fort Ratonneau*), we find a dramatic and illuminating story that expresses how the differences between the sexes can lead either to destruction or deliverance.[24] The story is about a crazed French soldier who for three days and nights single-handedly holds a harbor fort and terrorizes a city, but is saved from death and restored to sanity by the fearless love of his German wife. When the story opens, Francoeur, the soldier, has been captured by Prussian troops during the Seven Years' War and is lying in a hospital with a head wound. Here he meets his future wife who, inspired by pity, has come to minister to him. Her name, Rosalie Lilie, alluding to the rose (symbolic of love) and the lily (symbolic of grace), identifies her allegorically with the salvific *Liebe* and *Gnade* in the couplet that closes the novella and encapsulates the story's essential message: "*Gnade* löst den Fluch der Sünde, / *Liebe* treibt den Teufel aus" (Grace dissolves the curse of sin, / Love drives the devil out).

As the story develops, Francoeur, now Rosalie's husband, is still affected by his head injury. When he learns that Rosalie has persuaded the commandant to make his life more comfortable, his feeling of being betrayed by a patronizing wife is so intense that it causes his mind to snap. He then seizes the fort and threatens to destroy the entire city. His wife, however, is given permission to intervene, and in an extraordinary display of courage and self-sacrificing love, approaches her husband, who is stationed at his gunnery. At the sight of Rosalie's courage, a terrible struggle ensues in her husband's

[24] See John Whiton, "Der tolle Invalide", in *Crisis and Commitment: Studies in German and Russian Literature in Honour of J. W. Dyck,* Whiton and Loewen, eds. (Waterloo, Ontario: University of Waterloo Press, 1983), pp. 221–36.

heart. In a frenzy, he tears at his hair and in doing so reopens his old head wound. This action apparently relieves pressure on the brain and causes his madness to disappear. Having thus come to his senses, he rushes out to embrace and kiss his wife.

Rosalie's love is a medium of grace (not excluding the supernatural dimension) through which the devil of Francoeur's madness is driven out. Her self-sacrificial love has cured the illness that her patronizing love had caused. Francoeur's "curse" is connected with Rosalie's lack of confidence in both him and his love for her. But because of the union they experienced as husband and wife, her own lack of faith in her husband's love is inseparable from her confidence that she herself is a worthy object of his love. When she regains faith in her husband, she, in effect, dissolves the curse. The complementarity of this couple is evinced only when love is unambiguously expressed. When love is diluted by fear and distrust, the relationship threatens to erupt in a frenzy of violence. Here the social symbolism is irresistible: loving marriages benefit not only husband and wife but the whole community; this cannot be said of marriages where love is displaced by fear.

Perhaps no one has expounded more brilliantly and more extensively on the themes of the sacredness of marriage and the complementarity of the sexes than Pope John Paul II. Of central importance is his "Theology of the Body" (alternately referred to as a "theology of sex" and a "theology of masculinity and feminity", and published in four volumes by the Daughters of St. Paul), which the Holy Father expressed through 133 Wednesday audiences he gave from September 5, 1979 to November 28, 1984. Concerning this timely and invaluable contribution, one commentator has remarked, "This theology of the body does cast a ray of light, perhaps the most powerful ever shed, on that secret wound which has scarred the heart of every man and woman.[25]

---

[25] Marcel Clément, "The Modern Problem and the Pope's Response", *The Canadian Catholic Review,* vol. 1, no. 1, Jan. 1983, p. 14. The journal published a series of fifteen commentaries by Clément on the Pope's "Theology of the Body".

The Pope uses, for his starting point, the response of Christ to a question raised by the Pharisees: "Is it lawful to divorce one's wife? (Mt 19:3ff.). Christ answered, "Have you not read that he who made them from the beginning made them male and female. . . ." Reflecting on these words of the Divine Master, the Holy Father draws our attention to the expression "from the beginning", which Christ uses twice in the same Matthean passage. This "beginning" is recorded in Genesis 1:27 and 2:24, which set forth the principle of the unity and indissolubility of marriage as the very content of the Word of God, expressed in the most ancient revelation.

The Pope then goes on to explain that Christ has provided us with the grace we need in order to reestablish the original unity in marriage that our first parents enjoyed before the Fall. By redemption, Christ makes all things new. According to John Paul II, Christ urges man to return to the threshold of his theological history, that boundary between original innocence-happiness and the inheritance of the Fall. In doing so, Christ is outlining the path along which he is leading man—male and female—through the sacrament of Marriage. This path leads to recovering the real meaning of the human body as a means of establishing and expressing a "communion of persons".[26]

As a result of the Fall, man and woman began to lose sight of the conjugal significance of the body and started to view each other as objects, that is to say, as possessions that they could use to gratify selfish desires. No longer did they feel urged to give themselves as gifts to each other. Such a disposition toward mutual exploitation immediately gave rise to a profound sense of shame. The words of Genesis 3:10: "I was afraid, because I was naked; and hid myself", provide evidence of the first experience of man's shame, a shame that the Pope describes as "cosmic".

The notion of gift here is critical. Genesis 2:23–25 enables

---

[26] "Marriage in the Integral Vision of Man", *Original Unity of Man and Woman* (Boston: Daughters of Saint Paul, 1981), p. 177.

us to deduce that woman, who "is given" to man by the Creator, is "received" or accepted as a gift. But she is given and received in the way that conforms to her Creator's plan, that is, "for her own sake". She is not received as a possession but as a gift to be cherished for her own autonomous value.[27] It is precisely when she is received in this way that she attains the inner depth of her person and the full possession of herself. Thus, she finds herself through giving herself. Selfishness, therefore, would be a radical hindrance to her self-discovery.

Whereas the woman is given and entrusted to the man, he, on the other hand, is assigned the role of receiving this gift. He enriches her, but at the same time is enriched by her. They are gifts for each other. The man gives himself, but his giving is a response to that of the woman. As man and woman continue to give themselves to each other, they affirm their masculinity and femininity, while deepening their awareness of it. They establish a bond that is at once reciprocal and communitarian.

Thus, in marriage as it was in the beginning, the woman's vocation was to give herself to her husband to be accepted and cherished by him. In this act of giving, she discovered and deepened her awareness of self. The husband's vocation is to accept his wife as a gift and respond by giving himself, thereby establishing a complementary union of two human beings that accords with the Biblical notion of being two-in-one flesh. Together, as a union of male and female, they reflect the God who created man in his own image specifically as male and female. As Coventry Patmore has elegantly expressed it in *The Angel in the House:*

> Female and male God made the man,
> His image is the whole not half.

The immediate effect of the Fall is a severely diminished capacity for man and woman to regard each other as gifts. The

---

[27] Ibid., "Man and Woman: A Mutual Gift for Each Other", pp. 131–32.

man of lust, according to the Pope, does not "control his own body" in the same way as the man of original innocence did. And when the male and female yield to lust, they introduce an alienating conflict that separates them from each other and leads them to forsake their conjugal vocation. Hence, it is commonplace for people to believe that men and women are naturally incapable of getting along with each other, rather than understanding that it is the selfishness and concupiscence brought about by the Fall that has blinded the sexes to the original and complementary unity of male and female and to marriage as a communion of persons. Such a belief reminds one of the junk dealer who has spent all his life in a junkyard, and because he has never seen a car in its original condition or even in good working order, he automatically assumes that all cars are in disrepair. But Christ offers us not only a vision of the truth of marriage but the grace to put it into practice.

The disharmony between the sexes is a timeless tragedy. But it is also the world's longest-standing joke. "Wedlock is padlock", exclaimed Heinrich Heine. And George Santayana remarked that "the chief aim of liberalism seems to be to liberate men from their marriage vows." In his amusing and poignant *Diaries of Adam and Eve,* Mark Twain has Adam complain that Eve talks too much, eats too much, and has too much hair. Adam pines for the good old days when he muses: "My life is not as happy as it was."[28] When Eve informs Adam of her name so that he can use it when he calls her, he comments dryly: "I said it was superfluous, then." But in the end, Adam came to love his unavoidable companion so much that he could say:

> After all these years, I see that I was mistaken about Eve in the beginning; it is better to live outside the Garden with her than inside it without her. At first I thought she talked too much; but now I should be sorry to have that voice fall silent and pass out of my life. Blessed be the chestnut that brought us near

[28] New York: American Heritage Press, 1971, p. 11.

together and taught me to know the goodness of her heart and the sweetness of her spirit![29]

Mark Twain wrote these words mindful of the passing of his own dear wife, "Livy". His words, "Wheresoever she was, *there* was Eden", were composed as a joint epitaph to Eve and to her. The tragedy for so many, however, is to perpetuate the "mistake", believing that differences are obstacles and disharmony between the sexes is the norm.

Taking a page from the devil's inverted theology, Mephistopheles adjures Doctor Faustus not to marry. While threatening to tear him to pieces if he does not comply, Mephistopheles commands Faustus to "think with what unquiet life, anger, strife, and debate thou shalt live in when thou takest a wife".[30] He deems marriage intolerable, for "wedlock", as he says, "is a chief institution ordained of God."[31] Marriage, in this diabolical view, is essentially destructive to man since woman is not his helpmate but his adversary.

The Supreme Pontiff takes great pains in trying to explain how the differences between the sexes must be properly understood and expressed so that a loving communion is achieved and reciprocal appropriation is averted. He points out that if the man thinks or acts as if he were the woman's proprietor, it is inevitable that she, likewise, will treat him as an appropriated object. Lust elicits lust, just as egotism and pride beget their own repeated images. The key passage the Holy Father cites is Genesis 3:16: "Your desire shall be for your husband, and he shall rule over you." This describes the appropriation and domination that is a result of the Fall. The specific role of the husband, the Pope states, is to be the "guardian of the reciprocity of donation and its true balance".[32] This follows

[29] Ibid., p. 31.

[30] Christopher Marlowe, *Doctor Faustus* (New York: New American Library, 1969), p. 121.

[31] Ibid.

[32] John Paul II, *Blessed Are the Pure of Heart* (Boston: Daughters of Saint Paul, 1983), pp. 79–84.

from the fact that man's vocation is to accept woman as a gift and respond by offering himself as a gift to her. But man "condemns himself" if, in his relationship with woman, he considers her only as an object to gain possession of and not as a gift. It is the specific responsibility of the man to safeguard the equality of the reciprocal offerings that constitute the unique communion of persons.

This citation in Genesis seems to imply that man and woman have different radical weaknesses. On the part of the woman, her weakness is to be so ready to give herself to a man, so eager to please him, that she may do so precipitously, without sufficient reflection and discrimination. Hence, the words: "Your desire shall be for your husband . . ." The radical weakness on the part of the husband appears to be his temptation to take a woman by means of concupiscence, that is, to awaken desire in her in order to satisfy his own will egotistically. Hence, the words: ". . . and he shall rule over you." Thus, woman needs to be more circumspect, whereas man needs to be more respectful.

But these weaknesses border on strengths. The woman is inclined to precipitousness because of her instinctive generosity and willingness to give. The man is apt to dominate because he is in a guardianship position and may respond lovingly or react selfishly. A Christian marriage is dedicated to bringing the best out of husband and wife, overcoming their weaknesses and eliciting their strengths.

Christ provides us with an analogy by which we are able to understand marriage in Christian terms. The communion of husband and wife reflects the mystical union between Christ and his Church (Mk 2:19–20; Jn 3:29). John Paul reminds us that "marriage corresponds to the vocation of Christians only when it reflects the love which Christ the Bridegroom gives to the Church his Bride and which the Church attempts to return to Christ."[33] As Saint Paul writes: "Christ loved the

---

[33] John Paul II, *The Theology of Marriage and Celibacy* (Boston: Daughters of Saint Paul, 1986), pp. 192–93.

Church and gave himself up for her" (Eph 5:25), thus conferring on his redemptive love a spousal character and meaning.

Nonetheless, it would be a mistake to think that ecclesiastics always held marriage in high regard. At the passing of the great Catholic social thinker Antoine-Frédéric Ozanam (who founded the Society of Saint Vincent de Paul), a monsignor said to Cardinal Pecci (later Pope Leo XIII) that it was a pity Ozanam had "fallen into the trap of marriage". "Ah", said the Cardinal, "I did not realize that Our Lord established Six Sacraments and One Trap."[34]

It is because of the Cardinal's astute remark that this anecdote is remembered and worth retelling. Marriage is a sacrament and that is precisely why it is not a trap. But it may very well become a trap for those who do not treat it like a sacrament. Marriage inevitably becomes a "trap" when it is "privatized", cut off from its sacramental roots and converted into a private project, a solitary expression of the individual self. But a trap is not a marriage and therefore cannot begin to confer all the benefits—physical, psychological, sociological, emotional, spiritual, theological, and mystical—that marriage has the potential to provide.

The blessings and benefits of marriage are at once so basic and broad, so fundamental and far-reaching, that it would seem indisputable that so natural an institution would also be the normal vocation for most human beings. This normalcy of marriage has been acknowledged and applauded throughout the ages in more ways than we can possibly begin to enumerate. "Marriage," wrote D. H. Lawrence, as he reviewed some of its more resplendent features, "making one complete body out of two incomplete ones, and providing for the complex development of man's soul and woman's soul in unison, throughout a life-time. Marriage sacred and inviolable, the

---

[34] Quoted by E. Von Kuehnelt-Leddihn, "A Theist's View of Marriage", *The Human Life Review,* Summer 1979, p. 98.

great way of earthly fulfillment for man and woman, in unison, under the spiritual guidance of the Church." [35]

As further praise of Christian marriage, Edmund Burke stated:

> The Christian religion, by confining marriage to pairs, and rendering the relation indissoluble, has by these two things done more toward the peace, happiness, settlement, and civilization of the world, than by any other other part in this whole scheme of divine wisdom.

Marriage is our normal vocation, and we reap its benefits both personally as well as socially. It is the ordinary way in which ordinary people deepen their knowledge of life's meaning and mystery, most fully express what is immortal in them, and share in the life of the divine.

[35] *Sex Literature and Censorship*, H. T. Moore, ed. (New York: Twaine Publishers, 1953), p. 107.

Chapter Two

Creation, Procreation, and the Preservation of Parenthood

The story is told of a parish volunteer in Duluth, Minnesota, who was asked by his local pastor to paint the outside of the church. Having received a liberal supply of paint, the volunteer, who had more than a bit of Scotch in him, decided to add just enough turpentine so that he could paint his own barn as well and thereby save a tidy sum of money. After giving both the church and his barn a new luster, he went to bed and slept soundly, for he was most pleased with his shrewdness. But during the night there was a violent rainstorm. Upon waking the next morning, the volunteer was horrified when he looked out his bedroom window and saw fresh paint streaming from the walls of his barn. Realizing that the same thing must be occurring at the church—a calamity that would not escape the attention of the parish priest—he sped to the site of his place of worship only to confirm his darkest fears. Falling to his knees, the anguished volunteer beseeched heaven: "Dear Lord, what am I going to do?" Now the Lord, as might be expected, did not resort to cheap humor. He did not chastise the remorseful volunteer for committing "adulteration"; nor did he admonish him for an act of "moral turpentine". Yet, not wanting to brush the matter aside, he did say in thunderous tones: "Repaint and thin no more"!

It often happens that philosophical principles are more easily and immediately grasped through a joke than through a carefully developed line of reasoning. Currently, a widespread belief exists that by diluting things—that is to say, compromising their inner integrity—we can enlarge our freedom and multiply our options. It is difficult for many people to understand that dilution diminishes freedom, that the process of attenuation (or thinning) can rob something of its ability to hold, to stay in place, to serve in the manner intended.

A few years ago, a number of multinational corporations aggressively introduced powdered milk into Third-World countries. Through intensive promotion in hospitals, clinics, and on the radio, and by giving free samples of powdered milk to new mothers, they sought to get these women to abandon breast-feeding their babies in favor of using formula milk. In many cases the results were tragic. Mother's milk dries up if it is not used during the first few weeks after the baby's birth. By using the free samples, mothers became dependent on the commerical product. But many of them could not afford to pay for it on a continuing basis. In an attempt to stretch the formula, they diluted it with water. In some instances a four days' supply was stretched to last three weeks.[1] As a consequence, many babies died; of the many other who were severely malnourished, a significant number had become brain impaired. The resulting sicknesses and deaths among these babies who had been fed diluted powdered milk has been termed "commerciogenic malnutrition".[2]

Dilution expands things on a quantitative scale but can very easily, at a certain point, cause what is essential to be lost. It may prevent paint from holding, milk from "sticking to the ribs", or doctrine from providing nourishment for the mind or soul. Dilution offers the illusion of more, but the reality of less. One does not expect to improve the taste of a fine champagne by adding ice cubes. In this case, it is only too clear that addition is subtraction. By the same token, one should not expect that watered-down doctrine would better represent the mind of the Church or the will of God.

---

[1] Denyse Handler, "So What's Wrong with Formula?" *The Uncertified Human,* vol. 5, no. 11, April 1978, p. 3.

[2] Leah Margulies, "Exporting Infant Malnutrition", *Healthright,* vol. III, issue 2, Spring 1977.

In the recent revision of the New Testament of the *New American Bible,* the Greek word *adelphoi,* which literally means "brothers", is translated as such. Some critics of "exclusive" language, however, have found the retention of this traditional translation to be "indefensible".[3] They would prefer that "brothers" be replaced with a more "inclusive" expression such as "my dear people" (which is how *adelphoi* is rendered in certain other recent translations). When Saint Paul uses the word *adelphoi* in addressing his audience as "brothers", he uses this word to indicate that since they are the adopted children of God, they are members of the same family. Thus, the dilution of the word "brothers" results in a loss of the meaning of "family". By including too much, what is essential becomes excluded.

A dilution of the mode and meaning of human generation exists in our contemporary world of biotechnological innovation that is seriously undermining the traditional notion of parenthood. The attempt to enlarge parenthood by increasing the number of options people might have in the way they bring about new life is threatening the essential meaning of parenthood. Two examples suffice to illustrate the paradoxical nature of this problem.

The December 7, 1987, issue of the *Washington Post* carried a front page article entitled, "A Need Examined, A Prayer Fulfilled: Unmarried Priest Bears Child by Artificial Insemination". The article concerns Lesley Northrup, a woman priest in the Episcopal Church who had a child through self-insemination with sperm donated by three men, two of whom were priests of her own denomination. She chose these particular three men because they were willing to contribute their sperm without accepting any of the concerns or responsibilities that are normally associated with fatherhood. She felt that

---

[3] Msgr. Myles Bourke, "Justifying the Need for a Revised New Testament", *The Catholic Answer,* March 1989, p. 32.

none of these men were fathers in any sense. In her words, they were "donating a necessary element for something . . . not of creating a baby, not as potential fathers. . . . They were donating something rather than creating something".

In order to rationalize self-insemination as a morally acceptable option, it was necessary to abolish fatherhood and reduce the male role to that of mere donor. This particular dilution of sexual morality may create the illusion of freedom, but it does not spell freedom for the male, who is not free to accept his fatherhood, or for the child, who is not free to grow up with its father. It also contradicts the spiritual meaning of "father", the name by which the two priest donors are properly identified. The implication that the mother is the sole parent is a distortion of the facts and represents a refusal to acknowledge the true nature of human generation. Finally, self-insemination by a single woman is an offense against the consecrated meaning of marriage and conjugal intimacy.

In Maryville, Tennessee, a couple went through a divorce process that involved the contentious business of splitting up the seemingly unsplittable—their seven frozen embryos. The husband regarded them not as his own offspring but as "property" and saw himself as their "owner". The wife looked upon them in a somewhat nebulous fashion as "life". But the director of the in vitro fertilization clinic, where the embryos were stored, believed "they should be treated like children".[4]

In vitro fertilization, by initiating human life apart from the embrace of husband and wife, leads ultimately to so weakened a notion of parenthood that in specific instances the parents themselves are unable to recognize their own identities as mothers and fathers. And without such recognition, parents are unlikely to exercise their parental responsibilities. The various technologies that increase the number of ways human

---

[4] Ellen Goodman, "Ethics and Eggs Create a Legal Dilemma in Divorce Case", *Springfield Union*, March 10, 1989.

life can be initiated inevitably dilute the notion of parenthood. This dilution, at a certain point, renders parenthood either unrecognizable or meaningless. Biotechnology does not free people to become parents as much as it obscures the very nature of parenthood.

The critical question here is this: what are the fundamental principles by which we can understand parenthood in its original and undiluted form? We need to know this in order to do what is needed to ensure the preservation of parenthood.

Human beings do not "replicate", as cells do, or "reproduce", like machines, or "create", as God does. Properly speaking, human beings "procreate". In replication, daughter cells result when a parent cell divides. After division, there is no longer a parent cell as such since it is now the very substance of its offspring. By contrast, in mechanical reproduction, the machine that reproduces and the things that are reproduced are always external to each other. In creation, something is brought into being which was formerly nothing, a transition that requires the agency of an all-powerful God.

Procreation is not creation, because it begins with something, namely, the sex cells. It is not reproduction, because there is an intimate relationship between parents and offspring. Nor is it replication, because the progenitors retain their identity as parents after their progeny has been conceived.

The origin of the notion of procreation is in the Christian conception of the Trinity and owes its inspiration to a crucial distinction between *procreation* and *creation*. Scholar Paul Henry, S. J., believes that this distinction was prompted by Bishop Alexander of Alexandria, an early Church theologian whose Deacon was Athanasius. Father Henry is of the opinion that "throughout the entire history of thought no greater discovery has ever been made . . . than that of the distinction between 'procreation' and 'creation'."[5]

---

[5] *Saint Augustine on Personality* (New York: Macmillan, 1960), p. 14.

Pagans, understandably, see one thing causing another. Generation always appears to them as emanating from the *Kosmos,* the physical world, rather than from *Anthropos,* a personal reality. Hebrew tradition asserts that the creator of the universe is a God who is both personal and loving. Nonetheless, the Christian notion of the Trinity still posed formidable intellectual problems for early Christian thinkers, particularly with regard to the relationship between the Father and the Son.

The Arians, for example, argued that the relationship between the Father and the Son must be one of Creator to that which is created. They reasoned that the Father, who is Unbegotten (*agennetos*), is radically different from the Son, who is Begotten (*gennetos*). Therefore, the Father and the Son are not consubstantial, that is to say, of one substance, and the Father, being the Creator, must be superior to the Son.

The Arians saw God as creating the Son rather than procreating him, as the term *begetting* suggests. The doctrine of the Trinity as three distinct persons in one unifying substance could be understood and perserved only by grasping the meaning of "procreation".

The procreative relationship between the Father and the Son is timeless and proceeds from God's very substance. Therefore, the Son is consubstantial with the Father and is wholly equal in divinity with him. As Saint Augustine has remarked, "We understand equality to be in the Father, Son, and Holy Ghost, inasmuch as no one of them either precedes in eternity, excels in greatness, or surpasses in power".[6]

The Father has a procreative relationship with the Son inasmuch as this relationship preserves their unity in one substance, maintains the equality and distinctiveness of their personalities, and does not involve creation from nothing. It is a relationship that is one of procreation rather than reproduction, replication, or creation. The Father's Son is not in-

---

[6] *De Fide ad Petrum,* i.

ferior to him in any way but enjoys the same perfection that is in the Father. According to Aquinas:

> It belongs to the very nature of paternity and filiation that the Son by generation should attain to the possession of the perfection of the nature which is in the Father, in the same way as it is in the Father himself.[7]

Scripture uses a common language of "generation", "conception", "birth", and so on, to denote the similarities that exist between generations in the family of man and the generation in the Trinity of the Son from the Father. Human procreation is a similitude of the procession between the Father and the Son, which is its prototype. Saint Thomas writes:

> The Word proceeding therefore proceeds as subsisting in the same nature; and so is properly called begotten, and Son. Hence Scripture employs terms which denote generation of living things in order to signify the procession of the divine Wisdom, namely, conception and birth; as is delcared in the person of the divine Wisdom, *The depths were not as yet, and I was already conceived; before the hills, I was brought forth* (Prov. viii: 24).[8]

God's relationship with his creatures is creative. He is the ultimate cause of all things that are created. But in creating human beings in his own image, he creates them so that they themselves can be procreative and thus imitate his Triune Life. Therefore, the relationship of parent-to-child, on a human, biological level, must mirror the divine in honoring its intimacy, equality, and consanguinity.

Saint Augustine emphasizes the loving unity of the Trinity when he identifies the three Persons as *Amans, Amatus, Amor* (the Lover, the Loved, and Love). Thomas Merton calls our attention to the self-giving generosity within the Trinity when he writes:

[7] *Summa Theologica,* I, 42, 4.
[8] Ibid., I, 27, 2.

> In God there can be no selfishness, because the Three Selves of God are three subsistent relations of selflessness, overflowing and superabounding in joy in the Gift of their one Life.[9]

Contemporary attempts to rename the Trinity parallel the disunity between parents and offspring that biotechnological innovations have brought about. For example, a theologian at Vanderbilt Divinity School urges a trinity of "Mother, Lover, and Friend".[10] Such naming fails to convey the notion of unity. In fact, it brings to mind an image as discordant as a *menage a trois*. "Mother" exists without "child", "Lover" is at best ambiguously related to the other two persons, and "Friend" seems to serve as a third wheel. Neither procession, procreation, or prototype is even remotely suggested.

The procreative relationship that unites the Father with the Son—like that which unites parents with their children and one generation with another—denotes a form of transmitting life known as "propagation". Deprived of this life-to-life procreative vitality, the new models, such as "Mother, Lover, and Friend", are best understood by the word "propaganda".

The procreative relationship is simultaneously personal and familial. By *personal,* we refer to the fact that human beings are not mere individuals, but fulfill themselves in their loving relationships with others. By *familial,* we refer to the special intimacy that exists between members of the same family. The model of the Blessed Trinity instructs human beings to generate offspring in such a way that they are ever mindful of their personhood and their vocations as lovers, as well as their relationships with and responsibilities to other members of their families.

Human beings are better able to understand and preserve their role as parents when they understand the personal im-

---

[9] *Seeds of Contemplation* (New York: Dell, 1960), p. 45.
[10] P. Abramson, et al., "Feminism and the Churches", *Newsweek,* Feb. 13, 1989, p. 60.

plications of procreation. In the Trinity, the Father-to-Son dynamism is a loving relationship that affirms both their equality and natures as persons. Likewise, in human procreation, parents do not feel radically superior to their children but love them and in so doing, experience their own reality as self-giving persons and begin to awaken that same understanding in their sons and daughters. In this context, it is incongruous to regard one's children as "property", one's spouse as a mere "donor", or marriage as a temporary and optional "arrangement".

In order for there to be a family, there must be parents. In order for there to be parents, there must be a procreational capacity by which one establishes a personal and familial relationship with his progeny. The Trinity, particularly in the procession of Father-to-Son, exemplifies this personal and familial procreative relationship. Man is created by God in this Trinitarian image and is given a procreative capacity through which he is able to express personal and familial love to his own children.

The procreative model, which we find in the Trinity, has a much broader application than for biological procreation. Spiritual parenthood, the loving, personal concern for the souls of others, for all God's children, is the destiny of all human beings. Spiritual paternity and maternity are indications of a certain perfection of the person. The capacity for "procreation" in the spiritual sense, the ability to be lovingly and generously disposed to the care and formation of souls, requires a high degree of moral maturity.

In his masterful treatise, *Love and Responsibility,* Karol Wojtyla states that "human beings will come particularly close to God when the *spiritual parenthood of which God is the prototype* takes shape in them".[11] He goes on to identify the emergence of spiritual development with man's natural development:

[11] Translated by H. T. Willetts (New York: Farrar, Straus and Giroux, 1981), p. 261.

> Any attempt to diminish human beings by depriving them of spiritual paternity and maternity, or to deny the central social importance of maternity and paternity, is incompatible with the natural development in man.[12]

The loss of awareness of our procreative capacities, both in physical and spiritual senses, is also the loss of our awareness of our nature as persons, our role as family members, and our awareness that we have been created in the image of God.

For many people, our product-oriented, technological society, through its unremitting emphasis on man as a reproducer of products, has obscured the fact that man is a procreative being. Thus, man as "father" is replaced by man as "producer". It is increasingly common in the world of advertising for men to identify themselves by the products they produce or the services they perform. As biotechnology makes fatherhood increasingly tenuous, we find his commercial replacement in the form of Mr. Donut, Mr. Plumber, Mr. Razor, Mr. Goodwrench, Mr. Fixit, Mr. Clean, and so on. At the same time, communities of interpersonal relationships give way to large commercial networks such as Food City, Tie City, Radio City, Carpet City, Value Land, and Toys Я Us.

Biotechnology, with its various approaches to human generation that include self-insemination, in vitro fertilization, embryo freezing, etc., seems to enlarge the sphere of human freedom by multiplying options for those individuals who experience certain difficulties with having children. This enlargement of freedom, however, is an illusion. Biotechnology is assuming a more predominant role in the generation of human offspring at the price of diluting our notion of man as a procreating being. This dilution makes it difficult for man to remember his role as a responsible parent who has a personal nature and develops in the context of familial love. As a result, man begins to see himself more and more as an individual who stands apart from what he produces, rather than as a

---

[12] Ibid.

being who is created in the image of a Triune God whose inner life is dynamically procreative.

The cultivation of a sense of spiritual parenthood would reduce people's desire to resort to dubious and dangerous technological methods of initiating new life. Yet, in order to keep vibrant this notion of spiritual parenthood, it is necessary to honor and preserve the notion of procreative parenthood. This latter notion, in turn, is grounded on the procreative nature of the Trinity.

It is not a mere coincidence that at the very moment procreative parenthood is under assault, the appellations of Father and Son for the first two persons of the Trinity are also under attack. The Evangelist Lutheran Church in Canada has recently introduced a lectionary of "gender-free" Scripture readings[13] that go as far as striking male pronouns even when they clearly refer to a male. Fatherhood and motherhood, like sisterhood and brotherhood, are manifestations of personal identity. They are eminently real and are preserved and perfected through their alliance with God, who is preeminently real. God is not an abstraction. Indeed, as a loving Father, he is the corrective, *par excellence,* for the tide of impersonalism that is sweeping across our technological society.

[13] Virginia Byfield with Mathew Ingram, "Biblical Feminism: The New Gnosticism?" *Western Report,* Feb. 13, 1989, p. 28.

Chapter Three

Human Generation and the Place of Love and Power

The relationship between love and power has been a topic of perennial intellectual interest. In the practical realm, it has been a source of universal and continuing personal frustration. In one sense, love and power are antagonistic to each other. The desire to have power over another person is incompatible with love, just as love demands the renunciation of such power. At the same time, love has a power of its own; there is no such thing as an impotent love. Power, therefore, can be the crowning complement of love. Moreover, love presupposes power; love cannot flow from a source that is morally and spiritually bankrupt. From a theological point of view, God is both all-loving and all-powerful. Yet our age of power leads many people to suspect that love may be nothing more than power in disguise.

Perhaps nowhere is the confusion about the relationship between love and power more rampant than in the area of human generation. Now that certain biotechnical powers are available, should the source of human generation remain restricted to a loving act between husband and wife, or should we allow the power that science provides to occupy an equally prestigious place at the origin of human life? A single example from the daily press, which portrays an attitude that is winning more and more social acceptance, offers us a fair illustration of the depth of our current dilemma.

A twenty-seven-year-old woman has placed an ad in a newspaper indicating her willingness to "rent" her womb to a childless couple for $15,000. "My priority is the money", she states rather frankly. "In essence, I am selling a baby." Jacquelyn Burkhart, who has worked as a pregnancy and abortion counselor for five years, asserts that she "loves kids" and loves being pregnant, but regards the child she hopes to conceive as not hers. "I'm growing it for them", she declares. Ms. Burkhart married at seventeen and separated from her husband shortly after the birth of her first child. After her divorce, she wanted another baby, so she performed artificial insemination on herself using sperm donated by a friend. The result was her second child.

This example furnishes us with an attitude toward human generation that is remarkable for its moral and biological versatility. The *way* to have children does not seem to be of any particular importance. The main concerns here are *why*, which ranges from private desire to commercial interest, and *by what means*, which ranges from marital intercourse to artificial insemination using sperm from either friends or business partners.

What influence does so inconstant and arbitrary an attitude toward generating new life have on her children, her concept of self, the people she counsels? Such reproductive versatility may be welcomed by libertarians these days because it offers so many different "options", and thus paints an alluring portrait of freedom. Nonetheless, because it allows power to gain such a prominent and privileged place in the process of human generation, it inevitably raises very serious philosophical and theological questions.

The Biblical Model for Human Generation

Human beings are ambiguous and precarious creatures. As such, they have great need for moral guidance. Concerning the generation of human life, the Bible provides this guidance by setting the origin of human life in a sexual act that includes the loving power of God. The novelty of this Biblical revelation is most significant, for it liberates human fertility from mythical representations of the cosmos. The Bible makes it clear that it is God, not the material cosmos, that authors human life. According to *Genesis:* "God created man in his image, in the divine image he created him, male and female he created them" (Gen 1:27). It is important to note here that what the Bible makes evident about the first man and woman applies to all men and women.

Other passages in Scripture corroborate this notion that God has a hand in the formation of man. We read in Psalm 119:73, "Thy hands have made and fashioned me"; and in Psalm 139:13–15, "For thou didst form my inward parts, thou didst knit me together in my mother's womb . . . my frame was not hidden from thee, when I was made in secret, intricately wrought in the depths of the earth." And in the Book of Job (10:8–11), we find these words: "Thy hands fashioned me and made me; . . . thou hast made me of clay; . . . Didst thou not pour me out like milk and curdle me like cheese?"

The special role that God plays in the formation of man is contrasted with the manner in which he creates plants and beasts. The creation of the latter was brought about through a cosmic or earthly evolution. Accordingly, God said, "Let the earth put forth vegetation, plants yielding seed, and fruit trees bearing fruit in which is their seed, each according to its kind, upon the earth" (Gen 1:11) . . . "Let the earth bring forth living creatures according to their kind: cattle and creeping things and beasts of the earth according to their kinds" (Gen 1:24).

Man is not a mere product of cosmic or earthly evolution. He is made in God's image by a special intervention of God. Man is not a mere assemblage of DNA or genetic material. His existence requires a special act that issues from God's creative hand. Every appearance of a new human being represents something more than material evolution, or replication, or reproduction; it represents creation. And this is precisely why it is proper to say that human beings *procreate* (rather than reproduce), since the sexual act that invokes new life is in continuity with and proceeds from the power by which God is able to *create*.

The Bible combines this fact of the generation of human life with a moral obligation. The fact that God is involved in a special way in the creation of new human life means that the human context in which he operates must be worthy of his sacred power. Genesis specifies this worthy context as being the conjugal embrace of husband and wife who have "become one flesh" (Gen 2:24). For this reason, the Vatican Instruction on the *Respect for Human Life in Its Origin and the Dignity of Procreation* states that every human being has a right to come into being in a way that befits a person, that is, through loving sexual intercourse in marriage, not through manipulation in a laboratory.

The Bible presents procreation as an act that has sacred implications and, consequently, something that should be reserved for husband and wife. In this way the love the spouses have for each other and the power of their own fertility is united with God's love and the power of his creation. Human love and power are thus joined with divine love and power.

Saint Augustine captures the correlation between love and power in God's creative act in his most elegant phrase: *"Quia amasti me, fecisti me amabilem"* (Because you loved me, you have made me lovable). The primary relationship between God and man is one of love (*amasti me*). But love is not the same as power and, as such, cannot confer existence. God creates by virtue of his power (*fecisti me*). Love characterizes his essence which, when communicated to man, establishes him as lovable. It is because God loved man that he made him. He did not create man simply to display his power. His power is conjoined to his fundamental motive for creation, which is love.

This particular alignment of power and love stands as a model for man. Therefore, man should not try to separate power from love and try to initiate new life by power that is detached from love, specifically, that uniquely appropriate form of love expressed in the conjugal embrace. When man tries to make man apart from a motive of love, he is forgetting or is unmindful of how he himself is created. Thus, in trying to reproduce rather than procreate, man violates his partnership with God and as a result becomes alienated from himself, from God, and from his own offspring. It is in love, not power, that we are united. Power is that which gives love its expression and its efficacy. Power without love can be both ungodly and inhuman.

The employment of reproductive technology may appear to be continuous with a married couple's love for its prospective child. However, since one cannot love that which does not yet exist (or may never exist), it cannot be said that the couple truly and realistically loves that child. In using reproductive technology to initiate new life, then, a break in the continuity between love and life occurs, leaving power to remain by itself. In order to preserve the continuity between love and life, husband and wife must love *each other*, and the love they express in fruitful intercourse will naturally overflow into the child they procreate.

The Mechanical Model for Human Generation

The modern world, dominated as it is by materialism, technology, and the need for mechanical efficiency, has, to a significant degree, shifted the model of human generation from the Biblical notion of procreation to the mechanical notion of reproduction. As Cardinal Ratzinger observes:

> Until the present moment the origin of the human being has come to be expressed through the concepts of "generation" and of "conception", and the theology within which the whole process would be included, through the concept of "human procreation". Now it would seem that the word, "reproduction", is gradually describing the transmission of human life with greater precision.[1]

[1] Joseph Ratzinger, "A Theological Glance on the Subject of Human Procreation", *Avvenire,* May 14, 1988, translated by Robert Constable.

By extending the notion of reproduction to include human generation, man loses his noble status as a being whose creation requires the special intervention of God and is reduced to a being who has essentially the same kind of origin as plants and animals. "And if", as one moral theologian remarks, "a person is thus reducible to those hydrogen atoms that are the final components of DNA, then all our talk of rights is just a matter of sentiments and conventions, and not something inherent to nature, for hydrogen has no rights." [2]

An examination of the uses of current biotechnology indicates that the concept of "reproduction" is deeply ingrained in the modern consciousness. In fact, this concept is so deeply ingrained that new human life, now commonly referred to as a "product of conception", is often clearly treated as an object that can be subordinated to the desires of others. This kind of treatment is possible since the "product of conception" is not regarded as having rights and dignity of its own.

A number of medical doctors have expressed horror that East Bloc countries have been encouraging their women to get pregnant (through artificial insemination) and then have abortions in order to help them win gold medals. It is known that muscle power increases greatly during the early stages of pregnancy. Therefore, pregnancy in an early stage may give a female athlete an important competitive advantage in certain events, such as track-and-field. Once she is finished with her events, she terminates pregnancy through abortion. [3]

Such a practice makes it quite clear that new human life is regarded merely as matter and has value only instrumentally, inasmuch as it may help its mother win an athletic event.

Recent reproductive practices, which rely heavily on technology, also make it clear that what is produced is something that is appropriately treated as a product. It is, of course, im-

[2] David Williamson, "Persons and Embryos", *The Tablet,* August 1, 1987, p. 817.

[3] "Athletes Use Abortions to Chase Olympic Gold", *Edmonton Journal,* Tuesday, May 24, 1988, F1.

plicit in the very meaning of "reproduction" that a product is involved. In a well publicized surrogate motherhood case, a child was delivered who was seriously disabled. The biological father asked that medical treatment be withheld so that the neonate would die. The mother disowned the child, who then became a ward of the state. A *Time* magazine writer condemned the whole affair while directing particularly sharp criticism at the fact that "a procedure had been devised in which a human being is literally conceived as a manufactured product". "No child", he went on to say, "should be treated as a factory reject."[4]

On the in vitro fertilization frontier, America's most progressive IVF center (in Norfolk, Virginia) has proposed that "spare" embryos be used for research purposes. More specifically, these embryos would be used to develop new tests for a wide range of genetic imperfections in the human embryo. Thus, human beings who might have developed mental or physical disabilities, had they been allowed to live long enough, could be eliminated at the embryonic stage even before being transferred to their mother's womb. In this way, it is presumed, the genetically imperfect could be destroyed in a manner that would be less difficult and emotionally traumatic for the parents than the current practice of amniocentesis followed by second-trimester abortion.

In opposition to this proposal, Congressman Henry Hyde stated that it was a step toward making Aldous Huxley's *Brave New World* a frighteningly imminent reality, one in which "human beings are treated like products made to order, and quality-controlled by a technocratic elite that tries to make up in technical knowledge what it lacks in genuine humanity".[5] "By turning the process of procreation into something more like the manufacture of a product, the technique seems to in-

---

[4] Roger Rosenblatt, "The Baby in the Factory", *Time,* Feb. 14, 1983, p. 90.

[5] "Statement of the Honorable Henry Hyde", *Subcommittee on Human Resources and Intergovernmental Relations,* July 14, 1988, p. 4.

vite researchers to treat new life as a commodity subject to the most cavalier forms of 'quality control'."[6]

The Honorable Congressman Hyde's points are well taken. Where the husband and wife regard human generation as an act of *procreation,* the value of their offspring is intrinsic to their humanity. On the other hand, where a couple regards human generation as *reproduction,* the value of their offspring— who are seen as products—is extrinsic to their humanity. Thus, in procreation, a child is good in itself because it exists as a human being who is the image of God and comes into being out of love. In reproduction, the child is subject to quality-control testing and may be eliminated if it does not measure up to certain extrinsic standards. In procreation, the child is always *good* because it is created by God, and everything that he creates is good of necessity. In reproduction, since the parents themselves cannot install goodness in their progeny, they are prepared to destroy them and start over again if the kind of goodness they find in their children is regarded as inadequate. In procreation, love and power are never separated. Love always loves what love's power creates (and procreates). In reproduction, love and power are separable. The value or lovableness of what is made is dependent on how well it is made rather than, as in the case of procreation, how it is made as an expression of love.

Here we are confronted with the time-honored distinction between "making", which belongs to the sphere of art, and "begetting", which relates to the fathering or mothering of a child. With respect to art, its excellence is judged by the excellence of the artwork. With respect to the act of begetting, the main concern is not the excellence of what is begotten but the loving care and fidelity that is expressed between the parents and their offspring. Because the work that is made is not an intrinsic good, whatever extrinsic good it does possess must

[6] Ibid., p. 3.

be judged. Because children who are begotten do possess an intrinsic good, that good must be loved.[7]

Reproduction, therefore, follows a mechanical model and not a Biblical one in the matter of human generation. As a result, there is a twofold alienation: between the maker and the product, and between the maker and God. In the first case, the maker stands apart from his product. A baker stands apart from his baked goods. He is not their "father", nor are they his "babies". But if a couple stands apart from their own offspring in a similar fashion, they are alienated from each other. Likewise, if a couple believes, as is consistent with the notion of "reproduction", that they are merely making or producing children (with the assistance of technology), then they do not believe they are operating in a way that intimately unites them with God. Thus, they are alienated from God.

This twofold alienation leads man to lose his awareness of God, both as his own creator and as the creator of his children, as the one who sets his special seal of love on all the human beings he creates. This alienation is also manifested in the alienation of power from love. By separating power from love in the order of reproduction, man loses sight of the God of Love and seeks to become his own god, a god of power. The logic of reproduction, therefore, inevitably leads toward atheism.

Many contemporary defenders of technological reproduction argue that the new biotechnologies such as those involved in IVF, surrogate motherhood, extracorporeal gestation, cloning, and so on, actually enlarge man's freedom because they allow him to do things he could not do otherwise. This argument has a superficial validity on a purely material and quantitative basis. It is like saying that the Sixth Commandment restricts man's freedom because it discourages him from mul-

---

[7] See Oliver O'Donovan's book *Begotten or Made?* (Oxford: Clarendon Press, 1984).

tiplying his number of sex partners. On a moral and qualitative level, however, the argument breaks down.

The truth of man is that he is a being who is dependent on God for everything that contributes to his fulfillment. His freedom and perfection depend on how well he unites himself with God, how well he is able to allow the nourishing forces of God's love and power to flow into him. By separating himself from God or disacknowledging the intimate role God plays in his life, particularly in procreation, he is not enlarging but diminishing his freedom. A lamp is not free in any meaningful sense when it is unplugged from its electrical socket. It it free to be serviceable as a lamp and be a source of illumination only when it is connected with its source of electrical power. Man is not more free when he reduces himself to a material being that is produced mechanically, rather than procreated through Divine intervention. As Cardinal Ratzinger has pointed out, "man denies himself, that is, denies an incontrovertible reality, when he refuses in his thinking to go beyond the horizon of the laboratory".[8]

The Hebrew language illustrates this same point, namely that human freedom finds its fulfillment in harmony with the word of God, in a most interesting linguistic manner. The Hebrew word for "engraved" as used in Exodus 32:16 in reference to the commandments which God engraved on the tablets, is *choruth*. The Hebrew word for freedom is *cheruth*.[9] "Do not read *choruth* (engraved)", writes Rabbi Yehoshua ben Levi, "but *cheruth* (freedom), for no one can be considered free except the one who engages in the study of Torah".

The German poet Rainer Maria Rilke gives poetic expression to this need for man's freedom to fuse with God's will when he writes:

[8] Ratzinger, p. 10.
[9] Quoted by Gershon Winkler in *The Golem of Prague* (New York: The Judaica Press, 1980), p. 296.

Catch only what you've thrown yourself, all is
mere skill and little gain;
but when you're suddenly the catcher of a ball
thrown by an eternal partner
with accurate and measured swing
towards you, to your centre, in an arch
from the great bridgebuilding of God:
why catching then becomes a power—
not yours, a world's.[10]

The reduction of procreation to reproduction carries with it the imminent danger of reducing sex itself to a purely naturalistic function. For if human generation is merely the manipulation of matter, sex is equally imbedded in the material process. Cardinal Lustiger has warned that such a reduction is "a regression to pagan naturalism".[11] Procreation elevates human generation as well as human sexuality to the level of the sacred by uniting them with God's love and power. One might say, then, that it is difficult to be an atheist if one is a mother or father in the specifically procreative sense as outlined in Scripture. At the same time, it is discouraging to note that some Catholic writers who should know better reject expressions such as "fathering a child" and "mothering a child" as "sexist".[12]

God's love and power operate according to his Wisdom independently of man's particular attitudes. Atheistic parents who believe that their IVF child is a mere product of material manipulations have nonetheless procreated a human being who is a child of God's Love. In an ontological sense, all chil-

---

[10] Quoted by Carroll Guen, "Gadamer, Objectivity, and the Ontology of Becoming", *Dialogue, A Canadian Philosophical Review,* vol. XXVIII, no. 4, 1989, p. 608.

[11] Jean-Marie Cardinal Lustiger, "Bioethics & the dignity of the 'whole human person'", *National Catholic Register,* April 12, 1987, p. 1.

[12] Lisa Sowle Cahill, *Between the Sexes: Foundations for a Christian Ethics of Sexuality* (Philadelphia: Fortress Press, 1985), p. 96.

dren come into being through procreation. Applying the notion of "reproduction" to human generation is simply a misunderstanding of what actually takes place. It is a failure to discern and appreciate the dignity of initiating human life and the creative role that God plays in the process.

The Bible informs us that human generation involves pro-creation. In so informing us, it raises our awareness to a new height. But with this heightened awareness come increased moral responsibilities. It is like suddenly being told by an expert that the postage stamp you were about to use to send a letter is really worth $50,000. One takes greater care of things that have greater value. We should rejoice in the discovery that human generation involves a special partnership with God and accept the attending moral obligations with the natural eagerness that flows from a grateful heart. One should be grateful to anyone who points out that what we have is far more valuable than we could ever have thought it to be. How much more grateful should one be to the one who has created that value?

Nonetheless, the temptation persists that we would be better off guiding our affairs exclusively through our own powers. It is the temptation of our primal parents and one which we must continue to struggle against. We must learn again and again that love is primary, power secondary. In reproduction, power tend to eclipse love. In procreation, by subordinating the power of fertility to the act and expression of marital love, we are helping to ensure that our relationship to our children is more like the relationship God the Father has to his children, namely, one that is essentially characterized by love.

Chapter Four

Marital Love and the Genesis of Human Life

When contraception first won broad secular acceptance, few people could have imagined the amount of alienation this technology had inaugurated. Contraceptivists had envisioned a mere separation of procreation from intercourse. Nothing more than that. Failed contraception, however, then produced the demand for terminating the unwanted pregnancy, thereby alienating the child-in-the-womb from its mother. Subsequently, it became apparent that having babies without sex was just the logical flip side of having sex without babies. The contraceptive mentality had thus established an atmosphere congenial to enlisting a myriad of reproductive technologies in the interest of generating new life asexually.

Nonetheless, while reproductive technology separated making babies from having sex, it did not deny parenthood. Indeed, it was considered a way of helping infertile couples to become parents. But the recently developed art of embryo freezing has changed that, producing a set of unlikely and even startling alienations: parenthood from human generation and human generation from parenthood. In the first instance it appears that parents have lost their parental status toward their own prenatal progeny. In the latter, prenatal offspring have apparently lost their relationship with their own parents. The alienation of the unitive and procreative ends of conjugal intimacy leads to the unravelling of all the relationships that bind husband to wife and parents to children until everyone stands in unprotected isolation.

Consider the following two dilemmas that embryo freezing has brought about:

The York Case

Steven and Risa York, who reside in Southern California, decided in 1988 to end their semiannual flights to the Jones in vitro fertilization clinic in Norfolk, Virginia. Over the previous three years, doctors at the clinic had repeatedly failed in implanting in Mrs. York's uterus embryos that were formed when her husband's sperm had fertilized eleven of her eggs in a petri dish. The Jones Institute for Reproductive Medicine, as it is formally called, froze a twelfth embryo. In May 1988, after switching to an IVF clinic closer to home, the Yorks informed the Jones Institute that Steven, who is a physician, intended to collect the frozen embryo and hand-carry it in an insulated flask on an airplane flight back to Los Angeles. There, he would deliver the frozen embryo to his new physician, who would then try to implant it in Risa York's uterus.

Three weeks later, a Jones Institute physician informed the Yorks by mail that they could not take away their embryo, which the institute referred to as a "prezygote".[1] Dr. Howard Jones, founder of the institute, prepared a statement in which he specified some of the things that could go wrong if the "conceptus" were transported from one in vitro facility to another: (1) the first clinic might be held responsible for the competence of the second; (2) delays *en route* might exhaust the coolant and thereby thaw the embryo prematurely; (3) someone acting as an embryo courier might use the embryo for blackmail, destroy it deliberately, or hold it for ransom.

Outraged by the institute's refusal to release their own child, the Yorks filed a suit asking for $200,000 in emotional damages as well as for the immediate release of their frozen embryo.[2] The Yorks view the actions of the institute as tanta-

---

[1] Cynthia Gorney, "The Real-Life Dilemmas of Frozen Embryos", *The Washington Post,* July 26, 1989, p. 81.

[2] "IVF Clinic Sued for Holding Child Hostage", *Potomac* (Woodbridge, Virginia) *News,* May 11, 1982.

mount to kidnapping. The embryo has been frozen for twenty-six months. No successful implantation of an embryo which had been stored in liquid nitrogen for more than twenty-eight months has ever been made. The Yorks' concern, understandably, had a certain note of urgency.

A District Court judge, however, refused the Yorks' request for the immediate release of their embryo. The case is currently headed for trial. Meanwhile, legal counsel Lori Andrews claims that the Yorks should be able to get their embryo back both as its parents, and, if that does not work, as owners of their property.[3]

The distance that separates the Yorks from their prenatal child is so great, in time, space, as well as in manner of generation, that it may appear to the Jones Institute and other observers that they are not parents in any sense. In fact, the Jones Institute might regard itself as more of a parent or guardian of the frozen embryo than the Yorks, even though the Yorks contributed to the embryo's genetic makeup.

In an analogous sense, the law states that a wife whose husband has been a missing person for a number of years is no longer considered legally married to him and is therefore free to remarry. Similarly, various statutes of limitations allow the mere passing of time to dissolve one's right to make certain claims.

The Yorks undoubtedly look upon their frozen offspring in terms of a *moral* distance—a distance of the heart, so to speak—which brings to naught whatever physical and temporal distances there might be. At the same time, they have to endure a painful irony. Having eschewed adoption, presumably to have a child that is biologically theirs, they are now denied parental rights to the very child they did conceive.

[3] Gorney, p. 86.

The Davis Case

After Mary Sue Davis suffered through five tubal pregnancies, she and her husband, Junior Lewis Davis, enlisted the services of an IVF clinic. There, after several of Mary Sue's eggs were fertilized in a petri dish by her husband's sperm, doctors tried unsuccessfully to implant fourteen of the resulting embryos in her uterus. When the couple decided to divorce, seven fertilized eggs were left over, frozen in liquid nitrogen. Junior Lewis has listed the frozen embryos under joint property. Mary Sue, thinking in a less impersonal vein, regards them as "life".[4]

Now that the marriage has formally dissolved, the court must decide how to deal with embryos. If it judges them to be property, it must still decide whose property they are and how many belong to Mary Sue and how many belong to Junior Lewis. Alternatively, the court could decide "ownership" on the basis of what sociologist Barbara Katz Rothman describes as "sweat equity"—whose investment is greater on the level of sheer physiology. In addition, the court could view things from an economic perspective—who paid for them—or from a psychological one—which party is more eager to have them. If both Junior and Mary Sue agree to surrender all claims to their frozen progeny, the court could allow the clinic to offer them for adoption, to use them for experimental or research purposes, or to destroy them.

The ambiguity of the value and identity of the embryos correlates with the ambiguity of their progenitors' relationship to them. Mary Sue and Junior Lewis do not regard them-

---

[4] ABC's *Nightline*, Aug. 7, 1989. On Sept. 21, 1989, Circuit Court Judge Dale Young granted temporary custody of the seven frozen embryos to Mary Sue Davis. He said that the embryos were life and not property: "from fertilization, the cells of a human embryo are differentiated, unique and specialized to the highest degree of distinction. . . . Human life begins at conception." Junior Davis plans to appeal. ("Frozen Embryos Go to Woman, Judge Rules in Divorce Case", *Kitchener-Waterloo Record,* Sept. 21, 1989, A3.

selves as parents of their frozen offspring. At the moment, Mary Sue views motherhood as a future prospect, not as a present reality. She wants to be a "mother", but adds: "I'm not sure I can go through the program again. It's a very hard process, mentally and physically". [5] If she does become a mother "through the program", she would do so without any further assistance or contribution from her husband. In this way, the program would function as a kind of "father", since it would be the agency that would confer motherhood on her.

Junior Lewis has remarked that the embryos represent "his future" and has expressed a willingness to go on indefinitely paying the $150 a year storage fee to keep them frozen. In keeping with this viewpoint, he wants them kept out of the uterus of Mary Sue or any other woman who might, after implantation, become pregnant. Mr. Davis does not want to be forced into biological fatherhood. His lawyer agrees, arguing that feminists have won reproductive freedom for men as well as for women.

If Junior ever does decide to "father" any of the embryos, it would be, in his mind, a surrogate gestator, not his wife, who would make him a father. If this eventually did transpire, Mary Sue might feel that the surrogate made her a mother. She might then demand visitation rights to the child. On the other hand, the surrogate might see herself as the mother and may even want to keep the child and raise it as her own. And if she were married, her husband could become the "father". It is possible, therefore, that without voluntarily surrendering custody, neither the genetic mother nor the genetic father would be legally recognized as parents.

In addition to the confusion over the identity of the embryos and the meaning of parenthood is the confusion over the relationship between husband and wife or father and mother. When marital union results in new life, it is the husband who makes his wife a mother, and the wife who makes

---

[5] "A Battle over Frozen Embryos", *The Interim,* May 1989, p. 2.

her husband a father. In the Maryville, Tennessee, scenario involving the seven frozen embryos, the gap between the spouses is so wide that the impression is created that it is the IVF program that could make the wife a mother and a surrogate gestator that would make the husband a father.

The *alienation* of new human life from its normal genesis in marital love leads directly to a threefold alienation of crucial significance: the embryo from its identity as a human being, the husband and wife from their identities as father and mother, and the spouses from their relationship with each other as co-procreators who confer motherhood and fatherhood upon each other. Given this series of profound alienations, the moral void created by the absence of discernible identities, meanings, and relationships must be filled in ways that are not only arbitrary and willfull, but unsatisfactory, contentious, and subject to endless conflict.

In press coverage, the frozen embryos are repeatedly referred to as "pre-embryos". (The "pre-embryos" are also referred to as "eggs".)[6] This word is not found in pre-IVF embryological terminology. "Pre-embryo" came into being because a technique had been developed whereby new life could be initiated before it was placed inside the woman's body. "Pre-embryo" suggests a kind of life before life or a form of life that precedes human life. Designating new human life as "pre-embryo" makes it easier for the genetic mother to deny that she is its mother. It is far more difficult for a woman who wants to be a mother to make this denial if she knows that an embryo is growing within her body. Thus, the separation of the initiation of human life from marital union makes both the dignity of the embryo as well as the parenthood of the progenitors easier to deny.

Ellen Goodman has suggested that we might avoid future Maryville dilemmas by requiring couples to add "pre-

[6] Ibid.

conceptual clauses" to their IVF agreements. "Husband and wife would decide in advance," she writes, "which would control the fate of their biological merger if they uncouple."[7] Perhaps unconsciously, Ms. Goodman captures our threefold alienation in a nutshell. Husband and wife do not become parents as a result of initiating new life; their union is only a "biological merger". Such a "merger" would hardly be discerned as having the potential to form a new person since there is nothing personal about a "biological merger" in the first place. Moreover, husband and wife are not united in anything like a two-in-one-flesh intimacy. Marriage is merely "coupling", divorce is "uncoupling". Spouses engage and disengage like two railroad cars in a train yard. The use of the word "uncoupling" to signify divorce and the breakup of sexual partnerships has been made somewhat fashionable by Diane Vaughan's widely advertised book, *Uncoupling*.[8]

The human identity of human life in its origin, the beginning of motherhood and fatherhood, and the union of husband and wife in marriage are concepts that may be intelligible and realities that may be recognizable only within a perspective of love. Love unifies the partners within marriage and enables them to discern the dignity of their procreative act, the act by which they become parents to the child they have called into being. If love is not present, everything unravels. Marriage becomes "coupling", new human life is perceived merely as a "pre-embryo" or a "pre-zygote" or a synthesis of gametic cells, and parenthood gives way to "property ownership". Finally, parenthood itself and the human identity of human beings disappears. In the York case,

---

[7] Ellen Goodman, "Ethics and Eggs Create a Legal Dilemma in Divorce Case", *Springfield Union,* March 10, 1989. The "pre-embryos" are also referred to as "eggs". See also *The Interim,* op. cit. See also Sally Jacobs, "Couple Battles Over 7 Embryos: Divorce Centers on Status of Fertilized Eggs", *The Boston Sunday Globe,* August 6, 1989, pp. 8, 22.

[8] New York: Oxford University Press, 1986.

parenthood is alienated from progeny, as if the frozen embryo had no parents. In the Davis case, the progeny is alienated from parenthood, as if the Davis couple did not generate their seven frozen embryos. Both cases offer a dramatic confirmation of the Church's wisdom in teaching that love must precede life, that it must always be inseparably wed to it, and that the basis for respect for life in its origin is found in an appreciation of the dignity of procreation.

> The procreation of a new person, whereby the man and the woman collaborate with the power of the Creator, must be the fruit and the sign of the mutual self-giving of the spouses, of their love and of their fidelity. *The fidelity of the spouses in the unity of marriage involves reciprocal respect of their right to become a father and a mother only through each other.*[9]

The two aforementioned cases provide clear examples of the kind of calamities that can arise when the initiation of new human life has been sundered from its proper ground of marital love. But it would be a mistake to regard the situations involving the frozen embryos as isolated cases that are not likely to recur. Embryo freezing is a logical and inevitable extension of in vitro fertilization. A survey in early 1987 revealed that at least 41 IVF centers in the United States have added embryo freezing to their in vitro fertilization protocols.[10] Most of the other clinics surveyed plan to add it within two years. Although only an estimated 10 infants were born in the United States by 1988 after being frozen as embryos,[11] the number of frozen embryos in America nearly tripled from 289 to 824 be-

[9] *Instruction on Respect for Human Life in Its Origin and on the Dignity of Procreation: Replies to Certain Questions of the Day,* II A, 1.

[10] Andrea L. Bonnicksen and Robert H. Blank, "The Government and In Vitro Fertilization (IVF): Views of IVF Directors", *Fertility and Sterility* 49: 3 (March 1988), pp. 396–98.

[11] U.S. Congress, Office of Technology Assessment, *Infertility: Medical and Social Choices* (Washington, DC: U.S. Government Printing Office, 1988), p. 298.

tween 1985 and 1986,[12] and more than quadrupled to 3,715 by 1989.[13] In England, hundreds of frozen embryos have been abandoned by their natural parents.[14] In a laboratory in Atlanta, liquid nitrogen tanks presently hold 600 frozen embryos.[15] Given the current high rate of infertility and divorce, and the popular consensus that a couple has a "right" to have a child of its own through whatever technical procedures that are available to them, it is a virtual certainty that there will be a huge increase in the number of frozen embryos that will be either disowned, disputed, or destroyed.

Embryo freezing creates a profound contradiction in a couple whose natural desire to be intimately involved with a developing unborn child is frustrated by the fact that the child is alienated from them and exists in a state of suspended animation. Some women come to see their frozen offspring as babies. Some clients name them and request the petri dishes in which they were fertilized as mementoes.[16] This contradiction is particularly sharp when embryos die as a result of the failure of freezing equipment, when the wife becomes prematurely menopausal, or when she develops medical problems that would preclude pregnancy.

Couples who might want to abandon IVF attempts after a series of failures in order to explore adoption possibilities are frustrated when they feel a sense of obligation to their frozen progeny. In this way, embryo freezing can lock couples into

[12] Medical Research International, The American Fertility Society Special Interest Group, "In Vitro Fertilization/Embryo Transfer in the United States: 1985 and 1986 Results from the National IVF/ET Registry", Fertility and Sterility 49:2 (February 1988), pp. 212–15.

[13] Nightline, Aug. 7, 1989.

[14] Personal communication from Dr. Peggy Norris (M.D.) of England, Seventh Annual Human Life International Conference, New Orleans, Louisiana, April 22, 1989.

[15] Gorney, p. 81.

[16] Andrea L. Bonnicksen, "Embryo Freezing: Ethical Issues in the Clinical Setting", The Hastings Center Report, vol. 18, no. 6, December 1988, p. 27.

an IVF program, even when they have lost confidence in the program and want to seek some other solution for their child-lessness. Embryo freezing prolongs the experience of being a "patient", and thereby subjects couples to a series of painful decisions and disappointing consequences. Embryos are evaluated for their "freezability". A negative evaluation can affect the self-worth of clients for whom the pain of infertility is now compounded by the fact that their embryos have failed to pass the "freezability" test.

When there is a surplus of embryos, decisions must be made as to which ones should be implanted and which should be frozen. Should the stronger embryos be implanted and the weaker ones frozen? This is plausible since most of the embryos will not survive the freeze/thaw procedure. Or should the weaker ones be implanted? This is also plausible since the stronger ones have the best chance of surviving the freeze-thaw procedure. Clients are sometimes faced with vexing decisions concerning the donation of their frozen progeny to other infertile couples. They experience anxieties over the possible mix-up of ampules in which their embryos are stored, and go into mourning when their frozen embryos are lost.

The March 19, 1990, issue of *Newsweek* carried the story of a sperm donor mix-up that resulted in a black child being born to a white couple. DNA tests on the child and on the husband's remaining deposits at the sperm bank confirmed the absence of any genetic link between the husband and the child. The mother (whose husband died in 1989) is suing the sperm bank and one of its doctors for malpractice and breach of contract.

Another contradiction appears on the level of the patient-doctor relationship. Couples tend to personalize their embryos whereas the physicians tend to depersonalize them. The former describe them in humane terminology, referring to them by name or as babies or "twinnies", and so on. The clinicians are more accustomed to identifying them in scientific or even pseudo-scientific terms as "pre-embryo", "pre-zygote", or "sets of tissues". The embryo represents the hope that a couple will be able to have a child of its own. The medical personnel takes a more critical and clinical approach in evaluating the soundness and freezability of the embryo, bearing in mind that an abnormal child could bring unfavorable publicity to the program. To add to the contradiction, lawyers commonly advise couples to regard their embryos as joint property, while reminding them of a range of future possibilities that include divorce, death, or a change of mind. Some clinics offer their patients the option of overseeing embryo disposal in accordance with a death ritual.[17]

Separating the initiation of new life from a context of loving, conjugal intimacy exposes both the child and the procreating couple to an extraordinary number of physical and psychological dangers. Ironically, these dangers sometimes include the chance of suffering permanent sterility and lost opportunities for pursuing adoption or even having a child naturally. In the case where infertility is due to the husband's low sperm count, subjecting the wife—who may be perfectly healthy—to a protocol of hormone treatments, IVF, and unsuccessful implantations followed by embryo freezing and more implantation failures, could very well bring about medical complications that could produce permanent sterility. On a purely pragmatic level, therefore, IVF, with its inevitable accompaniment of embryo freezing, demands alienation and contradiction, divisive forces that are in direct conflict wih the unity of husband and wife that undergirds the very meaning and purpose of marriage.

Bio-ethicist Karen Lebacqz provides a list of scenarios in which people of widely varying moral dispositions seek to have a child utilizing modern reproductive technologies. These examples appear to be "exotic", but should appear

[17] Ibid., p. 29.

logical if one accepts the twin premises that people have a right to have a child and that life need not originate in the context of marital love. A sample from her list reads as follows:

8. A man and a woman are married. They desire to have a child, but the wife doesn't want to interrupt her career with a pregnancy. The husband's sister offers to carry the child for them.

12. An unmarried heterosexual couple wants a child "of their own", but neither can produce gametes. The woman's sister will donate ova and the man's brother will donate sperm.

16. A single man wants a child of his own. He purchases ova from an attractive woman to be fertilized by his sperm, and hires another woman for host gestation.

17. Two homosexual women, committed to one another for life, desire to have a child. To share the experience, one will contribute ova, the other her womb. Sperm will be provided by a donor.

19. Two homosexual males desire to raise a child. One man's sister donates ova, the other man donates sperm. Another woman is hired to bear the child.[18]

In each of these examples it is evident that the child is produced not as the fruit of the love between two people but by means of an impersonal mechanism. Also, the child is an object of desire, an object whose expropriation is justified solely on the basis of that desire. Regard for the child in its own right is not apparent.

The purely materialistic way in which the child is produced suggests that the spiritual dimension is not essential to parenthood. The fact that the child is something *for* the parents, rather than an autonomous being, places his preborn life in

[18] Karen Lebacqz (ed.), *Genetics, Ethics and Parenthood* (New York: The Pilgrim Press, 1983), pp. 26–27.

great peril if he exhibits certain defects or abnormalities. Were the child to be born, it is unlikely that he would be raised in an atmosphere of selfless love, especially if he failed to be the kind of child his parents originally had in mind.

The spiritualization of parenthood and the unconditional love of parents for their children are the two factors that are greatly undermined by technologized approaches to parenthood. These factors are essential for the proper functioning of parenting and child-raising. Without them, the family would be reduced to a travesty unworthy of human beings. Technologized parenthood is based on too materialistic a conception of both parenthood and offspring, as well as the mode of human generation itself. It rests on an inadequate anthropological view of the human being and fails to acknowledge that the spiritual and the bodily are both constitutive parts of the human person. As a result, it does not see the need to affirm a spiritualized, personal love between the spouses, or to encourage a disposition toward new life that welcomes it as a gift. In his remarks to the press, when the Vatican Instruction *Donum Vitae* was being released, Cardinal Ratzinger emphasized the significance of this point when he stated:

> Every person deserves unconditional respect and can never be reduced to an object to be used; this is valid from conception until death. Therefore the conjugal act by which the spouses specifically express their communion of interpersonal love is the only "cradle" worthy of the new human being.[19]

In the text of *Donum Vitae* we read:

> The origin of the human being thus follows from a procreation that is "linked to the union, not only biological but also spiritual, of the parents, made one by the bond of marriage".[20]

---

[19] "Cardinal Ratzinger Presents New CDF Instruction to Journalists", *L'Osservatore Romano*, 16 March 1987, N. 11, p. 8.

[20] Pope John Paul II, *Discourse to Those Taking Part in the 33th General Assembly of the World Medical Association*, 29 October 1983: *AAS* 76 (1984) p. 393.

Fertilization achieved outside the bodies of the couple remains by this very fact deprived of the meanings and the values which are expressed in the language of the body and in the union of human persons.[21]

Too much emphasis on biological parenthood and the material means of initiating new life tends to obscure the reality of spiritual parenthood and the personal value of the child conceived. The converse, however, is not true. In fact, the cultivation of spiritual parenthood leads to a proper understanding of biological parenthood. The reason for this is that spiritual parenthood, the protective and nourishing love for all God's children, provides a personal context within which the biological finds its proper role. Spiritual parenthood gives the biological a more expansive life and safeguards it from being confined to the material. Therefore, spiritual parenthood must precede biological parenthood. Similarly, love must precede sexual expression. Love gives sexual expression a loftier, more personal direction while safeguarding it from becoming a narrow, self-contained entity unto itself.

Spiritual parenthood is the root system that gives life and direction to biological parenthood, which is its flower. Without a spiritualizing force, the fruits of the biological soon wither. By cultivating spiritual parenthood, one experiences parenthood in a general way and is assured of enjoying at least some of its rewarding benefits. The transition from the spiritual to the biological, then, if it does take place, should be a natural progression. Learning how to become comfortable with a wide variety of children naturally prepares one for becoming comfortable with one's own children, whose individual identities, being always a surprise, can never be predicted and should never be presupposed. Spiritual parenthood also disposes a person to think favorably of adoption, and it helps one find personal satisfactions in the parent-like relationships he or she might have with younger members of the extended

[21] II B, 4b.

family, such as nieces or nephews. Should the transition to biological parenthood not take place, the spiritualized parent will not feel that he has been completely deprived of parenthood. But without a cultivated spiritual parenthood, one is prone to identify parenthood with the biological. As a result, when confronted with the misfortune of unwanted infertility, one might develop an obsessive desire to become a parent biologically, since that is the only form of parenthood he understands.

This obsessive desire is of particular moral significance not only because it threatens to place unreasonable demands on the prospective child to satisfy his parents' needs, but also because it makes the potential parent highly vulnerable to exploitation. Social critics have noted that the contemporary "obsession" with having a child of "one's own" is indeed rooted in a "naturalization of parenthood". One critic, for example, views this phenomenon as "an individualized biological understanding of parenthood", a concept of parenthood that is determined by one's genes.[22] Another describes it as a "fetishization of specifically biological traits".[23] These criticisms are well founded. One finds frequent mention in the literature, as well as in personal experience, of infertile couples who are "desperate" and "willing to try anything" to have a child. Infertile women commonly speak about the "ticking of their biological clock", which fills them with a sense of great urgency about getting pregnant. Nonetheless, the *argumentum ad misericordiam* remains a logical fallacy. One cannot justify the use of artificial techniques to have a child on the basis of desire alone. The state of "desperation" is a better indication of the need for counselling than for bringing new life into the world. In a parallel context, if a suitor proposed marriage by exclaiming to his prospective bride, "You must

[22] Verena Stolcke, "New Reproductive Technologies: The Old Quest for Fatherhood", *Reproductive and Genetic Engineering,* vol. 1, 1988, pp. 5–19.

[23] Emily Culpepper, quoted in H. Holmes et al. (eds.), *The Custom-Made Child* (Clifton, NJ: Humana Press, 1981), p. 276.

marry me. I'm desperate!" he would have provided her with sufficient reason to reject him.

Directors of IVF clinics that employ embryo freezing report that more than 90 percent of their patients consent to have their spare embryos frozen despite the fact that embryo freezing is an extremely hazardous procedure. Some observers find that such a high figure means that freezing is presented in a way that encourages patients' participation in the protocol (for example, by stating "our policy is to freeze embryos in excess of four").[24] In another study, 93 percent of infertile couples said that they would participate in "any innovative methods for achieving biological pregnancy".[25] Again, this is an indication of how susceptible infertile couples are to exploitation and how willing they are, despite low success rates, to expose themselves as well as their progeny to a variety of unknown yet significant dangers.

An infertile couple (or even a single person) that is determined to achieve biological parenthood makes itself, as well as the child, vulnerable to exploitation. The three essential factors that serve to prevent this dual exploitation from eventuating are the love that husband and wife bear for each other, the respect they share for the dignity of procreation, and their cultivation of a spiritual attitude toward parenthood. At the same time, these factors protect the integrity of marriage and help to ensure respect for the genesis of human life. Critics of *Donum Vitae*, and of Church teaching in general on marriage and procreation, appear to lose sight of the uncompromisable significance of these factors.

Michael Bayles, in his book *Reproductive Ethics*, argues that the law should not prohibit artificial insemination for single women. He offers five reasons for his position (1) that the enforcement of legal prohibition would be nearly impossible; (2) that single women can become pregnant through sexual

[24] Bonnicksen, p. 28.
[25] Thomas Shannon and Lisa Sowle Cahill, *Religion and Artificial Reproduction* (New York: Crossroad, 1988), p. 19.

intercourse; (3) that many single woman are better parents than some couples; (4) that no serious social consequences would result from single women becoming pregnant through artificial insemination; (5) that prohibition would represent discrimination on the basis of marital status.[26] His first two reasons are merely pragmatic observations and have nothing to do with the morality of the issue. In addition, they blithely disregard the cultural importance of the law as a teacher. His fourth reason is a gratuitous assertion that contradicts the facts. The third and fifth reasons are of particular interest inasmuch as they are based on a lack of sensitivity to the distinction between marriage in the legal, technical sense and marriage in the normative, fully realized sense. Two people can be married who neither love each other, have respect for the dignity of procreation, or have any notion of spiritual parenthood. Such a marriage should not be indiscriminately classified as a "marriage" alongside marriages that are what they should be. The nominal and the real do not belong to the same metaphysical category. While it may be true that some single women are better parents than some bad married parents, it is quite another thing to claim that these same women are better parents than good married parents or that the single-state of parenthood is superior to its marital counterpart. Such an assertion would be discriminatory against good fathers as well as against marriage itself. Marriage is ordered to parenthood, and the love between husband and wife is an indispensable factor in contributing to its proper perfection.

Bad marriages should not be used as a norm to justify approving the initiation of single parenthood. One form of parenthood that is morally defective should not be used to justify another that is substantially incomplete. The intelligent response is to overcome the moral defect rather than introduce a substitute that is deprived of an essential element. Further, one should be less concerned about discrimination against the

[26] Englewood Cliffs, NJ: Prentice-Hall, 1984, p. 19.

marital status of the single woman than about depriving the child of being born to two loving parents, a mother and a father. It is the child's rights that should be central in this issue, not those of the single woman. The mere "right" of a single woman to have a child through artificial insemination carries with it no assurance whatsoever that the child will be loved, cared for, and not abused or abandoned. Marriage in the true sense of the term does convey these assurances.

Bayles criticizes *Humanae Vitae* for holding that procreation should not occur except in loving sexual acts. He argues that the only reason reproduction should occur within the context of marital love is to provide nurturance for the offspring. He contends, however, that this nurturance has nothing to do with the sexual act and therefore charges the encyclical with confusing the biological act with the familial context.[27] *Humanae Vitae,* of course, does not argue that it is the sexual act and not the familial context that provides nurturance for the young. Bayles misses the point. The encyclical affirms the nurturing role of the family far more than he suspects. Its reason for holding that new life should be initiated only in the context of a loving sexual act is to assure that life follows love, that new life is initiated not from motives of selfishness but from a generous, unselfish act expressed between husband and wife whose incarnation is a life that is the fruit of their love. The Church wisely realizes that the child that is brought into being through an act of unselfish love is more apt to receive the nurturance it needs in the familial context than the child whose life is initiated to satisfy parental desires.

Bayles gravely misrepresents the mind of the Church when he equates a loving sex act with the "biological". Biology itself is not capable of a loving act. Love is always personal, whether it is expressed conjugally or familially. The crucial difference between conjugal and familial love has to do with its relationship with new life. Conjugal love is an intimate,

[27] Ibid., p. 15.

sexual expression between spouses that may be incarnated in the form of new life. Familial love is expressed within the family; it is exemplified by the love parents have for their children who already exist.

This distinction is missing in theologian Richard McCormick's criticisms of *Donum Vitae*. McCormick fully accepts the Instruction's position that the "procreation of a person should be the result of married love" and that "the one conceived must be the fruit of his parents' love". Indeed, it would be difficult for any reasonable person to reject such a position. But he does not accept the Vatican's contention that the child is "reduced to an object of scientific technology" when conceived as the product of an intervention of medical or biological techniques. "Sexual intercourse is not the only loving act in marriage", McCormick then asserts.[28]

Superficially, no one would disagree with him. But there is a fundamental, metaphysical point he overlooks. Love is both personal and realistic. It is not "biological" or "fantastical". Therefore, love is always the expression of a person for something that is real. But, a prospective child, or the child that may never be, is not real and therefore cannot be an object of love. Something that does not exist cannot elicit love. This is why infertility is such a peculiar affliction, since it represents the loss of something one never had.

Conjugal love (marital, sexual love) is directed toward people who do exist—husband and wife. This form of love has the unique capacity of invoking new life. But it is only when that life exists that it can become an object of love—of *parental,* not conjugal, love. The Church is clearly aware that sexual intercourse is not the only loving act in marriage. She fully recognizes the infinite variety of loving expressions proper to the domain of spousal love. But conjugal love is the only expression of spousal love that is ordinated to life. The

---

[28] Richard McCormick, S. J., "The Vatican Documentation on Bioethics: Two Responses", *America,* March 28, 1987, p. 248.

Church does not want to reduce all forms of love in marriage to the sexual; she does, however, want to remind people that all varieties of love must be realistic. She is saying, in effect, that parental love directed toward nonbeing—children who do not yet exist or who may never exist—is an illusion, and a very dangerous one at that, since the vacuum created by the absence of a love object tends to be filled by subjective and egoistic desires.

McCormick is trying to convince his readers that the Church is not loving enough, when the Church is only trying to ensure that all the different kinds of love are expressed realistically. He is also grossly unfair to Joseph Ratzinger when he dismisses as "sheer nonsense" the Cardinal's alleged charge that the use of IVF and embryo transfer is not a loving act but an "egoistic" one.[29] Cardinal Ratzinger's words were well chosen. He stated that "the Church's Magisterium cannot make even the slightest compromise with a viewpoint in which subjective desire is the sole and sufficient criterion to legitimate any medical intervention whatsoever."[30] This point, of course, is not peculiar to the Church and is enthusiastically endorsed by various agencies within the secular establishment.

Georgeanna Seegon Jones, cofounder of the Jones Institute for Reproductive Medicine, fails to appreciate how *Donum Vitae* not only welcomes all forms of spousal love (including its conjugal expression), but also protects them from illusion by always directing them toward someone who exists. Jones reduces all forms of spousal love to conjugal love and then accuses the Church of making her mistake. She writes:

> A definition which implies that intercourse *is* conjugal love, and that the sole function of intercourse is reproduction, does not differentiate between human beings and animals. It

[29] Ibid.
[30] Ratzinger, p. 8.

is unjust to burden Catholic couples with such a medieval definition. . . .[31]

The Vatican should redefine *conjugal love* between human beings in terms that emphasize all-encompassing *love* instead of limiting it to sexual intercourse.[32]

Mrs. Jones could not have interpreted *Donum Vitae* and Church teaching on these points more unjustly. Conjugal love is not narrow because it is expressed conjugally. Because of its nature, it cannot be expressed in any other way. Simply calling it "all-encompassing" does not free it from its conjugal nature and confer upon it the broad character of spousal love.

The Church, contrary to Jones's charge, has never taught that "the sole function of intercourse is reproduction." The very fact that the Church refers to the procreative act as "conjugal love" indicates that she recognizes that intercourse should be a loving act. Moreover, the immediate beneficiaries of the love expressed during conjugal love are the spouses. If the sexual union results in new life, that new life is now the object of parental love. The Church is far more sensible and realistic than Jones can imagine. She encourages the cultivation of multifaceted spousal love so that the sexual union husband and wife share will be truly loving. The loving conjugal expression, in turn, helps to ensure that any resulting progeny will also be loved. The Church is wise enough to realize that there should be no break in the continuity of love. Each love blesses and prepares the next: friendship leads to marriage, spousal love leads to conjugal love, which then leads to parental love and finally, familial love. The Church understands that a break in this line of continuity may very well be a break in the line of love. Love's arterial system must remain intact.

Other critics of *Donum Vitae* seem to think that the Church

---

[31] G. S. Jones, "Reply to the Vatican 'Instruction on Respect for Human Life in Its Origin and on the Dignity of Procreation'", *Fertility News*, 21(3), Feb. 1987, p. 4.

[32] Ibid., p. 5.

opposes babies rather than the artificial procedures that occasion their coming into being. An editorial in the *National Catholic Reporter,* for example, states that the Instruction is a "poor document for Catholics who want children and who know that, in their loving lives, a baby conceived in a test tube is still their baby".[33] Here again, the attempt is made to convey the impression that the Church is insensitive to love and opposed to babies. Similarly, Dr. Jesse Steinberg, who was a member of the Edwards–Steptoe team responsible for the world's first IVF baby, Louise Brown, states that all the infertile couples that come to his IVF clinic in California are thoroughly loving people. He angrily charges the Vatican with judging these people and "falling on its face" instead of helping them in a loving way. Confusing the Church's opposition to the procedure with the child produced through the procedure, he asks somewhat sarcastically whether the Church has ever stopped to consider that Louise Brown might someday want to enter the Church.[34] *Donum Vitae* is not a barrier to anyone's conversion. Furthermore, neither Church officials nor anyone else wants to judge the loving dispositions of Dr. Steinberg's clients. But their love cannot be directed toward babies who do not exist and, more than likely, will never exist. The Church does love Steinberg's clients and all the babies conceived through IVF, but in its realism, advises them to love what is real and consider the risks they assume when they choose IVF.

The Church holds that God is the author of life. Therefore, any involvement in procreation is an involvement with God the Creator, a being of supreme Holiness in whom love and life are inseparable. Such a realization should occasion a profound sense of humility in husbands and wives. In approaching God, one should be filled with a great sense of awe. In

[33] "Advice High on Theology, Low on Compassion", *The National Catholic Reporter,* March 20, 1987, p. 14.

[34] Radio broadcast, KGIL, NBC affiliate in Los Angeles, with host Carol Hemingway, Dec. 11, 1987, 6:30 P.M. EST.

communicating with God, the language of the imperative is always inappropriate. Whereas God can command man, man can never command God. In prayer, one petitions; in confession, one asks for forgiveness; in courtship, one proposes; in ignorance, one seeks enlightenment. So too, in sexual intercourse, the submissive posture must always be observed; one invokes new life but can never demand it. God must always reserve the right to say "yes" or "no". That right must always be respected. The Faustean desire to seize control of life at its origin is tantamount to attempting to usurp the role of the Creator, of trying to "play God".

Lisa Sowle Cahill criticizes the Instruction for reflecting a "siege mentality" and a form of "religious authoritarianism". [35] She also criticizes the document for opposing "both married couples who unite their own ova and sperm by means of technological substitutes for sexual intercourse and persons who go beyond the marital relation to use or act as donors and surrogates". [36] The document never suggests that these two different situations represent the same degree of illicitness. Cahill, however, appears to miss the principle that binds them together, namely, that they both represent a radical disruption in the continuity between love and life. The Vatican is merely consistent on this point and identifies it wherever it appears, whether within or outside of marriage. It should not be accused of reflecting either a "siege mentality" or of "religious authoritarianism".

Both Cahill and McCormick reject the Church's *principled* approach. They prefer one based on the *experiences* married couples have had with reproductive technologies. [37] They do

[35] "The Vatican Document on Bioethics: Two Responses", *America,* March 28, 1987, p. 247.

[36] Ibid.

[37] See also Richard McCormick, "The Vatican Document in Bioethics", *America,* January 17, 1987, p. 27: ". . . whether in vitro fertilization promotes or undermines the 'person integrally and adequately considered' awaits our experience and reflection upon it. It cannot be deduced."

not explain, however, why principles that protect life in its origin and the dignity of procreation are not valid principles. Principles are needed to protect couples from the unfortunate and sometimes even tragic experiences Cahill and McCormick seem to welcome in the interest of collecting data. But even if they had the data they desired, they would still be faced with the need for constructing principles. The Vatican bases its principles on an understanding of the nature of new human life and the meaning of human procreation. Its experiences went into the process of coming to know these realities. The experiences of individual couples cannot contradict these principles, although they can becloud them.

Cahill and McCormick may be allowing their legitimate and commendable sympathy for infertile couples to obscure their appreciation for the very principles that are designed to protect these couples. Nonetheless, their sympathetic concern itself is principled: "One should always be sympathetically disposed toward married couples who experience great suffering due to the fact that they cannot have children of their own." How could "experience" possibly contradict this principle? Could one ever come to the determination through experience that some of these couples do not deserve human sympathy? It would not seem so. Cahill and McCormick regard their own principle as exceptionless, but not those which *Donum Vitae* propounds.

Many people in contemporary society, where the ethic of hedonism prevails, simply assume that anything that causes people pain is by that very fact morally wrong. Conversely, they also assume that anything that brings pleasure is morally right.[38] Human sympathy is naturally directed toward people who are suffering. But to use sympathy as moral philosophy—to use sympathy to frame principles—is to lose sight of morality altogether. It is one thing to sympathize with people

---

[38] Dinesh D'Souza, "The Pope and the Petri Dish", *Crisis,* January 1988, p. 28.

who are confined to prisons. But one should not draw from this sympathy the conclusion that all prisoners should be released. In the process of moral maturation, suffering is sometimes necessary. Personal suffering is often a precondition to gaining a deeper awareness of the moral order. The Vatican holds that concerns for human dignity should predominate over those for technology and expediency. For many people, this is not an easy principle to accept.

In Shannon and Cahill's book *Religion and Artificial Reproduction,* the authors argue that the "occasional" use of contraception to avoid pregnancy and the "occasional" use of artificial means to bring it about should not be disapproved in principle, but judged in the light of the "committed love relationship of the couple in its totality". [39] This argument was repudiated in *Humanae Vitae* [40] and again in *Donum Vitae* when the Instruction advised that "the process of IVF and ET must be judged in itself and cannot borrow its definitive moral quality from the totality of conjugal life of which it becomes part nor from the conjugal acts which may precede or follow it." [41] Shannon and Cahill seem to forget that in defending life in its origin and the dignity of procreation, the Church is defending marriage in its totality. Contraception and artificial reproduction are in violation of this totality. The Church encourages married couples to achieve a wholeness of compatible elements rather than a "totality" consisting of elements that are mutually contradictory. God may judge people on the whole of their lives rather than on certain specific acts, but the important point here is that specific acts involving contraception and artificial reproductive technologies can deviate from a vision of the whole and can be radically incompatible with both marriage and personhood. In looking at the "texture" of married life rather than its substance, the authors ignore the moral quality of the very issues they are trying to

[39] p. 138.
[40] 14: *AAS* 60 (1968) pp. 490–91.
[41] II B, 5.

affirm. Secular law does not operate this way. Society does not permit a "solid citizen" to rob a bank "occasionally" (even if he needs the money to further the noble causes that solidify his social standing).

Donum Vitae reaffirms the traditional Church teaching that the genesis of human life should be in the embrace of marital love. This is an intensely realistic doctrine. The Church understands only too well that any break in the continuity of love provides a point of entrance for an assortment of unhealthy viruses, including pride, envy, greed, and competitiveness. The Church has no illusions about the human condition. It knows that giving license to desire leads logically to placing desperate infertile couples at the mercy of unscrupulous clinicians. It also knows that even with the best of intentions and the sternest of character, artificial reproduction inevitably compromises both the gift aspect of new life as well as the integrity of sexual love. This teaching may fall on many deaf ears, but it is worth stating and restating because it is a perennial truth—about man and the order of creation—that needs to be told as long as people confuse love with desire.

Chapter Five

The Politicization of Motherhood

Sociologist Kristin Luker makes an important observation in her book *Abortion and the Politics of Motherhood* when she points out that "the abortion debate is so passionate and hard-fought *because it is a referendum on the place and meaning of motherhood*." [1] The widespread acceptance of contraception and sterilization, as well as abortion, has done a great deal to compromise the mystique of motherhood, if not dethrone it entirely. The more society accords respectability to using these technologies in making reproductive choices, the more motherhood loses its status as a hallowed vocation and becomes merely another choice. Motherhood has become "politicized", according to Luker, because "feminists" and "housewives" are competing against each other for the right to assign the social place and moral meaning of motherhood that reflect their political viewpoints. The choices that reproductive technology has given women have thus turned motherhood into a political battleground.

The essential weakness in Luker's position is that in seeing all too clearly the politicization of motherhood, she has lost sight of the apolitical, objective reality of motherhood. She is correct in stating that "women come to be pro-life and pro-choice activists as the end result of lives that center around different definitions of motherhood." [2] But she is less than correct when she implies that all contemporary views of motherhood are political and none are realistic.

It may seem presumptuous, in a society that is as committed to relativism as ours is, to suggest that one definition may be right and another wrong, that one view is realistic and

[1] Los Angeles: The University of California Press, 1984, p. 193.
[2] Ibid., p. 214.

69

another illusory. Yet the pejorative connotation of the word "politicized", in speaking of motherhood being "politicized", suggests the distortion of a reality, its appropriation to popular taste. There is the reality, pure and objective, and there is the "politicization" of that reality. Politics has a way of subjectivizing reality, turning it into something that better accords with people's wishes. Women as well as motherhood have been and continue to be "politicized". What we need is a process of "depoliticization" in order to restore our understanding of women and motherhood to what they are in themselves rather than what rival factions would prefer them to be.

Margaret Atwood's novel *The Handmaid's Tale* offers a clear illustration of the politicization of both women and motherhood. In the novel, a regime of fundamentalist Christians overtakes the government, suspends the Constitution, and establishes a highly structured and restrictive society in which only the fertile women are valuable, and then only for their ability to be surrogate mothers, to bear children for an aging upper echelon of "Commanders" and their wives. As one handmaid describes her station: "We are two-legged wombs, that's all; sacred vessels, ambulatory chalices."[3]

Atwood's satire could not be appreciated if it were not for the fact that her readers had some understanding of women in their undistorted, unpoliticized reality. Radical Feminism complains vociferously about how women have been "politicized". Yet their remedy—more unfettered choice—is the very factor, enlarged by reproductive technology, that has intensified the politicization of women and motherhood. For if it is mere choice that determines the place and value of motherhood, then motherhood is caught in the web of subjective preference and loses its objective meaning. Once choice is severed from truth, the processes of "politicization" take over. Ironically, the real remedy for the politicization of women

[3] Boston: Houghton Mifflin, 1986, p. 136.

that feminists claim they are seeking is the very last thing they would be able to recognize. Freedom apart from truth inevitably leads to chaos.

Reproductive technology now makes it possible for a woman who lacks a uterus to have her own baby. This represents a "choice" on a level of reproductive freedom that was formerly reserved to the imagination of science fiction writers. By a combination of in vitro fertilization and embryo transfer to a surrogate gestator, the "infertile" woman can become the mother of her own genetically related child. But what about the host mother? According to Harriet Blankfeld, who directs a surrogacy program, "The host mother is truly, in every respect, an incubator."[4]

This extraordinary remark, a paradigm of extremism, would qualify Harriet Blankfeld for the role of a high-level Commander in *The Handmaid's Tale*. Yet, in her own mind, she sees it as heralding a new breakthrough for women's freedom. Have Ms. Blankfield and the host mother both become "politicized" without their even suspecting it?"

Dr. Robert Edwards, who teamed with Patrick Steptoe in supervising the world's first IVF baby, spoke these tender words after the birth of Louise Brown: "The last time I saw her, she was just eight cells in a test tube. She was beautiful then, and she's beautiful now."[5]

These are the words of the same man who would have directed the abortion of Louise Brown if there was but a "suspicion" that something might be wrong during the pregnancy, who stated that "fertilization is only incidental to the beginning of life",[6] and who proposed that human embryos be

[4] "New Method Makes Fetus for a Woman Who Has No Uterus", *The New York Times*, Nov. 22, 1985.

[5] P. Gynne, "Was the Birth of Louise Brown Only a Happy Accident?" *Science Digest*, Oct. 1978, p. 7.

[6] R. G. Edwards, "Fertilization of Human Eggs In Vitro: Morals, Ethics and the Law", *Quarterly Review of Biology*, March 1974, vol. 49, no. 1, pp. 13–14.

implanted in such animals as sheep, rabbits, and pigs.[7] His encomium to Louise Brown was more a political statement than a reflection of his inner convictions.

The recognition that women and motherhood have been politicized has led to an overreaction on the part of archfeminists who conclude that even personal activities, especially those of a sexual nature, including marriage, lovemaking, and orgasm are intensely political.[8] "The personal is political" has become a shibboleth for their movement. As political scientist Jean Bethke Elshtain points out, "Nothing 'personal' is exempt, then, from political definition, direction, and manipulation—neither sexual intimacy, nor love, nor parenting."[9]

The word "political", according to the feminist script, describes activities that exert power over individuals in an oppressive way that deprives them of opportunities for self-fulfillment. Impregnation, then, would be an evident political act since it is viewed as oppressing women. "Even if a woman wants to have children," writes Simone de Beauvoir, the intellectual matriarch of radical Feminism, "she must think very hard about the conditions in which she will have to bring them up, because child-bearing, at the moment, is real slavery."[10] According to Shulamith Firestone, whose books have been required reading in programs of Women's Studies, "The heart of woman's oppression is her childbearing and childrearing roles", functions that provide the ground for all the other inequities against women.[11] Monique Wittig speaks of libera-

[7] "Creating Monsters", *TFP Newsletter*, 4, 11 (1985), p. 10.

[8] See Susan Lydon, "The Politics of Orgasm", Robin Morgan, ed., *Sisterhood Is Powerful*, (New York: Vintage, 1970); John Leo, "On the Trail of the Big O", *Time*, March 3, 1986, p. 64.

[9] *Public Man, Private Woman* (Princeton, New Jersey: Princeton University Press, 1981), p. 217.

[10] "Talking to de Beauvoir", *Spare Rib* (March 1977): 2.

[11] *The Dialectic of Sex* (New York: Bantam Books, 1971), p. 72.

[12] "Paradigm", G. Stambolian & E. Marks, eds., *Homosexualities and French Literature* (Ithaca, New York: Cornell University Press, 1979), pp. 118–119.

tion from "the sexual economy imposed on us by the domi-
nant heterosexuality."[12] And to the eternal question, "Where
do children come from", Jeffner Allen, who sees motherhood
as the "annihilation" of women, states: "Children come from
patriarchal [male] sexuality's use of woman's body as a re-
source to reproduce men and the world of men."[13] Her escape
from male tyranny is through evacuation: "I am endangered
by motherhood. In evacuation from motherhood, I claim my
life, body, world, as an end in itself."[14]

Radical feminists reduce the complexus of society to a pair of
simple equations: (1) the personal is political, and (2) politics is
power. All human actions, then, revolve around the paradigm
case of Oppressor and the Oppressed. "There is nothing we
do," writes Nancy Henley, "no matter how individual and personal it seems—that does not reflect our participation in a
power system."[15] The only options people seem to have, according to Henley, are either dominance or submission.

This utterly cynical viewpoint can hardly serve the cause of
liberation. Defining the person in purely political terms and
casting him in the dual role of oppressor and oppressed rule
out the possibility of cultivating a society in which values
such as freedom, equality, and self-fulfillment could be realized. The identification of the person with power politics
leads directly to the disappearance of the person and, therefore, to the disappearance of any hope of establishing a society
where personal values reign. It also leads to the cognitive
disappearance of reality, that is, of the human ability to see
things as they are in themselves, undistorted by political ideologies and partisan viewpoints.

Politics is a system of social interactions that is devised by

---

[13] "Motherhood: The Annihilation of Women", Marilyn Pearsall, ed.,
Women and Values: Reading in Recent Feminist Philosophy (Belmont, California:
Wadsworth, 1986), p. 92.

[14] Ibid.

[15] *Body Politics: Power, Sex, and Nonverbal Communication* (New York:
Touchstone Books, 1986), p. 197.

persons. The person is prior to politics. The person also transcends politics, as evidenced by the fact that throughout history man has constantly been changing his various political systems. This is not to say that political structures do not influence people. They do. But the person and the political structure are distinguishable entities. They are dialectically related to each other, capable of mutual adjustment and correction. At times, when politics does not serve its primary purpose, it can be oppressive; at other times, when it does serve that purpose, it can be liberating. To say that the personal is political is to understand neither. It is to identify man with his political structures and to deny him his capacities for personal authenticity. Hegel identified the *real* with the *rational*. The folly of this position was amply demonstrated when he tried to explain the real solely from the perspective of the rational. The folly of the feminist dictum that what is *personal* is *political* carries a similar methodological danger since it implies that the personal can be adequately understood solely from the point of view of the political. This, of course, represents the dissolution of the personal.

The source of sexuality's politicization is not the fact of pregnancy, but the failure to honor and protect pregnancy with personal values. In the absence of personal values, pregnancy becomes a battleground for a host of impersonal concerns that include the political as well as the commercial, experimental, egoistical, carnal, and even diabolical. In order to avoid the first step toward the politicization of pregnancy, it is necessary to practice those personal values marriage embodies, namely, love, unity, and fidelity, together with all the other personal values that spousal and parental responsibility entails. Marriage is essentially and profoundly personal. It becomes vulnerable to politicization only when the personal values that protect it are compromised or withdrawn.

Reproductive technologies such as in vitro fertilization, embryo transfer, and surrogate motherhood represent threats to marriage and parenthood. In IVF, conception takes place apart from the woman's body and independent of the marital embrace. Embryo transfer may involve a third party, such as a donor or a surrogate gestator. Surrogate motherhood also involves third (and sometimes additional) parties; it also bifurcates maternity by separating the genetic mother from the gestational mother. These technologies compromise the personal values of love, unity, and fidelity that are needed to protect marriage from the impersonal processes of politicization. By exteriorizing human procreation and involving outsiders such as surrogates, brokers, businessmen, etc., several dangers arise. Among these are that power replaces love and that fundamental realities—especially the unborn child and the gestating woman—are no longer perceived as they are but are reinterpreted according to arbitrary and fluctuating demands.

Radical feminists need not look anywhere else than to their own rationalizations for abortion in order to find a model example of politicizing pregnancy. First, the unborn child is depersonalized; it is presumed to be only a part of the woman's body. Then the abortion procedure itself, which is an act of power that deprives another of his potential for self-fulfillment, is politically reinterpreted as merely a "choice". Hence, one is not pro-abortion, just pro-choice. Neither the victim nor the nature of the act are recognized or acknowledged for what they are. Personal values are extinguished, reality is distorted. Radical feminists are right about one thing, that the processes of depersonalization and power politics can go undetected by their own practitioners.

Technologized parenthood has its own built-in dangers. Against a social backdrop of abortionism, feminism, commercialism, capitalism, hedonism, and egoism, these dangers become greatly magnified. In Robert Coles's review of *Birth Mother: The Story of America's First Legal Surrogate Mother,* we find a candid and decidedly unflattering portrait of some of the professionals who were involved:

. . . a self-centered, arrogant, callous physician, eager as can
be to show himself off, pose for cameras, rake in cash while he
became known nationally as someone who arranges surrogate
pregnancies; a lawyer all too pushy and demanding; and worst
of all, a minister who not only was eager to be photographed,
to appear on television—nothing special these days—but was
willing to betray confidences, curry favor with reporters, strut
and pose endlessly at the expense of a vulnerable woman who
had turned to him for advice, if not consolation.[16]

Given the vicissitudes of power politics, surrogate motherhood, from the standpoint of valuating the unborn and its
gestating mother, is the opposite of abortion. In abortion, the
child is depersonalized while the mother is praised for her
courage to choose. By contrast, in surrogacy, the child is ele-
vated to the status of a "tenant" while its mother depreciates
to the status of an "incubator".

A few years ago a woman became a mother despite the fact
that she lacked a uterus. This incident offers a good example
of how human values rise and fall in accordance with the latest
technology. This woman's genetic offspring was transferred
from its origin in a petri dish to the body of the gestational
mother who gave birth to it.[17] The Court awarded custody to
the genetic mother, reasoning that the gestational mother
(who served as a surrogate gestator) functioned merely as a
"human incubator".[18] There was never any dispute over the
humanness of the offspring, either when it was in a petri dish
or when it resided in the womb of a surrogate incubator.

The arbitrary quality of the judge's decision in this case, the
fact that the adopting parents paid $40,000 to get the child
they wanted, and certain other actions of a disingenuous nature, have prompted George Annas of Boston University's
School of Medicine to make the following comment: "If we

[16] *The New York Times,* June 26, 1988, Sec. 7, p. 34.
[17] *Smith and Smith v. Jones and Jones,* 85–532014 D2, Detroit, Michigan, 3d
Jud. Dist., March 14, 1986, Battani, J.
[18] Ibid., slip op. at 9.

really believe money and contracts should rule, then the identity of the child's mother will depend upon contract and payment only, and both genetics and gestation (and therefore all biological ties) will be irrelevant."[19]

Annas is sensitive to the objective reality of motherhood and is less than eager to see it redefined according to terms established by the contracting parties. A well-known surrogate clinic on the East Coast illustrates how arbitrary surrogate contracts can be in valuating the mother and the child. This particular clinic has drawn up a contract stating that the surrogate gets $10,000 for the delivery of a healthy child and nothing for a "defective" child; further, she must pay the father $25,000 if she decides to keep the child. Is it reasonable, one might well ask, that the cost of the child leaps to $25,000 if the birth mother keeps it? Or is this higher fee to be construed as a way of punishing the mother for deciding to keep the child?[20]

When the *New York Times* wants to justify abortion, it has no difficulty valuating the unborn as less than human. But when it wants to advance the cause of surrogacy, that same pre-human is suddenly transvaluated into a person with a name. A *Times* editorial speaks about an unborn surrogate child named "Baby Thrane" who is "residing in a rented womb".[21] In this case, the unborn is humanized while the surrogate becomes a "rented womb". The rhetoric is most effective. Psychotherapists attest that surrogates identify themselves not as mothers but as incubators.[22] A surrogate is often indoctrinated into thinking that although she is carrying a precious little baby, she is not the real mother because she is carrying it for some-

---

[19] "The Baby Broker Boom", *Hastings Center Report,* vol. 16, no. 3, June 1986, p. 31.

[20] Robert Coles, "So You Fell in Love With Your Baby?" *The New York Times,* June 26, 1988, Section 7 (Book Reviews).

[21] April 1981.

[22] See Gena Corea, *The Mother Machine* (New York: Harper and Row, 1985), p. 222.

one else. This devaluation of the woman, which radically subordinates her to the child she carries, makes surrogacy highly susceptible to exploitation. A teenage Mexican surrogate, for example, testified that she was confined against her will in the house of a California sperm donor for the duration of her pregnancy.[23] The surrogate and the couple who hired her were granted joint custody of the child eight months after the baby was born. They were also ordered not to make disparaging remarks about one another in front of the child.[24]

In surrogacy agreements, the baby is paramount. But if the infertile parties who contracted for the child divorce or change their minds, or if the baby is not normal either before or after birth, they may direct the abortion of the child or reject it. The baby's value rests precariously on the couple's stability as well as on its own degree of normalcy. The baby that an infertile couple so desperately needs can easily become the "mistake" that nobody wants.

Another reproductive technique, known as "surrogate embryo transfer", introduces a slightly different set of values. In this procedure, a volunteer agrees to be impregnated through artificial insemination and then undergoes, a few days later, a treatment called lavage to wash the embryo out of her uterus. The embryo is then transferred to a second woman. This second woman is the one who wants to rear the child and be recognized as its legal mother. She is unable to produce fertilizable eggs and therefore is reliant on the volunteer's role. This method is safer for the volunteer than achieving conception through IVF because it avoids the very real hazards of egg retrieval through laparoscopic surgery.

In surrogate embryo transfer (SET), which is also termed "prenatal adoption", the baby and the gestating woman are

[23] *Surrogacy Arrangements Act of 1987: Hearings on H.R. 2433 Before the Subcom. on Transportation, Tourism, and Hazardous Materials of the House Comm. on Energy and Commerce,* 100th Cong., 2d Sess. (1987).

[24] "Surrogate Mom Gets Joint Custody", *The Kitchener-Waterloo Record,* February 24, 1987, A3.

highly valued, whereas the volunteer, who is the genetic mother, is regarded as a mere "donor". In terms of valuating motherhood, the SET procedure stands in sharp contrast with surrogate gestation. In surrogate gestation, it is the genetic contributor and not the gestator who assumes the mantle of importance.

Researchers at the Harbor–UCLA Medical Center in Torrance, California, were the first to devise the SET procedure. In advertising for volunteers, they requested "egg donors" for their "ovum transfer" project.[25] This conscious bit of deception lured 380 volunteers to the program. These young women were not, of course, simply requested to "donate an egg". Each was asked to endure repeated artificial insemination attempts in the interest of achieving conception, to undergo lavage to flush out the embryonic child, to submit to an abortion in the event the lavage procedure failed, to risk pelvic infection, venereal disease, and ectopic pregnancy, and to abstain from sexual intercourse in order to provide assurance that the child conceived was the client's.

The Center reported to the Press on February 3, 1984, that 10 volunteer "donors" were inseminated 46 times with sperm from the husbands of 13 wives who were prospective recipients. In 42 attempts at uterine lavage, 18 embryos were flushed out. Two recipient women had apparently normal pregnancies. Two women were impaired in the process. One suffered an ectopic pregnancy that led to the surgical removal of her right tube. The other woman, a donor, was left with an embryo inside her when it could not be flushed out. She spontaneously aborted nine days after her expected period.

The contrast between the status of the volunteer donor— who was deliberately deceived and duped into assuming unreasonable risks to her health and reproductive future—and the baby she was trying to conceive for an infertile couple is

---

[25] Corea, pp. 80–95. See also Shari O'Brien, "The Itinerant Embryo and the Neo-Nativity Scene: Bifurcating Biological Maternity", *Utah Law Review*, 1987: 1, pp. 6–9.

another striking example of the inverse evaluation of that which is found in the abortion picture. Pioneers of the SET project hired a California public relations firm to help them with their advertising. The firm came up with the idea of using the letters B-A-B-Y as the last four digits for the program's telephone number.[26] The "donor", it will be remembered, allegedly donated an egg. But the egg became a "baby", not when it was fertilized, but when it was transferred to the infertile mother who would gestate it.

Richard Seed, one of SET's pioneers, envisioned opening up a string of twenty to thirty embryo transfer clinics across the country. Expecting to win international acclaim for this work in this area, he stated in a 1980 interview: "I don't mind telling you that I expect to get a Nobel Prize." He believed that he would earn the coveted Prize if he could accomplish two things: (1) produce the first human pregnancy through embryo transfer (which he accomplished in 1983); (2) achieve pregnancy in a postmenopausal woman (which he is apparently still working on).[27]

Politics and pride have been an integral part of UCLA's SET project. In a March 1984 issue of the *Journal of the American Medical Association* (JAMA),[28] the author writes favorably about SET and makes the remark that we should worry less about the rights of SET children than about the desires of infertile couples. The article creates the impression that it is a non-partisan, scientific evaluation of SET. In truth, as George Annas points out, Marie Bustillo, who wrote the article, had been paid by the research team at UCLA to write a document, under contract, that helped them get their initial SET protocol through Harbor–UCLA's Institutional Review Board in 1981. Her JAMA article was based on that work. Thus, what was

---

[26] Ibid., pp. 86–87.

[27] Ibid., p. 95.

[28] M. Bustillo, et al., "Nonsurgical Ovum Transfer as a Treatment in Infertile Women: Preliminary Experience", *Journal of the American Medical Association* 251 (March 2, 1984), p. 1171.

prepared for the JAMA readership was not an evaluation of SET by a neutral observer.[29] It is no doubt true that the quest for promotion, tenure, and prizes is as much a deterrent to disclosing all the possible harmful effects of a particular reproductive technology as is the profit motive.

The politics of power have a decisive effect on the various and fluctuating evaluations of pregnancy, motherhood, fatherhood, and the child in the womb. Through the prism of self-interest, everything is distorted. It is only through the window of love that the values associated with human procreation are recognized for what they are, objectively and in accordance with their being. Love is often dismissed as a subjective experience. It is subjective, however, only in the sense that what the lover sees, he grasps in his subjectivity, that is, in himself as a subject. But what he sees is objectively discerned. As Chesterton has said, "Love is not blind; that is the last thing that it is. Love is bound; and the more it is bound the less it is blind." Power, however, is blind because the subject is more interested in his own subjectivity, in his own advantage, than in the good of the object. In this regard, love is more realistic than power.

Power is often said to be more realistic than love because, unlike the latter, it is willing to use deception, exploitation, pressure, and force in order to accomplish its aims. This Machiavellian sense of realism, however, is unrealistic in that it remains blind to the real, objective values of what it is trying to manipulate. Moreover, it is unrealistic in a more practical sense insofar as it incites other people to operate in a similar fashion, thereby bringing about a conflict or power that inevitably must be resolved either through force or through the force of law. The clash of divergent lines of power cannot be endured for very long.

Reproductive technologies—from contraception to surrogate embryo transfer—have greatly enlarged the horizon of

[29] "Surrogate Embryo Transfer: The Perils of Parenting", *The Hastings Center Report,* vol. 14, no. 3, June 1984, p. 26.

reproductive choice. Feminists, in general, have welcomed these innovations insofar as they have contributed to reproductive freedom and have given women greater control of their bodies. Nonetheless, this freedom is more an illusion than a reality. As motherhood becomes more and more dissociated from marriage, intercourse, conception, and gestation, its place in society and its moral significance grows increasingly arbitrary. Motherhood is now merely one of a number of choices a woman can make, and the particular way in which she becomes a mother is also a mere matter of choice. A woman no longer conforms to motherhood, she reinvents it.

Today, a woman can avoid marriage, intercourse, conception, and gestation and still have a child to whom she is genetically related. IVF in combination with surrogate gestation makes that possible. Or she can be married, conceive, gestate, and deliver a child and not be considered a mother. Surrogacy makes that possible.

Technology has freed motherhood from its traditional identity. But women are not enjoying their new opportunities to choose motherhood in the manner that suits their lifestyle. Rather, they are engaged in fierce and deeply emotional struggles both in and out of court over which mother is the real mother and who should have legal custody of which children. Dissolving the integral identity of motherhood has left it unprotected and vulnerable to new meanings and definitions. The struggle to project new meanings onto traditional motherhood is essentially a political activity, involving law, medicine, business, the Media, and public opinion. In this way motherhood has become politicized.

Chesterson once said that you can free a tiger of its bars, but if you free it of its stripes, you'll find that you no longer have a tiger.[30] Reproductive technologies have created the illusion

---

[30] *Orthodoxy* in *Collected Works of G. K. Chesterton,* vol. 1 (San Francisco: Ignatius Press, 1986), p. 243.

that you can free motherhood of its essence and still have motherhood, that you can politicize motherhood by assigning it a host of arbitrary redefinitions and somehow preserve its moral meaning.

Freedom that is not an illusion maintains its realism because it is anchored to what is true. The only freedom of choice that serves motherhood expresses itself in the form of recognizing what motherhood is and honoring and protecting its dignity, its nature, and its enduring moral significance.

Chapter Six

Marriage for One: Self-Insemination and the Expendability of Men

Einstein once said that he believed in making things as simple as possible, but no simpler. One of the enduring charms of the architect of relativity was his facility for making statements as valid for philosophy as for science. "Every two-legged animal is a metaphysician", he once remarked.[1]

What happens when we cross the Simplicity Barrier? Science offers instructive paradigms. We learn from chemistry, for example, that the simplest part of water that is still water is the molecule H_2O. Water is a neutral substance, which neither burns nor supports combustion; in fact, it is used to put out fires. But if water is reduced to its atomic components—hydrogen and oxygen—it ceases to be water and begins to exhibit antithetical properties. Hydrogen is highly flammable, and oxygen supports combustion. The two elements, when taken separately, make an explosive pair.

If we reduce married partners to two unrelated individuals, do we still have marriage, a "marriage for one"? Do we know what we get, or how antagonistic it could be to everything we are as human beings?

The current phrase "sex for one" borrows respectability from the world of restaurant etiquette. "Table for one" and "party of one" set the sophisticated tone. It is an attempt to make nature imitate art. The phrase is the title of a recent

---

[1] Quoted by Stanley L. Jaki, *The Absolute beneath the Relative and Other Essays* (Lanham, Maryland: University Press of America, 1988), p. 49. Fr. Jaki states that Einstein's greatest discovery was the discovery of metaphysics, that his metaphysics was steeped in realism, in the study of the physical, calling to mind Anteus of old who could not retain his strength except by touching the ground with his feet at regular intervals (p. 51).

book by Betty Dodson—*Sex for One: The Joy of Selfloving.*[2]
Dodson was the author of *Liberating Masturbation,* a popular
tract that recommended "intense love affairs with ourselves"
for women.[3]

It is questionable whether *Sex for One* is about sex at all. Is
talking to oneself (no matter how wonderful a talker you may
be) a real conversation? Is it possible to fall in love with yourself? And supposing it were, should you be trying?

Enthusiasts for this practice include people like Phil Donahue, the TV personality. In an advertisement for the book he
says, "In the age of AIDS, more and more people are having
sex with themselves. It's certainly a lot safer! It is quite a natural experience."[4]

The idea of "sex for one" is not mere narcissism. It is rather
narcissism with the pretense of humanism, solitude with the
illusion of community. Donahue could have said: "In a world
of alienation, the last thing humans need is a book that instructs them in how to use sex, whose purpose is communal,
to deepen their alienation and compound their misery." The
review of Francis Canavan, a political scientist, was more telling (if droll): "We may hail the book as signalizing the final
triumph of liberal individualism, a climax in which the self
communes with itself alone."[5] It was for such reasons that another critic once described masturbation as "the sexual equivalent of a Cartesian soliloquy".[6]

The word *joy* is frequently misappropriated by those in the
"respectable" sex trade, in books like *The Joy of Sex.* It is
worth observing that "sex for one" cannot bring joy, for joy
is an experience of the whole person. The hedonist tries to

[2] New York: Crown, 1987.
[3] Quoted in *The Next Whole Earth Catalog* (New York: Random House, 1981), p. 340.
[4] Book Review, *New York Times,* January 24, 1988.
[5] "Commentary", *Catholic Eve,* no. 54, March 17, 1988, p. 2.
[6] Gerald Runkle, *Ethics: An Examination of Contemporary Moral Problems* (New York: Holt, Rinehart & Winston, 1982), p. 107.

avoid the difficulties of life by confining its meaning to the pursuit of pleasure. Joy has a positive character. Hedonism is negative: a release from tension, an avoidance of pain and grief, a denial of human nature and human society.[7] It is a rejection of reality. Joy embraces reality: a person must have come to terms with the world, to be capable of positive joyfulness.

Hedonism has much in common with skepticism. Both represent a withdrawal of the individual from reality, though in the former the individual separates himself from society, whereas in the latter, the mind is severed from truth. In both cases, the individual isolates himself from moral realities and attempts to save himself at any price. Both attitudes fail because they deny human nature and the structure of reality. One can experience joy only on reality's terms.

Dodson and Donahue could not be so uninhibited about their public promotion of masturbation if they were not confident that significant forces in society were already on their side. Shere Hite and Barbara Seaman had paved the way for the acceptance of female hedonism in the seventies. The *Hite Report* argues that heterosexual intercourse is an inadequate substitute for normal masturbation. "Intercourse", according to Ms. Hite, "was never meant to stimulate women to orgasm". It may provide a "desirable form of release", but should not be used to substitute for "*real* orgasms".[8] In her best-selling book, *Free and Female,* Barbara Seaman celebrates the solitary act as signifying sexual emancipation from men:

> I think it's wonderful that women have discovered masturbation, because it will enable us to keep apart from men as long as necessary. . . . Some of the women I know are so pathetic. They run around looking for a man, any man, just because they don't know how to masturbate.[9]

[7] Kurt Goldstein, *Human Nature in the Light of Psychopathology* (New York: Schocken, 1966), p. 228.

[8] New York: Dell, 1976. See also "The Play's the Thing", *Time,* Oct. 25, 1976, p. 32.

[9] New York: Fawcett World, 1972, p. 69.

Ms. magazine was no less enthsuiastic over "sex for one", stating that "even if you have a lot of sex, you might feel like making love to yourself—every so often—or often".[10] Female masturbation has become an inseparable part of the feminist movement. "For all we know," writes *Time* essayist John Leo, "women who used to fake vaginal orgasms for their hubbies began to fake clitoral ones for the women's movement."[11] And its forms of promotion range from the lapel button ("Make love with someone you can trust") to the commencement address ("Think clitoris", as valedictorian Alix Shulman advised).[12] Men became the movement's inevitable casualties: ". . . once women discover the clitoris rather than the vagina as the source of the orgasm, man becomes sexually expendable and women are able to satisfy themselves or each other."[13]

Once the Simplicity Barrier is broken, the parts replace the whole. "Sex for one" provides the logical precedent for its correlative fragment—"marriage for one".

Earlier we mentioned the case of Lesley Northrup, a woman priest in the Episcopal Church. In addition to her priestly functions, she teaches liturgics at Virginia Theological Seminary and writing at the University of Maryland. When she was forty she experienced a "deep urge to create and nurture new life that would not be denied".[14] But she had no plans to marry and felt that adoption was beyond her means. On three successive nights in December of 1985, she introduced sperm

[10] B. Ehreinrich, E. Hess and G. Jacobs, "Re-making Love, the Real Sexual Revolution", *Ms.*, July 1986, p. 82.

[11] "On the Trail of the Big O," *Time,* March 3, 1986, p. 64.

[12] See Michael Levin, *Feminism and Freedom* (New Brunswick, New Jersey: Transaction Books, 1986), p. 265.

[13] Ann Koedt, "The Myth of the Vaginal Orgasm", *Notes from the Second Year: Women's Liberation* (New York: Radical Feminists, 1976), p. 41. See also John Vertefeuille, *Sexual Chaos* (Westchester, Illinois: Crossway Books, 1988), p. 60.

[14] Marjorie Hyer, "A Need Examined, a Prayer Fulfilled: Unmarried Priest Bears Child by Artificial Insemination", *Washington Post,* Dec. 7, 1987, p. 1.

into her body from three donors. Nine months later she gave birth to a girl, Evan Arandes Northrup. The mother does not know, nor does she wish to know, which of the donors is the biological father. Nor do *they* wish to know. Two of them are priests in her church. Their roles were formally restricted to making a sperm donation, receiving a birth announcement, and sending a christening gift.

Northrup believes she has done nothing to strain her vows or compromise any biblical command. She says that masturbation is not prohibited by the Episcopal Church, that none of the men are married, that there was no surrogacy, that the donors were unpaid volunteers. Her parents are "very supportive", her parishoners are "extremely supportive", and Bishop Paul Moore, who ordained her in 1981, has given her his unqualified support. "As her bishop," he comments, "I can affirm that which Lesley has done." In fact, things have gone so well that Lesley plans to have another baby by the same method.

She has been criticized by some men for planning a family in the absence of a husband, but she dismisses them, saying, "Building a family without a male being in it seems threatening to men." In her mind, none of the donors were fathers in any sense. They were merely "donating a necessary element for something, not of creating a baby, not as potential fathers".[15]

Fatherhood is a real value. Coming to its defense is not symptomatic of male insecurity but manifests a willingness to exercise responsibility. The male who eschews responsibility is the one more likely to be insecure. Mistaking responsible action, a willingness to care, for insecurity is indicative of a society that regards human alienation as a moral norm.

Miss Northrup's bishop and her parents may have supported her, but several other members of her denomination voiced outrage. After *The Washington Post* carried her story, a

---

[15] Ibid., A34.

number of severely critical letters appeared in a following edition. A rector in her church found Northrup's actions to be "another indicator of the discouraging dehumanizing drift in our society's perceptions of parenthood and family life". A second critic stated her view that "fatherhood is not simply a biological feat (rather easily accomplished), but a lifelong process of involvement with and commitment to one's children". A third expressed astonishment that Rev. Northrup, who is "empowered to solemnize marriage", sounds more like a "Philadelphia lawyer than a priest".[16]

Roe v. Wade in 1973 and *Planned Parenthood v. Danforth* in 1976 had stripped fathers of any legal status in coming to the defense of their own unborn children whose lives were threatened by abortion. Broad social support, rising even from Christian circles, for a view of self-insemination that is intolerant of any male responsibilities is a continuation of abortionism's depreciation of paternity. One lawyer reasons that given the "reproductive autonomy" *Roe v. Wade* granted women, the issue of obtaining a husband's consent for an act such as AID (artificial insemination by donor) on his wife's body "becomes less significant". He adds that a husband would "hope" that his wife would consult him about AID or self-insemination.[17]

Abortionism preaches that the father has no rights in protecting the life of his own unborn child. But it is not bent on dissolving the remaining strands that bind a husband to his wife. Nor does it repudiate the father's initial role as the progenitor of his offspring. If the self-inseminating woman decides to abort, because of displeasing amniocentesis results, for example, she still reserves the right to do so without so much as notifying the child's father. But the feminist ideology

---

[16] "Letter to the Editor", *Washington Post,* Dec. 12, 1987, A22.

[17] George P. Smith, "The Razor's Edge of Human Bonding: Artificial Fathers and Surrogate Mothers", *Western New England Law Review,* vol. 5, no. 4, Spring 1983, p. 643.

of self-insemination goes far beyond abortionism and rules that women do not need husbands in order to raise a family, and mothers do not need fathers to initiate new life (only donors who contribute a "necessary element for something"). Once society decrees that it is acceptable to fragment the male's relationship with marriage and the family, it is not likely that it will want to apply the brakes.

One may learn about the art of self-insemination from the pages of a widely circulated Random House catalogue. Its "Community" section advertises two instruction manuals. They explain how such convenient household utensils as eye-droppers, syringe stalks, and turkey basters can be used to achieve conception without sex and inaugurate families without fathers. One book is promoted with a picture of a smiling young woman holding her one-year-old baby. The woman had inseminated herself using a joint sperm donation from three homosexual friends. The caption expresses "thanks to the growing expertise in amateur insemination by the San Francisco gay community", for "the possibilities for person-making".[18] The ad for the other book advises: "If you know that you don't want the donor in your future, the safest route is to use anonymous donors".[19]

The titles of the two manuals—*Woman Controlled Conception* and *Lesbian Health Matters*—are morbidly, if unconsciously, ironic. Given the specter of AIDS, the use of joint sperm donations from San Francisco area homosexuals makes a farce of "health" and "control". The blurb authors were oblivious, taking refuge in this curious defense of amateur inseminations: "The root word for 'amateur' is love."

Dr. Norma Wikler, who teaches sociology at the University of California, Santa Cruz, says that the incidence of self-insemination is increasing, and she estimates that hundreds of

---

[18] *The Next Whole Earth Catalog* (New York: Random House, 1981), p. 345.
[19] Susan Stern, "Amateur Insemination", *The Next Whole Earth Catalog,* op. cit.

babies have started in this way.[20] "For one reason or another," she notes, many women "may not be in a relationship with a man . . . and they don't want to forego having children." She first encountered the turkey baster phenomenon in 1978 while interviewing women for her book, *Up against the Clock: Career Women Speak on the Choice to Have Children.*[21]

As male expendability increases, the phenomenon of one-gender marriages increases along with it. According to a *New York Times* report, thousands of lesbians are inseminating themselves.[22] Informal networks have been established to help them find sperm donors; support groups sponsor picnics, parties, and other social events to keep lesbians who have children from feeling isolated. A Columbus, Ohio, lawyer says that she knows at least thirty lesbian mothers in and around Columbus. About 40% of the women inseminated at the Sperm Bank of Northern California identify themselves as lesbians—twice as many as in 1982 when the sperm bank opened. The director of the Gay and Lesbian Parents Coalition in Washington, D.C., states that one in twenty lesbians had babies through artificial insemination; three years ago, they estimated one in fifty or a hundred.

Dr. Richard Green, a professor of psychology at UCLA is well aware of the growing phenomenon of husbandless marriages and fatherless families, although he is not particularly disturbed by it: ". . . the issue of children raised without a man in the family has not been studied to be able to predict whether that could lead to other problems."[23]

Do we need studies to affirm the importance of a father to his children? What could these "other problems" be if being

---

[20] Robert Cooke, "Some Single Women Inseminating Selves Artificially", *The Boston Globe,* April 5, 1984.

[21] Ibid.

[22] Gina Kolata, "Lesbian Partners Find the Means to Be Parents", *The New York Times,* January 30, 1989, p. 1.

[23] Ibid.

born and raised without a father is not a problem itself? And how could we recognize these other problems?

Bioethicist John Fletcher remarks that "a physician can act ethically to help a lesbian couple with AID, if the partners show a prevailing pattern of responsibility."[24] Would it be un-ethical to deny AID to such a couple? Is not Fletcher himself, as well as the AID physicians, also depreciating the male role in marriage and parenting?

Gloria Steinem tells us, in her best-seller, *Outrageous Acts and Everyday Rebellions,* that she had come to "replace" her fa-ther who abandoned her when she was ten years old, leaving her to care for his emotionally unstable wife. In addition, she boasts of fulfilling the role of husband, an accomplishment she presumes to share with many of her feminist colleagues: "Now we are becoming the men we wanted to marry".[25] But these roles do not exhaust her Protean versatility. She is also her own mother: "I either gave birth to someone else", she explains, "or I gave birth to myself."[26] In choosing the latter, she was able to realize, in a single person, all the essential roles of the nuclear family—father, mother, and child. It is the ul-timate triumph of liberal individualism—the individual as Triune!

Steinem often dismisses men as expendable, and cynically views traditional marriage as "the only gamble women take . . . or a way of reducing two people to one and a half".[27] By marrying a man, a woman reduces herself by one half. Lesbian liaisons apparently do not produce such existential shrinkage.

---

[24] "Artificial Insemination in Lesbians", *Arch Intern Med,* vol. 145, March 1985, p. 420.

[25] See Michael Jones, "What Happens When Dad Walks Out?" *Fidelity,* July, 1985, pp. 4–7.

[26] Martha Smilgis, "The Dilemma of Childlessness", *Time,* May 2, 1988, p. 88.

[27] See Betty Steele, *The Feminist Takeover* (Richmond Hill, Ontario: Tercet, 1987), p. 59.

One celebrity implies as much when she points out that in the relationship she has with her live-in female lover neither feels any diminishment of her personhood since neither feels obligated to cook meals, clean the house, or do the laundry for the other.[28]

The notion that men are expendable both as husbands and as fathers finds its echo throughout the world of self-insemination. In *Test-Tube Women,* for example, Francie Hornstein states that in seizing the right to donor insemination, lesbians "have taken back a little more of what is rightly ours. . . ."[29] Renate Klein, in an article entitled, "Doing It Ourselves: Self Insemination", discusses how the Feminist Self Insemination Group in England helps in procuring semen from homosexual men. She praises "women-controlled" insemination for breaking out of the stereotype of the "one child–one mother relationship". As a testimonial to the benefits conferred by this form of fecundation, she cites little Catherine, who proudly declares that she has three mothers: "Mum Pauline, Mum Claire and Mum Ann."[30]

In Canada, former *Chatelaine* editor Doris Anderson, in a prominent piece in the *Toronto Star,* glibly promotes single motherhood as if it were a fashion that any trendy sophisticate would be proud of emulating:

> Catherine L. is one of a growing number of women in their 30s—more than three times as many as in 1974—who have opted to have and raise a child on their own. . . . [She is] a well-established accountant five months pregnant through artificial insemination, and planning to raise her baby by herself . . . confident that she can manage both physically and financially. . . .

[28] Uta West, "Forget the Devil—Meet Miss Jones", *Viva,* Nov. 1973, p. 92.

[29] "Children by Donor Insemination", Rita Arditti, et al., eds. *Test-Tube Women: What Future for Motherhood* (Boston: Pandora Press), p. 379.

[30] Arditti, et al., eds., op. cit., p. 388.

> Nancy S., 34 years old, a Ph.D. and a university lecturer, has had three miscarriages and is trying once again. . . . She has never met the prospective father of her child.[31]

The "rights" of offspring conceived by single women through donor insemination to know their fathers or benefit from association with a male parent are not included in the Chapter of Rights in the Canadian Constitution.

Proponents of the "right" of single women to have children of their own argue that society permits mothers to continue to raise their children when their husbands are no longer available. Therefore, there is no reason to prohibit choosing single parenthood, since many single parents are doing their job as well if not better than some married parents who are raising their children together. This argument, however, fails to recognize that the two-parent family is *normative*.

A single mother, in a particular instance, might prove to do a better job of parenting than a given tandem of mother and father. But it is prejudicial to say that this woman would not have become an even more effective parent if she were wedded to a loving and responsible husband. Raising a family remains the kind of job that requires a complete set of parents. And it is precisely the kind of job childrearing is that should always be kept in mind. A particular father might fail to fulfill his role. He might even be a liability in the rearing of his children. This does not mean that his role is not critical or that he can be replaced. It serves only to underscore the serious moral obligation a man assumes when he takes on the role of fatherhood. There is no adequate replacement for fatherhood. Certainly not the well-meaning support groups that organize picnics, parties, and the like. The partners of a loving marriage are more likely to be successful at parenting than a single mother because they more adequately conform to the needs

---

[31] "Women Are Choosing to Go It Alone as Mothers", *The Toronto Star,* Oct. 19, 1985.

that rise from the very nature of child-rearing. They embody the norm and the standard upon which social policy concerning child-rearing should be based.

It is normal for a pianist to have two hands. Paul Wittgenstein, who lost his right arm in World War I, acquired notable facility in performing works written exclusively for the left hand. Ravel, Prokofieff, and Richard Strauss were among the composers who wrote especially for him. Wittgenstein made the best of a bad situation. But no pianist with dexterity in two hands would either disable one hand or restrict his repertoire to concertos for the left hand. Despite Wittgenstein's success, no musician would deliberately put himself under his handicap. Having two hands is normative for a pianist, although being restricted to one does not necessarily put him out of commission. Even Wittgenstein himself would not have chosen to inactivate his right hand.

Another problem concerning the deliberate choosing of single motherhood is that it disparages both fatherhood and husbandhood. To suggest that the presence of a man who is a father to his children and a husband to his wife could not improve the family, is a highly discriminatory judgment against men. It also represents an unconscionable disregard for what must be done so that marriage and parenthood fulfill their destinies.

However successful single-motherhood might be in a particular instance, it would be greatly improved with the presence of a good father who is also a good husband. To think otherwise is to depersonalize certain men and reduce them to the mindless, bodiless, loveless role of sperm donors. In this regard, it is supremely ironic that feminists who object to pornography's reduction of women to their sex parts can champion the reduction of men to their sex cells. In making men microscopic, they may feel they have protected themselves against male villainies. The larger truth, however, is that they have deprived themselves of an invaluable helpmate.

Choosing single-motherhood disparages all men because it presupposes that men are not an essential part of either marriage or the family. In effect, it disenfranchises them from their most natural home. It also disparages marriage and the family themselves, setting lower expectations for them and asking less of what they were instituted to provide.

One should not choose something inferior because what is normative sometimes fails. It is critical to understand what a successful family needs and to subordinate one's energies in the direction of its attainment. A bowman is much more likely to hit the target when he aims at it. "Marriage for one", and its exclusion of men, is essentially aimless, though it cannot avoid wounding parenthood.

Chapter Seven

IVF and the Technologies It has Spawned: A Ten-Year Retrospective

July 25, 1988, commemorated the twentieth anniversary of *Humanae Vitae*. It also marked the tenth birthday of Louise Brown, the first baby conceived in a laboratory dish. The two events this date recalls represent the antipodes of the moral discussion concerning the inseparability of the unitive and procreative dimensions of human sexuality. For many people, the very existence of Louise Brown is the definitive refutation of *Humanae Vitae's* essential message. At the same time, however, the extraordinary technical innovations that in vitro fertilization has demanded and ushered in over the past decade have convinced many that initiating new life apart from the conjugal embrace is not only wrong in itself, but sets into motion attitudes concerning marriage and the family that are even more pernicious.

Doctors Steptoe and Edwards, the gynecologist and physiologist who did the pioneering work that made the birth of Louise Brown possible, displayed an unusual amount of persistence before they finally achieved their desired result. It is estimated that over a period of twelve years they discarded 99.5% of the ova fertilized in their laboratory.[1] These embryos had been judged unfit for reasons as various as obvious abnormality or development beyond the optimum stage for implantation in the uterus. In a report to the Royal College of Obstetrics and Gynecologists, the doctors detailed the final countdown to their success: sixty-eight women who underwent laparoscopy (a method of egg retrieval), forty-four

[1] Eugene Diamond, "A Call for a Moratorium on *In Vitro* Fertilization", *Linacre,* Nov. 1979.

yielded appropriately mature eggs, of which thirty-two were fertilized, and four were successfully implanted, resulting in two live births. Louise Brown was born in July 1978. Steptoe and Edwards's second success, Alastair Montgomery, arrived the subsequent January.[2]

The Media, which more often prefers bad news to good, hailed the arrival of Louise Brown, and paid scant attention to the failures that preceded her. The public embraced the idea that in vitro fertilization could bless infertile couples with children of their own. In August 1978, *Parents' Magazine* published a Harris poll in which eighty-five percent of the women who responded found in vitro fertilization an acceptable procedure for couples otherwise unable to have children. A Gallup poll showed sixty percent of men and women "in favor". *McCall's* captured the spirit of the time with a heartwarming article titled "Our Miracle Named Louise". In vitro fertilization clinics sprang up around the world. Within a few years, the United States had two hundred of them, and entrepreneurs were calculating that by 1990, every city would have one.

There was a problem, however; it was the same problem Steptoe and Edwards had encountered: an extremely high failure rate between egg retrieval and child delivery.

The biological root of this problem is the fact that, during her reproductive career, a woman produces, on average, only one fertilizable egg per month. The high cost of in vitro attempts (financial, physiological, psychological) demands a faster pace of natural egg production. Thus women are superovulated to produce as many eggs as possible for each in vitro fertilization trial.

Howard Jones, the director of what has become the most successful IVF clinic in the Western Hemisphere, in Norfolk, Virginia, failed to achieve a single success in his first ten months of operation. During this period he had allowed his patients to ovulate naturally. His first success occurred when,

---

[2] Gena Corea, *The Mother Machine* (New York: Harper and Row, 1985).

on the advice of Australian fertility experts, he decided to "control ovulation" by using hormones. Dangers are associated with ovulation-inducing drugs, but they may spare the woman further exposure to the trauma of anesthesia and laparoscopic surgery.

Ovulation-inducing drugs have stimulated the production of as many as twenty eggs in one cycle; more commonly, from four to seven. The additional eggs offset failures during fertilization, implantation, and gestation, and thus help to ensure that at least one egg makes it through fertilization to birth.

Surplus eggs may be donated to infertile couples of whom the wife is unable to provide her own eggs or if her eggs may have a genetic defect. Concerns are expressed, however, about the possibility of immunological rejection of donor eggs as well as the risks assumed by a woman in her 40s (or even older) whose pregnancy is initiated by a donor egg. Further, donor eggs create the possibility of bifurcating maternity since the genetic mother who provides the egg is not the same woman as the gestational mother who carries the pregnancy to term. There are legal problems here.

When inefficiency is expected, and even planned for, efficiency then becomes undesirable. Doctors at the IVF unit of Toronto East General Hospital were somewhat unpleasantly surprised when all five fertilized eggs they implanted in one of their patients survived. In this case, Mrs. Wayne Collier, of Holland Landing, Ontario, gave birth to quintuplets.[3] Thanks to ovulation induction, multiple births are a common feature of in vitro fertilization. It is currently estimated that as many as 15–20% of pregnancies where multiple IVF embryos are involved may result in multiple gestation.[4]

[3] Lawrence Surtees, "Collier Quints Stable: New In Vitro Method to Cut Multiple Births", *The Toronto Globe and Mail*, Feb. 9, 1988, A2.

[4] The Ethics Committee of the American Fertility Society, *Ethical Considerations of the New Reproductive Technologies,* September 1986, p. 538 (hereafter referred to as ECAFS).

The Collier babies were the world's third "test-tube quints". Toronto East General has had twenty-one sets of twins and six of triplets among the one hundred and twenty babies born since the unit opened in 1983. The Collier babies were delivered by Caesarian section, eleven weeks prematurely. The lightest was one pound twelve ounces, the heaviest two pounds ten ounces. All five were put on respirators.

A technology that remedies one problem sometimes creates another. Ovulation induction remedies nature's low rate of egg production at the risk of multiple pregnancies. Like anesthesia and laparoscopic surgery, the superovulating drugs are traumatic to the reproductive system and can permanently reduce its capacity to achieve pregnancy.

Embryo freezing was developed to offset the problems of multiple pregnancies and post-operative trauma. It provides a temporary storage for surplus embryos and allows the woman to recover her strength so that in a subsequent cycle successful implantation is a greater likelihood.

Some IVF clinics do not employ embryo freezing. At these centers the "surplus" embryos that cannot be donated are routinely destroyed. Dr. Robert Casper, however, who heads the Division of Reproductive Sciences at the University of Toronto, an IVF center that does not freeze embryos, is careful to point out that at his center "we don't just throw them [the 'surplus' embryos] away." As he explained to Canada's Royal Commission on New Reproductive Technologies, the "surplus" embryos are "destroyed naturally" by placing them in the mother's vagina where they are absorbed into her body.[5]

The world's first frozen embryo baby was born in Melbourne, Australia, in March 1984. Her mother had produced eleven eggs when superovulating. Ten of these were fertilized.

---

[5] Hearing held in Toronto in the Frontenac Room of the Harbour Castle Westin, November 20, 1990. Some might understand Casper's practice of destroying embryos "naturally" as ritual killing.

Three were lost in unsuccessful implantation attempts; seven were frozen. Of these seven, one was rejected as unsuitable, and four did not survive the freezing. The remaining two were implanted; one survived, was delivered by Caesarian section, and was named Zoe Leyland.[6]

Embryo freezing has been criticized on the ground that a doctor should not create a situation in which he has more patients than he can possibly keep alive. Some have expressed outrage that human embryos are treated as "industrial waste".[7] But the aim of freezing embryos is neither reckless nor malicious. It is a logical extension and an inevitable refinement of in vitro fertilization.

The success rate in freezing, thawing, and implanting embryos is low, as might be expected with a new technology that involves a delicate subject. Dr. William Karow, director of the Southern California Fertility Institute, where embryos are routinely frozen, estimates the chances of producing a "freeze-thaw" baby at two to three percent. He is nonetheless optimistic: "My philosophy has always been to try everything that's humanly possible."[8]

Embryo freezing allows a woman to avoid the hardship of carrying many children at one time. In 1987, a British woman delivered a baby eighteen months after the birth of its twin sister. One embryo was implanted and the resulting pregnancy was carried to term. The twin was frozen, then thawed and implanted eighteen months later. The frozen embryo remained on hold, as it were, until its mother gestated its sister and then recovered from the experience. It was thus born twenty-seven months after conception.

Because the frozen embryo is kept in a metal cylinder, its welfare is not directly linked with the welfare of its mother. It

---

[6] Jo Wiles, "The Gift of Life", *Star World,* April 24, 1984, pp. 24–26.

[7] Roger Rosenblatt, *Time,* February 14, 1983, p. 90.

[8] "Baby Craving: Science and Surrogacy", *Life,* June 1987, p. 41.

would not be affected if its mother were to die. One might even construe this independence as a possible advantage for the frozen embryo.

An extraordinary case occurred in Australia that illustrates what can happen when a frozen embryo is orphaned. In 1981, Elsa Rios of Los Angeles had several of her eggs fertilized in vitro with sperm from an anonymous donor. The IVF team at Australia's Queen Victoria Medical Centre froze two of them and tried to implant some of the others in Mrs. Rios. The implants failed. Shortly thereafter, Mrs. Rios and her husband were killed in a plane crash in Chile.

Mario Rios, a fifty-seven-year-old Californian, was a millionaire property developer. The Rios couple had no other heirs. Australian law had no provision for dealing with frozen embryos whose parents were dead. There was public speculation that a surrogate mother could rescue the embryos and claim a share in the millionaire's estate.

The legal uncertainties of the situation provide excellent grist for a fiction writer's imagination. Could a woman become an heir by serving as the gestational mother of the two children? Once having secured this title, could she then exercise her prerogative and abort the children without forfeiting her claim on the estate? Or could she hold the children hostage in the womb, to assure getting what she wanted? Would a woman be entitled to a sizable share of the fortune if complications during pregnancy left her infertile? Should there be two gestational mothers? If so, on what grounds should they be selected?

A "scholarly committee" studied the matter and recommended that the embryos be destroyed. State officials accepted the recommendation.[9] Lawmakers in the State of Victoria, however, rejected it and passed an amendment calling for an attempt to have the embryos implanted in a surrogate mother

[9] "Australians Reject Bid to Destroy 2 Embryos", *The New York Times*, Oct. 24, 1984, A18.

and then placed for adoption.[10] Scientists held little hope for the orphans' survival.[11]

Nonetheless, Laura Horwitch, the lawyer representing the Rios estate, was not taking any chances. She declared that the orphaned embryos could not be heirs under California law since Mario Rios was not their natural father. Mrs. Rios' eggs had been fertilized by donor sperm.[12] This judgment, however, is at odds with other instances involving AID and IVF where the consenting husband of a wife whose egg is fertilized is always presumed to be the father of the newly formed embryos.

If the orphaned embryos were victims of legal discrimination, they would have no one to defend them since no legal guardian was appointed to act in their behalf.[13] As things turned out, these legal questions became a moot point. The attempts to implant the embryos failed.

Despite various snags, there is progress at the frontier of embryo freezing. Recently Toronto East General Hospital established embryo freezing as an extension of its in vitro fertilization service, as part of its LIFE program.

The modern world moves at dizzying speed; it is not easy to keep up, and efforts are made to make many things easier and faster to assimilate. For motorists, "through" becomes "thru" and "crosswalks" become "X-walks". Newspapers replace sentences with truncated expressions called "headlines". Commercial advertising employs slogans and jingles to by-

---

[10] George P. Smith, "Australia's Frozen 'Orphan' Embryos: A Medical, Legal and Ethical Dilemma", *Journal of Family Law*, 24 (1), 1985–86, pp. 26–41.

[11] Keith Dalton, "Dead Couple's Embryos to Be Thawed", *The Washington Post*, Dec. 4, 1987, A38. See also "Quickening Debate over Life on Ice", *Time*, July 2, 1984, p. 68; "Embryos' Future in Question", *The New York Times*, June 18, 1984, B10.

[12] "Attorney Dismisses Embryos' 'Claim'", *Record-Journal* (Meriden, Ct.), June 21, 1984.

[13] Ibid.

pass reason and go straight to the emotions. There is simply not enough time to analyze and reflect upon the passing scene.

The most radical form of linguistic contraction is found in the acronym, where complex identities that take so long to articulate they would be taxing to the memory are neatly compressed into a single word. A well-chosen acronym not only saves time, but carries a built-in moral endorsement. Perhaps nowhere is this more evident than in the field of bioethics, where VIP stands for Voluntary Interruption of Pregnancy, and its equivalent, MR, is Menstrual Regulation. In hospital slang, GORK abbreviates God Only Really Knows, and describes a patient who (the doctors suspect) has no hope of recovery. In the world of reproductive technology, GIFT is a gift of life through Gamete Intrafallopian Transfer, and TOT, through Tubal Ovum Transfer.

C. S. Lewis, in his science fiction novel *That Hideous Strength,* created the acronym N.I.C.E. to represent the National Institute for Coordinated Experimentation, a malefic bureaucracy possessing the power to destroy society, showing the moral distance that may exist between an acronym and the reality it camouflages—the acronym as inacuronym.

The LIFE acronym stands for Laboratory Initiated Fetal Emplacement. "Laboratory Initiated" conjures the distracting and infelicitous spectacle of promiscuity among the test tubes, unless the laboratories themselves are understood to be amorous. The word "fetal" is wrong, since it is an "embryo" that is transferred to the uterus. "Emplacement" is misleading: the desired end is "implantation".

A booklet for the LIFE Program calls the freezing of embryos "cryopreservation". It presents this procedure as a "therapy". The terms suggest optimism rather than realism, since the technique is more likely to kill the embryo than preserve it.

To freeze an embryo, the temperature is slowly reduced to below freezing. But when the temperature reaches minus-six to minus-eight degrees centigrade, ice crystals begin to form. This damages the embryo's cellular structure. In order to prevent this, chemicals are introduced to diminish the size of the crystals or dehydrate the embryo so that ice will not form in and around it. These chemicals are called "cryoprotectants". Their effect on the human embryo is not yet established. About half of the thawed embryos will not survive in culture. One-tenth of these, or one in twenty of the embryos originally frozen, are expected to be born.

While the proportion of embryos that survive freezing, thawing, and implantation is small, the results are cumulative. The more embryos frozen, the better the chances. By September of last year, one hundred and fifty babies had been born from thawed frozen embryos; innumerable others are on the way.

A couple who has a child through the LIFE Program may not want another. Husband and wife may have frozen embryos they do not want kept. In this case, LIFE offers several options. The couple may donate these embryos to another patient, donate them to research, or have them destroyed. A woman can give surplus eggs to the clinic's new ovum donation program for the use of a patient who has produced an inadequate number of eggs, or who does not wish to use her own eggs because she carries some genetic disorder.

On the other hand, new circumstances may arise after freezing. If the husband and wife change their minds or simply disagree about having a child, if there is a divorce, or if either dies, the LIFE Program is empowered to dispose of the embryos. The embryos may be destroyed if the parents fail to communicate their intentions for six months, or if they fall six months behind on the storage payments, or if the mother turns forty, or if the program itself goes out of business and cannot transfer the frozen embryos to another IVF center.

Here is an unintended and paradoxical effect. Techniques designed to help a woman have her own child, and thus give her more control over her reproductive system, end up giving her less authority over her progeny. Under the present laws of most Western countries, a pregnant woman can abort or carry a child to term without the approval of the child's father: her will is sovereign. But when her embryo is frozen in liquid nitrogen, joint consent is needed if she hopes to give birth to the child, for the father has a veto power he would lack were the child in the womb. Further, the clinic may override the couple's decision, though both husband and wife wish to keep their embryos alive. With embryo freezing, disposal rights shift from the woman to the father and to the clinic, giving them "pro-choice" options previously reserved to the pregnant woman, this shift of rights limits the authority she has over her own pregnancy to the kind of power a minority stockholder has in determining company policy. The more the woman is enmeshed in reproductive technology, the more rights she must surrender to external agencies.

Embryo freezing is a logical response to particular problems created by in vitro fertilization: surplus embryos, multiple pregnancies, and the repeated, traumatic effects of ovulation-inducing drugs, anesthesia, and laparoscopic surgery. It improves the chances for infertile couples to have their own child, but without guaranteeing the elimination of these problems. For example, a woman who has six fertilized eggs may choose to freeze three and have three implanted. She need not worry about giving birth to sextuplets, but, whether she wants them or not, she might still have triplets.

The final solution for the redundant embryo has been designed by a four-man team of doctors at the University Hospital in Leiden, the Netherlands. It is a technique called "pregnancy reduction". A needle is inserted through the woman's abdominal wall, and under ultrasonic guidance is directed to the embryos in the uterus. A solution of potassium chloride is injected into the hearts of those judged to be supernumerary. In due course, these embryos dissolve and are absorbed into the mother's body.

While pregnancy reduction is going on in the uterus, attempts at inducing twinning are being conducted in the petri dish. Carl Wood of Australia's University of Monash has been trying to stimulate embryo division at the zygote stage, in the hope that another viable embryo may be produced who is the identical twin of its parent zygote. One-celled protozoans reproduce in a similar fashion. The intention is to improve a woman's chance to have a child in vitro when she begins with only one fertilized egg.

Each of the many technologies that IVF has spawned is consistent with its original purpose of serving the needs of the infertile couple. Despite this apparent tidal wave of progress, the overall "take-home-baby-rate" is, according to the international weekly *Medical Tribune,* a disappointing 5.6 percent.[14] And there is reason to worry for the babies themselves. A survey conducted by the Australian government in 1985, of nine hundred pregnancies, found in vitro babies four times as likely to be stillborn and twice as likely to have congenital abnormalities than babies conceived in the traditional way. One in vitro pregnancy in twenty was ectopic (the child developing outside the uterus), and one in four ended in miscarriage. Premature delivery was common, and forty-three percent of deliveries were by Caesarian section.[15]

A later study revealed that of 4,507 treatment cycles reported, 11.2% of the women experienced preclinical abor-

[14] Rick McGuire, "Charge Baby Biz Programs Still 'Oversold and Overrated'", *Medical Tribune: International Medical News Weekly,* June 21, 1988, p. 17. See also "Procréatique et désinformation", *Le monde* (Paris), December 17, 1987 which puts the average birth rate per total IVF attempts at very much below 7% ("très inférieur à 7%"). It should be remembered that a small percentage of couples would have conceived naturally had they not employed IVF. Such a figure, obviously, is indeterminable.

[15] Ann Pappert, "Critics Worry Women Not Told of Fertilization Program Risks", *Toronto Globe and Mail,* Feb. 6, 1988. See also "In-Vitro Fertilization Pregnancies in Australia and New Zealand", *The Medical Journal of Australia,* vol. 148, May 2, 1988.

tions, 5.2% had ectopic pregnancies, 23.1% suffered spontaneous abortions, and 2.2% bore babies who were dead.[16]

Outcomes such as ectopic pregnancy, spontaneous abortion, preterm delivery and perinatal death are consistently more common in in vitro fertilization pregnancies than in pregnancies after natural conception.

In an editorial entitled "In-Vitro Fertilization—A Gift for the Infertile or a Cycle of Despair?" appearing in *The Medical Journal of Australia,* Fiona Stanley details the high cost of IVF and its low success. She concludes by making the sensible suggestion that it would be more practical to spend less on IVF and more on preventing the causes of infertility. She writes:

> However, at present, while these large amounts of money are spent on in-vitro fertilization, study of the causes of infertility or its primary prevention in Australia virtually is neglected—a gross imbalance. There may be very important preventable factors, for example, the use of intrauterine contraceptive devices, pelvic inflammation, and venereal diseases such as chlamydial infections.[17]

For reasons such as these, some IVF specialists have abandoned their work. Dr. Jacques Testart, who facilitated the first French test tube pregnancy and was involved with freezing human embryos, made the following statement in an interview with the Paris newspaper *Le Monde:* "I will not go on in this. One cannot apply the logic of progress to something which will become a grave danger to humanity."[18]

Patrick Steptoe once remarked that in pioneering IVF, all he wanted to do was "help women whose child producing mechanism is slightly faulty." The mistake was to view the woman's

[16] National Perinatal Statistics Unit and Fertility Society of Australia. IVF and GIFT pregnancies, Australia and New Zealand. Sidney: NPSU, 1987.

[17] "In-Vitro Fertilization—A Gift for the Infertile or a Cycle of Despair?" *The Medical Journal of Australia,* vol. 148, May 2, 1988, p. 426.

[18] *Lifelines,* vol. 14, no. 2, April 1988, pp. 18–19.

procreative power as consisting of an assemblage of mechanisms in the first place.

Several years ago Edward Grossman wrote in *Atlantic* that a day would come when a woman's two laparoscopy scars will be as commonplace as our smallpox vaccination mark. At age twenty, every female will be superovulated, and her eggs will be collected and frozen, since babies conceived by women of that age are less likely to suffer from Down's symdrome and other congenital defects. Thereafter, whenever a woman wants to become a mother, she will simply have one of her eggs thawed, fertilized in a dish, and gestated in an artificial incubator. The uterus will become vestigial, though the ovaries will remain important. No woman will lose her figure in childbearing.[19]

According to such a scenario, the only part the woman plays in the development of her motherhood is in furnishing the egg (which she accomplishes with a complete absence of conscious effort). Everything else transpires independently of her. Thus, she does not grow into motherhood; motherhood is prepared for her, apart from her. When she becomes a mother, she does so instantly. But the nagging question remains: will women be ready for instant motherhood when it is ready for them? Will they be able to cultivate maternal feelings and responsibilities while their children are developing away from them? IVF inaugurates a pattern that progressively externalizes procreation. As this process develops, incarnate motherhood progressively diminishes.

The scenario Grossman depicts appears relatively tame when compared with what other prognosticators envision. Following the first stage of human life, the zygote, is *cleavage,* during which the single initial cell undergoes successive equal divisions with little or no intervening growth.[20] The resulting cells—or blastomeres—become progressively smaller, while

[19] "The Obsolescent Mother: A Scenario", *Atlantic,* May 1971, p. 49.
[20] ECAFS, 26S.

the size of the total aggregate remains approximately the same. After three such divisions, the aggregate contains eight cells.[21] In experiments with mice, it has been shown that if two such eight-cell aggregates, each of different parentage, are fused into a sixteen-cell unit, the resulting single organism can develop to adulthood. In this instance, the adult has four genetic parents. One social commentator has remarked: "If multi-mouse is here, can "multi-man" be far behind?"[22] If such a technique could be developed, it would offer hope for a lesbian couple to have a child of its own, though two other male parents would also be involved in contributing to the genetic makeup of the child. Two zygotes would be formed in vitro in separate dishes by four different progenitors. At the eight-cell stage, the two embryos would be fused into a single entity, thereby establishing a sixteen-cell embryo who would develop to adulthood, bearing the traits of each of his four genetic parents.

All women ask of in vitro fertilization is motherhood: not surplus embryos to be frozen or disposed of or donated for one purpose or another; not multiple pregnancies to be reduced or carried to term at much risk; not the maturation of a prodigality of eggs that are frozen or donated.

A bare desire cannot be directed into the organic network that commands the initiation of life without disturbing at that moment a myriad of ancillary operations. The body does not restrict its responses to our desires. It has a mind of its own, so to speak; it is not wholly submissive to our will. And so, reproductive technology is an excursion into unpredictability. The myth of progress creates the illusion that technology can grant our desires without burdening us with unrequested tribulations. Reality remains stubbornly organic; touch a nerve and the whole system trembles. We choose what is con-

---

[21] N. Le Douarin and A. McLaren, eds., *Chimaeras in Developmental Biology* (New York: Academic Press, 1984).

[22] Alvin Toffler, *Future Shock* (New York: Random House, 1970), p. 205.

venient, and what is inconvenient chooses us. It is the central irony of our modern technocracy.

Conquering nature and yoking human generation to our desires will continue to elude us. And well it should since within the body is ingrained a balance and a wisdom we disregard at our own peril. The ten years that elapsed since Louise Brown should have reeducated us to the fact that motherhood and fatherhood are uncompromisingly personal. But it has tempted us to believe that they are replaceable. The new world of technologized parenthood must indeed be brave, for it ventures into *terra incognita* with more faith in reason than reason would find reasonable. By contrast, *Humanae Vitae* contains a message of perhaps unexpected wisdom, namely, that preserving the integrity of the unitive and procreative ends of intercourse also preserves the integrity of parenthood and personhood.

Chapter Eight

Reproductive Technologies and Social Justice

Reproductive technologies, such as IVF (in vitro fertilization), GIFT (gamete intrafallopian transfer), ET (embryo transfer), SET (surrogate embryo transfer) and the emplacement of freeze/thawed embryos, represent a deviation from the traditional aims of medicine inasmuch as they treat a desire rather than a disease. Even successful interventions do not restore fertility. The man, woman, or couple have exactly the same fertility problem as they had prior to treatment.

At the same time, cosmetic medicine, which is also not disease-related (though in a more general sense it may be regarded as health-related), is enjoying increased popular acceptance. Although breast augmentation and reduction, plastic surgery, liposuction, the surgical removal of cellulite, and the like are not entirely free of controversy, they now appear to be part of an established branch of medicine.

The new controversy that reproductive technology has created is not confined to a particular sphere, such as medical ethics. There is widespread infertility in North America. The costs of reproductive technology are very high—financially as well as psychologically and physiologically—and its success rates are extremely low. Moreover, this unhappy state of affairs prevails in a milieu where abortion is routine and adoption often problematic. At the same time, the exorbitantly high cost of reproductive technology conflicts with opportunities for providing poor people with basic health care. The new controversy reproductive technology poses has, quite clearly, important moral and sociological ramifications. It is, indeed, a *social justice* problem.

The rate of infertility in North America is said to have reached "epidemic" proportions.[1] Nearly three million couples—approximately one in every six—in the United States cannot conceive during the woman's childbearing years.[2] And the proportion is on the rise.[3] The infertility rate among women age 20–24 has tripled since the 1960s to 11%; among those between 35 and 39, it has increased by 25%.[4] Male sperm count has fallen more than 30% in the last half century and is continuing to fall. Presently, 25% of American men have sperm counts so low that some fertility specialists consider them to be functionally sterile.[5]

Many factors have brought about this escalation of infertility, including contraception, abortion, sterilization (male and female), and sexually transmitted diseases. There are 88,000 women who are infertile because of infections from IUDs.[6] An official for the Venereal Disease Action Coalition in Detroit estimates that by the year 2,000, 15–20% of all women in the reproductive range will be infertile due to sexually transmitted disease.[7] Some women are infertile as a result of experimental drugs, such as *diethylstilbestrol* (DES).[8]

---

[1] Robert H. Blank, "Making Babies: The State of the Art", *Futurist,* 19 (1), Feb. 1985, p. 17.

[2] Patricia M. McShane, "In Vitro Fertilization, GIFT and Related Technologies—Hope in a Test Tube", E. H. Baruch et al. (eds.), *Women and Health,* 13 (1/2), 1987, p. 31. Approximately 5 million married couples in America are clinically infertile, which is defined as the inability to conceive after one year of noncontraceptive intercourse. See Anita Diamant, "The Baby Quest", *The Boston Globe,* April 16, 1989.

[3] Blank, p. 17.

[4] Lewis Lord et al., "Desperately Seeking Baby", *U.S. News and World Report,* Oct. 5, 1987, p. 59.

[5] Blank, p. 17.

[6] Lord, p. 59.

[7] Gena Corea, *The Hidden Malpractice* (New York: Harper and Row, 1985) p. 129.

[8] Mary Sue Henefin, "Introduction: Women's Health and the New Reproductive Technologies", in Baruch, op. cit., p. 4. This drug was given to

Infertility is also linked to women's increased athletic and business activities and to the common practice of postponing one's first pregnancy because of career or status considerations.[9] Environmental causes have also played an important role in contributing to the present problem. Some clinical ecologists recommend freezing the sperm of young men who are likely to be exposed to chemical and radioactive mutagens in the environment and in the workplace.[10] Given the current situation, it is not in the least surprising that many infertile couples claim a right to use any reproductive technology that offers them hope for having a child of their own.

The Right to Have a Baby

A number of important judicial rulings in recent years are based on notions of individual rights to privacy and reproductive freedom. These rulings, which embrace the rights to contraception and abortion, have been interpreted by many specialists within the field of jurisprudence as implying the additional right to have a child. They reason that the rights to prevent life and to terminate prenatal life suggest a right to begin life. Dr. John Robertson, for example, the Marrs MacLean Professor of Law at the University of Texas Law School, believes that people have a "constitutional right" to have children. According to Robertson, such a "right" should not be controlled by the "moralistic rhetoric"[11] that would restrict it to married people.

---

women for the purpose of preventing miscarriages. Tragically, however, it produced vaginal cancer in female offspring and breast cancer in mothers. See also Aral and Cates, "The Increasing Concern with Infertility", *Journal of the American Medical Association,* 250 (1983), p. 2327.

[9] Blank, p. 17.

[10] Paul Bagne, "High-Tech Breeding", *Mother Jones,* 8 (7), Aug. 1983, pp. 23–35.

[11] Walter Goodman, "New Reproduction Techniques Redefine Parenthood", *The New York Times,* Nov. 16, 1984.

> If reproductive technology makes it possible for the unmarried person to have her own child, it is discriminatory and socially unwise to deny that person the right to procreate simply because she or he "may be unable to find a suitable spouse, be unwilling to marry, or object to heterosexual intercourse".[12]

Robertson argues that the individual's right to control conception (through contraception) and pregnancy (through abortion) should extend to childbirth (through reproductive technology regardless of marital status).

A significant number of lawyers agree with Robertson's position. Some argue that procreation is a "constitutional right" consistent with one's right to privacy and "intimate association";[13] while others view it as a "constitutional right" equivalent with the right to "family autonomy":

> Unmarried women have a right to bear children and to raise those children in the family environment of their choice. The constitutional rights of procreation and family autonomy protect the single woman's right to choose a nontraditional family unit.[14]

The notion that the "right" to have a child is protected by the Constitution would be most welcomed by infertile couples who want to employ reproductive technologies to remedy their pain of childlessness. But it would also be welcomed by unmarried people and homosexual couples who would also like to have children through technological means. There is at

---

[12] Procreative Liberty and the Control of Conception, Pregnancy, and Childbirth", 69 *Virginia Law Review,* 1983, pp. 418, 424. See also "Reproductive Technology and the Procreation Rights of the Unmarried", *Harvard Law Review,* 98 (3), Jan. 1985, pp. 669–85.

[13] Lisa Ikemoto, "Providing Protection for Collaborative, Noncoital Reproduction: Surrogate Motherhood and Other New Procreative Technologies, and the Right of Intimate Association", *Rutgers Law Review,* 40 (4), Summer 1988, pp. 1273–1309.

[14] Kristine Roszak, "Mother Knows Best: A Constitutional Perspective on Single Motherhood by Choice", *Southern Illinois Law Journal,* 1984 (7), 1985, pp. 329–48.

least one program in the United States that already uses sperm donated by homosexual men to impregnate lesbian women through AID.[15] The right to have children through various reproductive technologies, therefore, would extend to the nonfertile in addition to the infertile. (A homosexual couple is not infertile, but simply nonfertile. The privative prefix "in" does not apply to a couple that by nature lacks any capacity for procreation. One would not describe a rock as insensitive since it is not deprived of a natural capacity for sensation. A homosexual couple, then, is not fertile in the same sense that a rock is not sensitive. There is no privation involved.) This consideration raises an additional ethical point. Should technology provide children for couples who were never intended by nature to have the capacity for having children?

The Costs

In 1989, the average cost of diagnostic and medical treatments for infertility was more than $2,500 per couple.[16] Common diagnostic procedures include ultrasound or sonography, in which sound waves are used to detect blockages or irregularities in the reproductive organs, and laparoscopy, in which a small viewing scope is inserted into the fallopian tubes. Costs can soar, however, if the couple elects IVF. According to Blue Cross–Blue Shield, the median cost for each attempt is between $5,000 and $6,000. The fertility drug Pergonal alone costs $1,000 per month.[17] In 1987, some 14,000 IVF attempts were made, at a cost of about $66 million.[18]

[15] Betty Rothbart, *Frontiers in Fertility, Report on the Symposium on Human Fertility Regulation: Technological Frontiers and Their Implications* (New York: Planned Parenthood Federation of America, 1985), p. 18.

[16] According to a report by the Congressional Office of Technological Assessment. See Julie Johnson, "Insurance and the Cost of Infertility", *The New York Times,* March 5, 1989.

[17] Lord, p. 63.

[18] Alan Otten, "Study Cites Lack of Success with In Vitro Fertilization", *The Wall Street Journal,* May 18, 1988, p. 33.

The government of Ontario, the only government in the world to finance IVF clinics, has spent more than $6 million in two years on just four of its clinics. During that time, approximately 200 babies were born, at a cost to the Province of $30,000 per child. Patients in other provinces pay up to $4,400 for each IVF attempt.[19] An Ontario health policy analyst has estimated that the cost of providing IVF for all eligible Canadian women would be $135 million. Costs have risen appreciably since this estimate was made in 1985.[20]

The 660 babies born in the first five years of IVF programs in Australia cost an estimated $25 million, or slightly less than $37,500 per birth.[21] The World Health Organization amended this estimated cost in its report on IVF issued in 1989. According to WHO, the cost per IVF baby is at least $50,000 because twice as many IVF babies than average die within the first month, and more than an average number have to be put into newborn intensive care units, where they spend longer than average amounts of time.[22]

Life magazine did a feature on a couple who spent more than $40,000 in an unsuccessful attempt to have a child through IVF in combination with a surrogate gestator. The wife, 41, was born without a uterus. Though she and her husband have two children through adoption, a boy 17 and a girl 12, they have an intense craving for a biological child of their own. Three of their embryos, fertilized in a petri dish, were frozen. Problems arose when doctors attempted to produce—through hormone injections in the surrogate gestator—a uterine condition suitable for the transfer of the embryos. Though the director of the fertility program informed the husband and wife that the chances of producing a baby through IVF using the

---

[19] Ann Pappert, *Toronto Globe and Mail*, Feb. 8, 1988, A 2–3.

[20] Ibid.

[21] *Melbourne Age*, Nov. 12, 1987.

[22] Jackie Allender, "WHO warns IVF a $64,000 Risk", *The Australian*, May 16, 1989, p. 8.

embryo-freezing technique is only 2 to 3 percent, they remained undaunted. In the highly unlikely event that an embryo survives the freezing and thawing and is successfully implanted in the surrogate, the couple have agreed to pay her an additional $9,000. They will pay $2,400 more for the six weeks' salary she would lose on maternity leave.[23]

But there are additional costs, not only financial and psychological ones for the infertile couple, but also physical costs for the child conceived through IVF. A survey conducted by the Australian government in 1985 examined 900 IVF pregnancies and found in vitro babies four times more likely to be stillborn and twice as likely to have congenital abnormalities than children conceived through conjugal intimacy.[24] The study also found that ectopic pregnancy rates for IVF were 5% and miscarriages 25% of total pregnancies. Premature delivery was common and 43% of all deliveries were by Caesarian section. All these rates were 3 times the national average for Australia.

In 1987, *Lancet* reported an unexpectedly high rate of two types of congenital malformation—spina bifida and transposition of the great vessels—among IVF and GIFT babies in Australia and New Zealand.[25] This finding was subsequently corroborated by several doctors in the Netherlands, who found a correlation between ovulation-inducing drugs, such as clomiphene, and neural tube defects in IVF babies and those born to subfertile women who underwent super-ovulation. "These data", the doctors report, "suggest once more an enlarged risk of NTD [neural tube defects, particularly anen-

[23] T. Cutner and G. H. Colt, "Baby Craving: Science and Surrogacy", *Life*, June 1987, pp. 36–42.

[24] Pappert. See also *Medical Journal Australia*, May 2, 1988.

[25] Paul Lancaster, "Congenital Malformations after In-Vitro Fertilization", *Lancet*, Dec. 12, 1987, p. 1393. See also "Australian In Vitro Fertilization Collaborative Group. High Incidence of Preterm Births and Early Losses in Pregnancy after In Vitro Fertilisation", *British Medical Journal*, 1985, 291, pp. 160–63.

cephaly] in pregnancies established with the aid of ovulation stimulating drugs."[26]

The woman is also at risk. The medical literature has documented instances of IVF-related cancer. In one case, a 25-year-old woman in England developed virulent cancer of her reproductive system. Doctors associated the cancer with the drugs used in her IVF regimen.[27] An Israeli IVF center reports two cases in which physicians may have been responsible for damaging previously healthy fallopian tubes.[28] It should also be noted that reproductive technologies can *cause* female infertility. This is apparent in the case where a healthy woman is subjected to invasive surgery when the infertility problem lies exclusively with her husband.[29]

Consent forms for IVF, embryo transfer, and embryo cryopreservation frequently detail the numerous adverse consequences that these technological procedures can bring about. The form prepared by the *IVF Australia Program–Boston* enumerates the following risks and consequences: the development of ovarian cysts; puncture of the bowel, bladder, uterus, intestine, ovaries, blood vessels, and other abdominal organs; infection; damage to sperm, eggs, and fertilized egg(s); miscarriage, ectopic pregnancies, or stillbirth; multiple pregnancy; premature delivery; neurological defects including but not limited to cerebral palsy; thawed embryos will be examined for apparent viability and transferred only if they appear to be viable; mechanical support systems are subject to failure,

[26] M. C. Cornel, et al., "Ovulation Induction and Neural Tube Defects", *The Lancet,* June 17, 1989, p. 1386.

[27] D. W. Cramer and W. R. Welch, "Determinant of Ovarian Cancer Risk", *Journal of the National Cancer Institute,* 71, pp. 717–21.

[28] M. E. Carter and N. N. Joyce, "Ovarian Carcinoma in a Patient Hyperstimulated by Gonadotropin Therapy for In Vitro Fertilization: A Case Report", *Journal of In Vitro Fertilization and Embryo Transfer,* 1987, 4 (2), pp. 126–28.

[29] Ibid.

possibly resulting in the inadvertent thawing of an embryo or in an embryo that will not grow, or appears abnormal.[30]

The Australia–Boston program is indemnified against "any and all liabilities, claims, actions, damages, expenses and losses of any nature whatsoever alleged to have arisen out of the provision of IVF services, including but not limited to any claims based on negligence of any person or institution associated in any manner with the IVF Program." It will, however, perform abortions at its own expense where the examining obstetrician recommends such action.

Low Success Rates

The *Medical Tribune*'s survey of 54 of 108 clinics registered with the American Fertility Association shows an overall success rate in terms of live births of 5.6%[31] The survey also reveals that half of these centers never produced a live birth. These zero-success clinics had been operating from one month to three years and treated more than 600 women. Despite their absence of success, they collected, by conservative estimate, more than $2.5 million in patient fees. Other reports have indicated that of 150 IVF clinics in the United States, half have yet to achieve a pregnancy and even fewer have produced a live birth.[32] Moreover, while no American clinic produced a live birth in the first year of its operation, some of these clinics were boasting of a 25% success rate.[33] "Success", in their

[30] Informed Consent Forms #1a and #2a. *IVF Australia Program–Boston* at Walthamweston Hospital and Medical Center.

[31] R. McGuire, "Charge Baby Biz Programs Still 'Oversold and Overrated'", *Medical Tribune: International Medical News Weekly*, Jan. 21, 1988, p. 17.

[32] Lord, p. 6. See also Richard Strauss, "Fertility Clinics Plan to Disclose Results", *The Boston Globe*, Nov. 20, 1989.

[33] Jalna Hanmer, "Reproduction Trends and the Emergence of Moral Panic", *Social Science Medicine*, 25 (6), 1987, pp. 697–704.

view, was computed in terms of the likelihood of pregnancy as determined by chemical testing.[34] Gary Ellis, project director for the Office of Technology Assessment in Washington, reports that most couples come away from an IVF clinic without a live baby, despite outlays of $22,000 or more per couple.[35]

Surveys throughout the world yield comparable figures. IVF specialist Jacques Testart and his colleagues studied the results of 40 of France's best IVF centers. They concluded that the average birth rate per total IVF attempt is very much below 7%. They also point out that an undeterminable number of women who come to the centers are not infertile and conceive naturally through intercourse during the IVF cycles. Nonetheless, their conceptions and deliveries are numbered among the IVF successes.[36]

In Australia, the IVF success rate leading to live birth has been reported as 8.9%[37] This figure does not take into account the percentage of "natural" conceptions that may have taken place during IVF cycles; nor does it reflect the number of reproductively healthy women who may have been rendered infertile as a result of the IVF procedure.

In England, where success rates are comparably low, Professor R. Winston states, "In vitro fertilization remains the most disappointing and expensive of all treatments."[38]

GIFT appears to show a somewhat higher success rate than IVF. However, the rates are usually computed in terms of pregnancy, not live births. Other techniques have not been particularly satisfactory. LTOT (low tubal ovum transfer) had

[34] "IVF Raises False Hope", *Interim,* July/Aug. 1989, p. 10.

[35] Otten, p. 33.

[36] Jacques Testart et al., "Procréatique et désinformation", *Le Monde* (Paris), Dec. 17, 1987.

[37] "Australian In Vitro Fertilization Collaborative Study", *Medical Journal of Australia,* May 2, 1988.

[38] *British Medical Journal,* Sept. 5, 1987. See also Dr. Peggy Norris, *In Vitro Fertilization and Population Control* (Liverpool: The Medical Education Trust, 1988–89).

no success at all, while TOTS (tubal ovum transfer with sperm) has succeeded in only a few instances. Other reproductive technologies, such as PROST, ZIFT, POST, VISPER, etc., have been performed too infrequently for meaningful success data to be available. These procedures are specialized versions or variants of IVF and GIFT. Therefore, it would not be expected that their success rates would be appreciably higher.

Exploitation

The significant discrepancy between real success rates and those that are advertised, together with approaches to advertising that are often manipulative, have raised the issue of exploitation. One fertility clinic has placed an ad in a newspaper featuring a fuzzy photograph of a newborn with a subliminal stork on the blanket. The caption reads: "Before you let go of the dream, talk to us." The message below the photograph is more an abuse of sentiment rather than an accurate representation of the slim chances of having a baby that this particular fertility clinic really offers its clients:

> There's no other perfume like it, the smell of a newborn: a milk-scent, warm-scent, cuddle essence.
> Her skin a kind of new velvet. Toes more wrinkled than cabbage, yet roselike. Tender, soft, totally trusting; a blessing all your own.
> That dream might still come true for you. New techniques can resolve infertility problems, including some that were previously considered hopeless.[39]

It exemplifies, writes one commentator, the reemergence of "medical hucksterism".[40] Dr. Kathleen Nolan, a bioethicist

---

[39] Ellen Goodman, "The Ethics of Marketing Babies", *The Boston Globe,* April 13, 1989, p. 7.

[40] Ibid.

at the Hastings Institute, adds, somewhat more cautiously: "It seems wrong to play upon the pain of infertility in order to sell fertility services."[41] In the same manner and with the same sizzle that an ad man would use in advertising an automobile, the ad sells the hope of having a child. Needless to say, no mention is made of the possibility of an anecephalic child or a spina bifida baby.

"There's no question that some couples are exploited", writes Dr. Robert Rebon of Northwestern University's School of Medicine. "But you have to ask," he adds, "'Are they intentionally exploited?' When the couple says they'll do anything to have a baby, it's very difficult for the doctor to say it's time to stop."[42]

Doctors are trained to treat, not to stop treatment. An infertile couple determined to have a child through a particular reproductive technology is also indisposed to terminating the treatment. "It had begun to feel like getting pregnant was the only thing in life", states one IVF patient. "That if we didn't get pregnant, the rest of our lives would be useless and meaningless."[43] A California woman who tried to have a child over a period of 6 years and at a cost of $25,000 states that she is still on "an emotional roller coaster, the worst thing in my life . . . I resent seeing a pregnant woman."[44] These developments are not unusual. One finds the pain and desperation of infertile couples expressed time and again in books that document their ordeal, such as Mary Martin Mason's *The Miracle Seekers,* and Ellen Sarasohn Glazer's *Without Child.*

An editorial in *Fertility and Sterility* asks the question, "Are we exploiting the infertile couple?" The editors analyzed the issue along three lines: the inappropriate use of credentials,

---

[41] Ibid.
[42] Quoted in Lord, p. 63.
[43] Diamant, p. 66.
[44] Lord, p. 63.

the misuse of new reproductive technologies, and truth in advertising. While acknowledging that the medical profession might be at times guilty of exploiting infertile couples on each of these levels, it also presented a case for being exploited by infertile couples themselves:

> [I]n a consumer-driven medical care system, the physician is often in a precarious position of having to offer premature or indiscriminant therapy to those who demand it, or risk losing the patient to a more accommodating competitor.[45]

A number of feminists are not as protective of the medical profession as are the editors of *Fertility and Sterility*. Gena Corea, for example, in her extremely well-documented book, *The Mother Machine*, claims that the medical profession encourages us to focus our sympathy for the infertile woman in such a way as to increase its control over her. "We do not believe", she writes, "that encouraging an infertile woman to hand over her body to the pharmacracy for manipulation and experimentation is a truly sensitive response to her plight."[46]

A number of lawsuits have been brought against fertility specialists who defrauded or abused their patients.[47] In one scandalous case, a prominent geneticist was found guilty of defrauding six women who paid him up to $5,000 for each fertility treatment. He repeatedly lied to these women, first telling them they were pregnant and later informing them that their fantasy babies had been reabsorbed into their bodies. This charlatan had prescribed several injections of a chorionic gonadotropin for his female patients. This hormone caused urine samples to test positive for pregnancy. When he stopped

[45] "Are We Exploiting the Infertile Couple?" *Fertility and Sterility*, 48 (5), Nov. 1987, p. 737.

[46] New York: Harper and Row, 1985, p. 173.

[47] Neal Allen, "Woman Sues Fertility Doctor", *The Record*, (Hackensack, N. J.), Oct. 30, 1986.

the injections, signs of pregnancy disappeared, but many of his patients returned to him for repeated treatments.[48]

Children as Commodities

Another moral problem that reproductive technologies have created is the tendency to view children not as gifts that result when husband and wife express sexual love to one another, but as commodities that are produced in a laboratory through the skill of technicians. Traditionally, care for the child began with the care parents expressed for each other. Husband and wife expressed love for each other and out of their union a child was conceived. But the child was not conceived for the sake of the parents. Rather, parenthood was recognized as being for the child who is an end in himself and not a means to an end, such as fulfilling his parents' wishes or making them happy.[49]

Reproductive technologies have reversed the order of things, so that an IVF child, for example, appears to exist for the sake of the parents to satisfy their wants, rather than to exist in his own right. The interest of the child, which was completely obnubilated in *Roe v. Wade,* is also overshadowed in the current technological approaches to reproduction. The child is lost amid the scramble on the part of adults to assert and satisfy their "rights" either to have a child who does not exist or not have one who does. Nonetheless, justice demands that the child be free from a context that treats him as a means to an end.

Writing in the *Texas Tech Law Review,* Timothy White makes the interesting observation that greater foresight on

[48] Susan Carleton, "Allegations Highlight Fraud Potential in Lucrative Treatment of Infertility", *Physicians Financial News,* April 15, 1989. See also Mary Jordan, "Va. Doctor Lied to Patients: Women Told Pregnancy, 'Loss' of Fetus", *Washington Post,* Jan. 28, 1989, A1–A13.

[49] Daniel Overduin, *Babies Made in Glass: The Christian Response* (Adelaide, South Australia: Lutheran Publishing House, 1986), p. 143.

this issue makes strange partners, including the Roman Catholic Church and the feminist movement, "both of whom have seen the adverse socio-humanitarian effects which these agreements precipitate".[50] No person should be regarded as the object of another person's rights. The converse of this moral axiom states that no person should regard another person as an object of his rights, that is to say, no person has a right to another person. The question concerning when human life begins seems immaterial here since what the infertile couple wants is not an embryo or a fetus but a child that they can hold in their arms.

In affirming the position that the end does not justify the means, that no one, not even a prenatal child, should be used as a means to an end, professors Sherman Elias and George Annas offer a few applications of this moral principle. Accordingly, the desire to have a child does not justify kidnapping another's child, or forcibly removing an embryo from an embryo donor (or "ovum donor", as she is sometimes erroneously called) who has changed her mind.[51] It may also not justify placing a healthy embryo at risk, either by freezing it or allowing its formation to take place in the unnatural and hazardous environment of a petri dish. Nor may it justify placing a prenatal child in a situation where it may be fought over for custody by a multitude of individuals who claim to be its parents.

Nancy Davis, a philosopher at the University of Colorado, refers to the new reproductive technologies somewhat bluntly as "child-acquisition techniques". She fears that their widespread use would magnify and reinforce some of the less admirable attitudes people have toward children, especially those that regard them as gratifying parental needs. We should en-

[50] Timothy L. White, "Toward a Dignified Theory of Children: Prohibition of Collaborative Reproduction", *Texas Tech Law Review,* 19 (3), Spring 1988, pp. 1091–139.

[51] "Social Policy Considerations in Noncoital Reproduction", *Journal of the American Medical Association,* Jan. 3, 1986, 255 (1), p. 64.

courage the adoption of a social policy, she urges, that places a greater emphasis on children's need for love, regardless of their "quality".[52] There have been instances where the employment of reproductive technology has resulted in a defective child whom the infertile couple rejected.

In fundamental agreement with Professor Davis is Katharine Bartlett. Writing in the *Yale Law Review,* she advocates a social policy that would reinforce parental dispositions toward generosity and other-directedness. She strongly opposes looking upon children in terms of satisfying individual rights. Such an attitude, in her view, implies a conceptualization of parenthood in individualistic, possessory terms. Rather than encourage attitudes of "parental possessiveness and self-centeredness", Ms. Bartlett would prefer that society emphasize "benevolence and responsibility".[53] She recognizes that love and generosity transcend the *quid pro quo* tendency of legal arrangements. Therefore, she argues that the parent-child relationship should receive a higher status in law than fairness and individual entitlement, which are based upon principles of reciprocity and exchange.[54]

Closely connected with a possessory attitude toward children is the reductive notion that parenthood is essentially genetic. While the genetic connection between parent and child is objective and prototypic, it neither exhausts the full nature of parenthood nor does it guarantee the best interest of the child. The gestational, caring, nurturing, and rearing dimensions of parenthood, though lacking the procreative originality of genetic parenthood, represent its moral and spiritual fulfillment, while centering on what is best for the child. Genetic parenthood is the prototype, but spiritual parenthood is the archetype. In the final analysis, it is in the realm of the

---

[52] "Reproductive Technologies and Our Attitudes towards Children", *From the Center* (The Center for Values and Social Policy), n.d.

[53] "Re-Expressing Parenthood", *Yale Law Review,* 98 (2), Dec. 1988, pp. 293–340.

[54] Ibid., p. 337.

moral and spiritual that one is likely to make a lasting impression on his children. "One should not forget", writes Joan Heifetz Hollinger, "that the reproduction of self that so many hope to achieve through their children is more evident in the long term relationships of rearing and nurturance than in the single act of genetic procreation." [55]

Too much emphasis on the genetic aspect of parenthood can easily obscure the needs that orphaned babies have for the loving home that adoptive parents can provide. One social critic reminds us that "new reproductive technologies permit parents to have a genetic link with their children. But by doing so, they decrease the number of potential adoptive and foster parents." Mindful of the hidden social justice element involved, she goes on to say: "We emphasize genetic parenthood but we turn away from the plight of children in need of parents, languishing in institutions." [56]

Current reproductive technologies have spawned the highly impersonal phrase, "noncoital collaborative reproduction". [57] The phrase brings to mind an assembly-line approach to human procreation. David Weaver and Luis Escobar have specified twenty-four different ways of having a child, only one of which is natural. [58] Their inventory is incomplete, however, since the ways enumerated are limited to no more than four collaborators. It is possible for twice as many collaborators to be involved in the conception, birth, and legal guardianship of a child. Consider the following example: A married couple is infertile due to its inability to produce healthy gametes. The wife also has occlusions in both fallo-

[55] "From Coitus to Commerce: Legal and Social Consequences of Noncoital Reproduction", *University of Michigan Journal of Law Reform*, 18 (4), Summer 1985, pp. 865–932.

[56] Henifin in Baruch, p. 5.

[57] W. Goodman. Lori Andrews remarks that one of the shortcomings of existing law "is its failure to define maternity and paternity in all possible circumstances".

[58] "Twenty-four Ways to Have Children", *American Journal of Medical Genetics*, 26 (3), March 1987, pp. 737–40.

pian tubes. Donor gametes are brought together through the GIFT technique and placed in the fallopian tube of a surrogate. An implantation problem requires the washing out and transferring of the embryo to a second surrogate, who completes the period of gestation and gives birth to the child. In the meantime, the infertile couple divorces and the child is adopted and reared by another couple. Thus, eight different people are involved, three men and five women, in the conception, gestation, birth, and rearing of the child. But in this scenario, the meanings of motherhood and fatherhood have been strained to the point of virtual meaninglessness. In our brave new world of high-tech baby-making, parents give way to a conglomeration of parent-like participants—"matroids" and "patroids", "momoids" and "dadoids".

It may not be possible to secure the right to have a child through reproductive technology without at the same time losing the integrity of parenthood. The procreative relationship between parents and offspring must be based on a most generous and unselfish love if both parties are to preserve their proper identities. The obverse of the commodification of children is the attenuation of parenthood. If motherhood and fatherhood are to remain personal and meaningful realities, children must not be viewed as objects of rights or instruments of gratification.

"Noncoital collaborative reproduction" obscures parenthood, commodifies offspring, promotes selfishness, destroys meaningful relational identities, and creates no end of contentious legal battles. It is unwise, from the standpoint of the integrity of marriage and the family as well as the health of society, to promote this impersonal, collective approach to human procreation.

Social Justice

The exploitation of infertile couples, the low success rates, the commodification of children, the attenuation of parenthood, and the inability of law to keep pace with evolving reproductive technology form an aggregate of interrelated problems strongly indicating that something must be wrong on a fundamental level. Perhaps the claim that one has a "right" to a child, and the accession on the part of the medical profession to that claim, are not possible without creating adverse reverberations through the whole of society, even to the point of infringing on the rights of others to have their basic health needs met. Perhaps there is no such thing as a "right" to have a child and that one may only desire, hope, and pray for one, and seek medical assistance to correct whatever fertility problem one might have. It seems contrary to individual as well as social ethics to claim that one has a right to procreate another human being.

Society has a duty to respond to people's basic health needs, since people have a right to have those needs met. *Needs* are universal and as such are appropriately discussed in the framework of rights. *Wants,* on the other hand, are private rather than universal. An individual may have any number of wants peculiar to him. These wants, no matter how intense, are not the same as needs and consequently are not the subject of rights. An individual may want a high income, pleasurable vacations, and a second car. He may also want contraception, sterilization, and access to an in vitro fertilization program. At best, these are privileges rather than rights. But when society allows the medical profession to deprive some poeple of their basic rights to health care in order to try to satisfy the wants of others, the issue of social justice is brought into sharp focus. Social justice demands that rights be given a certain priority over wants.

The need a baby has for parents is unambiguous and grounded in the child's absolute dependence. It is impossible to imagine that a child's need for parents could be confused with a need for something else. The "need" on the part of adults for babies is not so clear. As the husband of one infertile couple has declared, "We realized that a lot of other yearnings were loaded onto the wish for a child."[59] An infertile couple is not in a position of dependence merely because it is infertile. It is not dependent on a baby. Nor should it be. Similarly, poor people depend on others, and not *vice versa*. Thus, the relationship between babies and parents, poor people and their more affluent counterparts, is one of *need* and not mere *want*. And just as babies have a right to have parents, the poor have a right to basic health care. These rights are solidly grounded in fundamental human needs.

The ideology of choice, so popular in contemporary America, fails to take into consideration the fact that some people's "choice" for hazardous and expensive reproductive technologies that are neither medically indicated nor likely to succeed, sets up a chain of causal relationships that ultimately denies other people of their "choice" for appropriate health care.

The claim that all people in a society have a right to basic health care has a long and respected tradition. According to St. Thomas Aquinas:

> A man has the obligation to sustain his body, otherwise he would be a killer of himself . . . by precept, therefore, he is bound to nourish his body and likewise we are bound to all the other items without which the body can not live.[60]

Pope John XXIII's encyclical *Pacem in Terris* is most explicit in outlining every man's right to basic health services: "[E]very man has the right to life, to bodily integrity, and to the means which are necessary and suitable for the clothing, shelter, rest, medical care, and finally the necessary social services."[61]

Finally, the Catholic bishops of the United States reaffirmed this teaching in their 1981 pastoral letter on health care when they stated that every person has a basic right to adequate health care, and that this right implies "that access to that

[59] Diamant, p. 66.

[60] *Super Epistolas S. Pauli* (Taurini-Romae: Marietti, 1953), II Thess., Lec. II, N. 77.

[61] April 11, 1963, #11.

health care which is necessary and suitable for the proper development and maintenance of life must be provided for all people, regardless of economic, social or legal status. Special attention should be given to meeting the health needs of the poor."

An inordinate preoccupation with individual rights, including the right to privacy and the right to reproductive freedom, may have obscured the larger notion of social justice and the primacy of basic health needs as well as realistic attitudes toward maintaining health. Society hardly noticed the connection between the anti-fertility mentality that demanded contraception, sterilization, and abortion, and the ensuing epidemic of infertility it ushered in.[62] People have taken health for granted and have lost sight of the fact that a price must be paid on a social scale for the accumulation of irresponsible acts committed on the private level.

The World Health Organization has calculated that "[f]or the cost of one live IVF baby, it is likely that 100 women could be prevented from ever becoming infertile in the first place through programs to prevent sexually transmitted diseases".[63] It is estimated that sexually transmitted diseases account for 20% of all cases of infertility.[64] If something could also be done to prevent the infertility caused by other avoidable factors, such as contraception, sterilization, and abortion, an even greater percentage of women and men would be spared the hardship of infertility. Each year 15,000 American women request surgical reversal of a previous voluntary sterilization.[65]

"The growing preoccupation with IVF–ET and other new

[62] Robert Marshall, "Alternative Reproductive Technologies: Implications for Families and Children", *U.S. House of Representatives Select Committee on Children, Youth and Families,* May 21, 1987, Panel 2.

[63] Allender, p. 8.

[64] Otten, p. 33.

[65] B. Freedman and P. Taylor, "Government Funding for Surgical Reversal of Voluntary Female Sterilization: Ethical Points of Reference", *Journal of Reproductive Medicine,* 27 (6), June 1982, pp. 334–44.

reproductive technologies", writes Mary Sue Henifin, a lawyer specializing in women's rights and public health, "diverts attention from primary prevention of infertility. This is particularly harmful to poor and minority communities, which have little access to medical care and experience high rates of infertility." [66] While putting money and effort into the preventing of infertility is unassailably prudent and sensible, it is not always easy to win support for a prevention campaign. The disease one is suffering from always seems to be incomparably more important than the one that has not yet arrived. Therefore, prevention seems to involve the hypothetical and the abstract, factors that are less urgent than the affliction one is experiencing. Nonetheless, such a view, understandable as it is, flows from an individual perspective rather than from one broad enough to take into consideration the good of society and the needs of the future. A prevention policy, needless to say, is not antagonistic to one that administers immediate relief. Rather, it should be viewed as harmonious with it, while, in the long run, proving to be most practical.

In addition to shedding light on the importance of prevention, social justice considerations also illuminate the need for equitable allocations of funds. More than 30 million people in the United States—11 million of them children—have no health insurance whatsoever. When these people get sick, they often receive care, but frequently the care is late, may not be of the best quality, or is too costly. [67] At the same time, as William Woodside has pointed out, "No one in this country should be denied reasonable access to health care because he is too poor to buy insurance on his own." [68] The possibilities of providing health insurance for more poor people, however, will be greatly diminished if insurance companies decide to

[66] Baruch, p. 4.
[67] William S. Woodside, "Health Care for the Poor: How to Pay for It", *The Wall Street Journal,* May 29, 1987.
[68] Ibid.

increase their coverage for reproductive technologies, at costs that could easily run into the billions of dollars.[69]

Pat Schroeder, a Democratic representative of Colorado, has planned to introduce legislation in Congress that would mandate full-infertility coverage in the health insurance package offered to three million government workers. Ms. Schroeder's proposal mandates that health plans for federal employees cover a wide range of reproductive technologies, which she refers to as "family building activities".[70] Speaking against this proposal, a spokeswoman for the Employee Benefits Research Institute in Washington remarked: "When you have 37 million uninsured, covering in vitro fertilization is not on the priority list."[71]

Given the organic relationships between the government and insurance companies (and also taking into account the sharply rising costs of health care),[72] the increased costs of covering highly unsuccessful reproductive technologies would seem to conflict with expanding basic health insurance coverage for the indigent. At any rate, the funding issue should force more directly a discussion of whether reproductive technologies are genuinely therapeutic or are treating individuals' wishes. It should also force the more practical question concerning reproductive technology's potential for creating more health problems than it solves. The words of a senior official of WHO are worth reiterating: "What we do know is that, at great cost, about 8 per cent of couples in any country can be helped by in-vitro fertilization with considerable risk of not ending up with a healthy baby."[73] We should also not forget the considerable risks to the woman herself.

[69] Thomas Shannon, "In Vitro Ethical Issues", in Baruch, p. 161.

[70] Johnson.

[71] Margaret W. Newton quoted in Ibid.

[72] Spencer Rich, "U.S. Health Costs Continue Steep Rise: 8.4 Percent Increase Far Outstrips Inflation, Growth of Economy", The Washington Post, Oct. 11, 1987, A8.

[73] Dr. Marsden Wagner quoted in Interim.

David Ozar, director of the M. A. Program in Health Care Ethics at Chicago's Loyola University, argues that making reproductive technologies available to everyone who wants them "would almost certainly draw significant resources away from other pressing health care needs or from other uses of resources within the larger community". [74]

Another societal cost involved in providing reproductive technology for infertile couples is that medical expertise is directed away from the needy and toward society's more affluent members. Observers have pointed out that the enormous effort in time and manpower that has gone into establishing IVF units alone has produced a "brain drain in many departments of obstetrics and gynecology". [75]

Last, viewing reproductive technology against a conflicting background of abortion, Ronald Lawler asks whether the medical profession is conducting a battle against itself, unmindful of its most fundamental obligation to life:

> Is it right for us to encourage an atmosphere in which obvious and subtle pressures create an abortion industry that destroys a million and a half unborn babies every year, and then begin to establish another industry to create babies for people who are induced to believe that the baby someone manufactures for them will be more appropriate than a baby already living? [76]

Social justice considerations in the area of reproductive technology draw attention to five subjects of human rights: (1) infertile couples, who have a right to be protected from exploitation as well as the right not to be subjected to nontherapeutic procedures that are hazardous to their health; (2) members of the medical profession, who have a right to practice medicine without being unduly pressured to treat pa-

---

[74] "The Case against Thawing Unused Frozen Embryos", *Hastings Center Report,* vol. 15, no. 4, Aug. 1985, p. 12.

[75] Dr. Tulchinsky, *Intelligence Reports in Ob-Gyn,* March 6, 1986, p. 9.

[76] "Moral Reflections on the New Technologies: A Catholic Analysis", in Baruch, p. 174.

tients' desires; (3) children—prenatal, orphaned, or abandoned—who have a right to have parents; (4) poor people, who have a right to affordable basic health care; (5) all naturally fertile people, who have a right to know how certain procedures, devices, and activities can cause infertility.

Public Policy Recommendations

1. *That infertile couples be protected from exploitation arising from the media, from manipulative advertising, or from the medical profession.* Because infertile couples are a highly vulnerable group, action should be taken to protect them from the potential deception that exists on a variety of cultural levels. Success rates should be unambiguously and accurately reported. Risks to clients and offspring should be made clear. Advertising should fairly reflect the scientific aspects of reproductive technologies and not be manipulative or try to take advantage in any way of couples who are already in a vulnerable position. The media should report failures and successes in a more balanced way.

2. *That prenatal human beings, even at the earliest stages of life, be treated with appropriate respect as members of the human family and not viewed as commodities.* A human being is destined for autonomy and thus should never be regarded as a means to an end. No human being, prenatal or prospective, should be viewed as an object of someone else's rights. No one has a right to another human being. Moreover, viewing children as commodities that can be purchased and sold, returned or exchanged, would inevitably prove detrimental to the well-being of children, since it would regard them as goods of a determinable value. Primary consideration should always be given to the welfare and "best interests" of the child.

3. *That society encourage the cultivation in both prospective and actual parents of attitudes toward their offspring that are benevolent and nonpossessory.* A generous and other-directed love is the only appropriate attitude parents should have for their chil-

dren. They should not view their offspring as objects of rights. Love transcends the level of an exchange of rights. Babies need parents far more than parents need them. The role of the parent is essentially to be *for* the child.

4. *That the traditional presumption according legal motherhood to the birthing mother be deemed irrebuttable.* She may later agree to give up the child for adoption, or relinquish her parental rights and responsibilities. But those decisions would be hers alone to make. In this way, the child's mother will always be readily identifiable. If the mother is married, her husband would be acknowledged as the child's father. This would be done in the interest of the integrity of marriage and would spare the child any stigma of illegitimacy. It would also recognize the importance of establishing a consistent and unambiguous notion of motherhood.

5. *That more effort and money be directed toward preventing infertility and toward the research and development of techniques which provide genuinely therapeutic interventions, i.e., those that are aimed at restoring fertility.* This would encourage doctors to treat diseases rather than desires, and to be less vulnerable to media and patient pressure. It would also allow more medical resources and personnel to be available to serve the basic health care needs of poor people.

Chapter Nine

The Baby M Case
and Other Arguments
against Surrogate Motherhood

The Current Misapplication of the Word "Surrogate"

A surrogate is a person who substitutes for another. That person may be a *vicar* who represents another in an official capacity, such as an episcopal-vicar, or a *proxy* who is deputized to act for someone who cannot be present. He may be a *stand-in* who takes the place of an actor while the film crew prepares for shooting, or a *stuntman* who executes a difficult and dangerous maneuver that someone else cannot perform. Or he may be a *pinch hitter* who fills in for another in an emergency. In all of these examples, the surrogate is involved in an activity that is task-oriented. One cannot think for another, will for another, or love for another; these are not tasks, but immanent or non-transient activities. Moreover, in none of these instances does the surrogate experience any confusion about his personal identity. He may have less authority, receive less pay, and enjoy less prestige than the person he replaces, but he knows exactly who he is and is properly acknowledged for the surrogate role he plays.

Confusion of identity enters the picture when the presumption is made that the surrogate's activities realize direct, personal benefits for the individual on whose behalf he is acting, rather than for the surrogate himself. Making such an assumption is tantamount to believing that a person can lose weight by having a surrogate diet for him. Dieting, obviously, is a non-transferrable activity. Here, the confusion is twofold: the surrogate believes he is not what he is, and the person for whom he acts believes he is what he is not.

Until the recent misapplication of the word "surrogate" to the domain of sexuality, such confusion of identities was largely restricted to the province of literature. In *The Courtship of Miles Standish,* for example, John Alden makes a feeble attempt to play the role of surrogate suitor. His effort proves unsuccessful, chiefly because Priscilla Mullens is able to read his heart. With exquisite simplicity, she poses her immortal question: "Why don't you speak for yourself, John?" For Priscilla, John was a diamond trying to interest her in a zircon. In the kingdom of love, there can be no substitutes.

This highly celebrated scene held much more than mere literary meaning for its author, Henry Wadsworth Longfellow. The events he described were family legends; he was descended, on his mother's side, from John Alden and Priscilla Mullens. A contemporary version of the poem, however, would have Miles Standish paying John Alden handsomely for his surrogate services, Priscilla Mullens accepting Miles's offer of marriage, and then eloping shortly before the wedding with his attorney.

One of America's most beloved humorists, Fred Allen, cleverly illustrates the folly of carrying surrogacy beyond its natural limitations with his creation of the "Allen Relaxation Society". This imaginary organization existed for tired businessmen who did not have the time to follow their doctor's advice to take a long rest. Allen provided surrogates to take the relaxation for these busy tycoons, thereby leaving them free to overwork themselves to death or to their hearts' content. "We took care of one magnate", Fred recalled, "whose doctor warned him to go off with his wife for a long, health-restoring cruise. We produced a man who not only took the cruise for him, overate for him, undertipped for him, and got seasick for him, but flirted so shamelessly with a cute blonde for him that his wife went into a huff all the way from Cherbourg to Juan-les-Pins."[1]

[1] Bennett Cerf, *The Life of the Party* (New York: Random House, 1956), pp. 242–43.

When "surrogate sex partners" came into vogue within certain supposedly enlightened circles as a form of therapy,[2] the notion of surrogacy passed from realism to surrealism. A person cannot be both sexually intimate and professionally distanced from the same person at the same time. By entering into sexual intimacy with someone, a "surrogate" cannot help but represent herself. She cannot leave her personality entirely outside of the situation and function as a mere surrogate, acting solely with a third party's interest in mind. Sexual intercourse fosters intimacy between the participants, not between one participant and another person who is not present.

Surrogates, in the realistic sense, are asked to perform objective tasks for someone else. But sex is not an objective task; it is an intimately personal relationship. It is an organic unity—involving two specific people—that is violated when one partner is replaced by a "surrogate". The intimate and personal nature of sex precludes surrogacy. The fact that the loved ones deem each other to be irreplaceable is rooted in the very essence of love. For love focuses primarily on the lovers and not on what they do or how well they do it. Love is first and foremost a phenomenon of *being,* not *doing.* And the good that two people *do* as man and wife should spring from who they *are.*

Society makes a critical mistake when it reduces marriage to a set of tasks. In doing so, it loses sight of the "being" element of marriage. Sexual intercourse between husband and wife is a manifestation of the *being* of their married state and as such does not permit surrogate partners. One can find a maid or a machine to do the dishes, but not a surrogate to replace one's wife because a wife is part of the husband's being (as the two-in-one-flesh unity implies). One's spouse is irreplaceable.

Indeed, every human being, because he is uniquely lovable, is irreplaceable. A loving husband or wife could no more accept a surrogate sex partner than a grieving mother or father could accept a surrogate child to replace the one they lost. By

[2] "Therapy Can Be Fun", *Time,* Sept. 10, 1973, p. 63.

the same token, the notion of "surrogate motherhood" contradicts the unity of marriage and creates the impression that partners should view each other not as irreplaceable persons, but in terms of the tasks or functions they can or cannot perform.

Confusion over the Meaning of Surrogate Motherhood

The term "surrogate mother" originally referred to a "host" mother who carried a child conceived through in vitro fertilization from the egg and sperm of a married couple.[3] In this case, the "surrogate" was furnishing the gestational phase of motherhood, which the genetic mother could not provide. She was a mother continuing the work of the original mother who was unable to be pregnant with her child. The first conception-delivery by means of this procedure took place at Mount Sinai Hospital in Cleveland in 1986.[4] In another case, doctors extracted the egg of a woman who had no uterus, fertilized it outside her body with her husband's sperm, and implanted it in a surrogate.[5] This method is a difficult and complicated one and has a very low rate of success. Nonetheless, it has not yet been abandoned.[6]

In a second method, a child is conceived in vivo through

[3] Maggie Gallagher, "Womb to Let", *National Review,* April 24, 1987, p. 27.

[4] Nancy Blodgett, "Who Is Mother?" *American Bar Association Journal,* June 1, 1986, p. 18.

[5] *New York Times,* Nov. 21, 1985, B22, col. 1.

[6] See "Surrogate Case a Canadian First", *Kitchener-Waterloo Record,* May 12, 1987, p. 1. This news item describes a Canadian married couple who have paid $10,000 to an American lawyer and have provided another $10,000 for an American surrogate. They have also set aside $8,000 to cover medical costs of two attempts at implantation. See also "Woman Bearing Daughter's Triplets Viewed as Heroine in South Africa", *Toronto Globe and Mail,* April 8, 1987, A5. A 48-year-old South African woman carried IVF triplets for her daughter whose uterus had been removed after the birth of her son because of a complication.

sexual intercourse and then, about five days later, extracted from the woman and implanted in a surrogate. This technique is also known as "surrogate embryo transfer".[7] With both methods, there is a bifurcation of maternity into *genetic* and *gestational,* in which the genetic mother is the rearing mother and the gestational mother is the surrogate mother.

In addition, there are two modes of surrogacy in which there is no bifurcation of maternity. In these instances, the surrogate *is* genetically related to the child. In the first mode, the woman is artificially inseminated by the sperm of a man whose own wife is either infertile or chooses to avoid conception; the surrogate carries the child to term. This is how society and the media understand surrogate motherhood. Nonetheless, because this surrogate does not continue the work of the genetic mother but, rather, replaces the wife who cannot be or chooses not to be a mother in any natural or biological sense, it may be said that she is really a "surrogate wife". In order to bring home the practical significance of this point, we may refer to an incident which Noel Keane recounts in his book, *The Surrogate Mother.* Keane, a lawyer who is in the business of matching infertile couples with surrogates, put a Manhattan couple in touch with a potential surrogate from Brooklyn. The husband and the surrogate went to a motel to attempt artificial insemination but decided to effect the conception in "the old-fashioned way". In Keane's words: "They liked it so well they ran off with each other." Keane then received a call from "a hysterical wife" who complained that not only did she not get her baby, but she lost her husband.[8]

In the second mode, the surrogate is involved neither with reproductive technologies nor with men to whom she is not married. In this instance, the woman conceives a child through marital intercourse, carries it to term, and relin-

---

[7] Lori Andrews, *New Conceptions: A Consumer's Guide to the Newest Infertility Treatments, Including In Vitro Fertilization, Artificial Insemination, and Surrogate Motherhood* (New York: St. Martin's, 1984), p. 254.

[8] New York: Everest House, 1981, p. 139.

quishes it to the adopting parents who initially bargained for the child. Here, the wife who bears her own husband's child and surrenders her parental rights to it is usually called a "domestic surrogate".[9]

Surrogate mothers are also identified as "host mothers", "mercenary mothers", "incubators", or simply as "breeders".[10] And to make matters even more confusing, the natural father of the child in the typical surrogate arrangement is sometimes referred to as the "surrogate father".[11]

One factor that all four types of "surrogate mothers" have in common is that they are the ones who give birth to the baby. Traditionally, this impressive fact was sufficient to establish "real motherhood". According to American law, the mother as "the one from whose womb the child came"[12] carried an unshakeable presumption that until recently had been considered so absolute as to have generated no controversy. According to the British House of Lords, maternity is in law "based on a fact, being proved demonstrably by parturition".[13]

The presumption that the father of a child born to a married woman is that woman's husband is said to be one of the strongest known to the law. In some states the presumption is said to be conclusive.[14] A California appellate court has declared that this presumption exists to protect "the integrity of the family unit and to protect the child from the social stigma

[9] Moira Wright, "Surrogacy and Adoption: Problems and Possibilities", 16 *Family Law*, April 1986, pp. 110–11.

[10] Gena Corea, *The Mother Machine* (New York: Harper and Row, 1985), p. 214.

[11] Angela R. Holder, "Surrogate Motherhood: Babies for Fun and Profit", 90 *Case and Comment*, no. 2, March–April 1985, 4.

[12] Andrea E. Stumpf, "Redefining Mother: A Legal Matrix for New Reproductive Technologies", *Yale Law Journal*, Nov. 1986, p. 187.

[13] *Ampthill* Peerage Case (1977). A.C. 547, 577 *per* Lord Simon of Glaisdale.

[14] Barbara Cohen "Surrogate Mothers: Whose Baby Is It?" *American Journal of Law and Medicine*, Fall 1984, p. 266

of illegitimacy".[15] According to Section 5 (b) of the Uniform Parentage Act, adopted by several states, this presumption applies even where artificial insemination is involved: "The donor of semen provided for use in artificial insemination of a married woman other than the donor's wife is treated in law as if he were not the natural father of a child thereby conceived."

What tradition saw no reason to doubt, concerning the definition of real motherhood, contemporary society now views with great uncertainty. One commentator has described the surrogate mother as "a prenatal wet nurse who supplies nourishment to a developing fetus".[16] One surrogate herself likened her maternal capacities to those of an "incubator" and managed to convince herself that she would "just be nest-watching".[17] An advocate for surrogate motherhood states in a law review: "Use of the surrogate method, manifesting procreative intent, should invoke the legal presumption that the child belongs to the intenders."[18]

But the uncertainty surrounding the meanings of "real motherhood" and "surrogate motherhood" is largely artificial, originating in the commercialization of procreation where the names of things are falsified in the interest of pleasing the consumer. From a realistic (non-commercial) perspective, it is the adoptive mother who is truly the surrogate, since it is she who rears a child born by another. "Surrogate motherhood" is a contradictory notion (like "childless parent") because it suggests that a woman can both be and not be a mother at the same time. In particular instances, such as the Baby M episode, the natural mother is caught in a contradiction between her contractual obligation that tells her she is not a mother, and her lived experience that tells her she is. In this particular case, it was Mary Beth Whitehead's existential ex-

---

[15] *Vincent B. v. Joan R.,* 126 Cal App. 3d 624, 179 Cal. Rptr 11 (1981).

[16] Avi Katz, "Surrogate Motherhood and the Baby-Selling Laws", 20 *Columbia Journal of Law and Social Problems,* no. 1, 1986, pp. 23–24, f.n. 115.

[17] Corea, p. 222.

[18] Stumpf, p. 196.

perience of motherhood that convinced her that she was indeed Baby M's mother. This case offers a dramatic and instructive testimony of the contradiction that surrogacy poses and the great personal hardships it can impose.

The Baby M Case

The Baby M case is the first custody dispute involving a surrogate mother ever brought before an American court. The case was well publicized, attracting news teams from as far away as Sweden and the Soviet Union. The details, announced each day in the media, formed the substance of a continuing national soap opera.

Early in 1985, William and Elizabeth Stern of Tenafly, New Jersey, contracted with Mary Beth Whitehead, a resident of Brick Township in that same state, for her to conceive a child through artificial insemination and carry it to term for them. Mrs. Stern, 41, had been reluctant to have a child of her own since she was diagnosed in 1979 as having "a probably mild case of multiple sclerosis".[19] The soundness of avoiding pregnancy because of this disease, however, has been debated. Phyllis Shaw, a spokesman for the National Multiple Sclerosis Society, has said there is no reason for a woman with multiple sclerosis to avoid pregnancy unless she is so disabled she cannot care for a newborn infant.[20]

After reviewing and rejecting the applications of 300 women, the Sterns chose Mary Beth Whitehead, age 29. Mrs. Whitehead appeared to be the perfect candidate. She did not drink or smoke, and she even bore a facial resemblance to Mrs. Stern. She was a housewife with two school-age children by her husband, Richard, and asserted that she wanted

[19] Lacayo, p. 62.
[20] "Pregnancy Could Have Been Risky, Custody Hearing Told", *Kitchener-Waterloo Record*, Jan. 10, 1987, p. A8.

no more children of her own. Richard himself had undergone a vasectomy.[21]

After their first meeting in a New Jersey restaurant, the Sterns and the Whiteheads became friends. When Mrs. Whitehead signed the surrogate contract, she promised among other things that she would not "form or attempt to form a parent-child relationship" with the resulting child. The Sterns agreed to pay Mary Beth $10,000 plus medical expenses.

As the pregnancy developed, William Stern insisted that Mrs. Whitehead undergo amniocentesis to help ensure that the child was not abnormal. This she did, though it was contrary to the advice of her private obstetrician. She retaliated, however, by not telling the Sterns the baby's sex.[22] Stern also held that he had a right to insist on an abortion if the amniocentesis report was unfavorable.[23] If Mary Beth miscarried during the first four months, she would receive no payment; if she miscarried later, she would receive $1,000.

Achieving pregnancy was not easy. After the failure of the first attempt, at a New York sperm bank on February 6, 1985, a regular routine followed. Several times a month, William Stern and Mary Beth Whitehead drove together from New Jersey to New York for further insemination attempts. Mrs. Whitehead finally conceived on July 2, 1985.[24]

The baby was born on March 27, 1986. When the newborn child smelled her mother's milk and drew closer to Mary Beth Whitehead, a court-appointed chaperon stationed at the hospital interceded to prevent her from nursing. The court did

---

[21] Elizabeth Kolbert, "Battle for Baby M: Fierce Emotions and Key Legal Issues", *The New York Times,* Aug. 23, 1986.

[22] B. Kantrowitz, "Who Keeps 'Baby M'?" *Newsweek,* Jan. 19, 1987, p. 49.

[23] Michele Landsberg, "Baby M Decision Gives Legal Backing to Inhumane Practice", *Toronto Globe and Mail,* April 4, 1987, p. A2.

[24] Kantrowitz, p. 49.

not want a mother-child bond to be formed because the state of New Jersey had not yet decided whether Mary Beth Whitehead would be allowed to be Baby M's mother.[25] Nonetheless, the bonding that had developed during the pregnancy had had its effect. Mrs. Whitehead changed her mind. She decided to reject the money and keep the child. As she later told the court, the experience of childbirth "overpowered" her. "Something took over. I think it was just being a mother", she said. "I was completely devastated having the child taken from my arms", Mary Beth wrote after the fact. "I felt like I was used for one purpose and was no longer needed or wanted."[26] Her husband, Richard, had also expressed doubts about giving up the child. He said that he was troubled by the thought of taking $10,000 and selling the sister of his two children.[27]

The Whiteheads took the newborn child home with them. Three days later, the Sterns arrived and took the child back with them. But after surrendering her child to the Sterns, Mary Beth cried hysterically, asking, "Oh God, what have I done?"[28] The very next morning, she went to the Sterns' home and begged for temporary custody. A two-hour emotional battle arose, which ended when Mrs. Stern, who feared that Mary Beth was suicidal, gave in to her demand. Two weeks later, the Sterns tried to regain custody of the child, but the Whiteheads refused to cooperate.

A month later, after obtaining a court order and having a lien placed on the impoverished Whiteheads' property, the Sterns returned with five policemen to recover the now five-week-old infant.[29] In the ensuing confusion, Richard White-

[25] Maggie Gallagher, "Womb to Let", National Review, April 24, 1987, p. 27.

[26] Ellen Goodman, "Whose Baby Is She?" The Boston Globe, Sept. 2, 1986, p. 15.

[27] Kantrowitz, p. 49.

[28] Lacayo, p. 60.

[29] Landsberg, p. A2.

head escaped with the child through a bedroom window. The Whiteheads then fled to Florida with the infant and took up residence with the child's maternal grandparents. The Sterns then responded by hiring a private detective, at a cost in excess of $20,000, to track down the Whiteheads.[30]

From her parents' home, Mary Beth telephoned William Stern on July 15. In a conversation that was taped and later presented before the court, she said: "I'd rather see me and her dead before you get her." In a subsequent telephone call, she threatened to accuse Stern of sexually abusing her oldest daughter, if he continued to seek custody of Baby M.[31]

After 87 days, authorities finally located the Whiteheads. Catherine Messer, of Holiday, Florida, Mary Beth's mother, testified that about six police officers came to her home on July 31. She said that one of the officers grabbed her by the arm, threw her on the floor, and asked where her daughter was.[32] The authorities apprehended the child and returned her to New Jersey, and Judge Harvey Sorkow granted temporary custody to the Sterns. Judge Sorkow allowed Mrs. Whitehead to spend two hours twice a week with Baby M on the neutral turf of a local children's home.

Early in the custody phase of the trial, Lorraine Abraham, the court-appointed lawyer for Baby M, urged the judge to award custody to her biological father and to deny visitation rights to Mrs. Whitehead, the woman who had conceived, carried, and delivered the child.[33] This was a somewhat surprising move since it was made before testimony had been presented. The Sterns' attorney enumerated 35 reasons why Whitehead should not gain custody. He pointed out that the

---

[30] Kantrowitz, p. 49.

[31] "Surrogate Mom's Chilling Threat: 'I can take her life'", *The Toronto Sun*, Feb. 5, 1987, p. 3.

[32] "Woman Tells How Police Seized Baby", *Kitchener-Waterloo Record*, March 6, 1987, p. A12.

[33] "Lawyer Acting for Baby Urges No Visitation Rights for Surrogate Mother", *Kitchener-Waterloo Record*, Feb. 3, 1987, p. E8.

Sterns, both professionals with a combined annual income of $91,000, would provide the child with a more stable home and a better future than Mary Beth and her husband, a garbage collector, could.[34] A lawyer representing the Whiteheads furnished an expert witness who claimed that the baby would benefit by growing up with the surrogate's other two children and by having grandparents for additional emotional support. On the other hand, another expert witness disparaged Mrs. Whitehead's skills as a mother because she did not play pat-a-cake the right way[35] and was pathologically narcissistic because she dyed her prematurely white hair black.[36] Mary Beth's competence as a mother was also brought into question because she had acquired as many as four stuffed panda bears.[37]

At the end of the 32-day trial, Judge Sorkow read his 121-page ruling. He upheld the surrogate contract and awarded full custody of the child to the Sterns. He was particularly severe in his appraisal of Mrs. Whitehead, describing her as manipulative and exploitive, untruthful in her testimony and unwilling to accept that her husband's problems, especially his alcoholism, are also her problems. He ruled that surrogate parenting is not the same thing as selling a baby because Bill Stern "cannot purchase what is already his."[38]

Thus, Baby M, whom the Whiteheads called Sarah and the Sterns, Melissa, finally received a permanent name, a fixed address, and an identification with specific parents. This came about on March 31, 1987, four days after her first birthday. Four months later, Mary Beth and her husband separated.

---

[34] "Surrogate Mother 'Guilty of Too Much Love'", *Kitchener-Waterloo Record,* March 13, 1987, p. B15.

[35] "In the Best Interests of a Child", *Times,* April 13, 1987, p. 50.

[36] Landsberg, p. A2.

[37] "Nothing Surrogate about the Pain", *The New York Times,* March 9, 1987.

[38] "Surrogate Mom Loses Baby M", *Kitchener-Waterloo Record,* April 1, 1987, p. A1.

According to their lawyer, the separation "merely confirms one piece of evidence during the trial, that there was marital instability in the Whiteheads' marriage in the past, and we predicted there would be instability in the present and the future".[39] Less than three months after the separation, Mary Beth moved in with Dean Gould, a man four years her junior whom she met while on vacation in St. Thomas. She soon became pregnant by him.[40] Once her divorce from Richard Whitehead became final,[41] she married Gould, a comptroller for a company that manages condominiums on Long Island. About five months after the arrival of their first child, a boy, Mary Beth became pregnant again. A few months thereafter, she commenced a 22-city, $100,000 publicity tour to promote her new book— A Mother's Story: The Truth about the Baby M Case.[42]

On February 4, 1988, the New Jersey Supreme Court invalidated the surrogate contract between the Sterns and Whiteheads. The Court stated, "We invalidate the surrogacy contract because it conflicts with the law and public policy of the State."[43] In granting custody to the natural father, it also recognized and ratified the corresponding rights of the natural mother: "[W]e void both the termination of the surrogate mother's parental rights and the adoption of the child by the wife/stepparent [Mrs. Stern]. We thus restore the 'surrogate' as the mother of the child."[44] It also denounced the commercial aspect of surrogacy: "Its [the contract's] use of money for this purpose—and we have no doubt whatsoever that the

[39] Joseph F. Sullivan, "Whiteheads Announce Separation", *The New York Times,* Aug. 5, 1987, p. 81.

[40] "Baby M's Mother Pregnant", *The Boston Herald,* Nov. 1, 1987, p. 9.

[41] "Surrogate Mother Granted a Divorce", *The Kitchener-Waterloo Record,* Nov. 13, 1987, B12.

[42] "A Surrogate Tells Her Story", *The Boston Globe,* Feb. 27, 1989.

[43] Family Law Reporter, p. 2008. See also Thomas Shannon, *Surrogate Motherhood,* (New York: Crossroad, 1988), pp. 139–41.

[44] Ibid.

money is being paid to obtain an adoption and not, as the
Sterns argue, for the personal services of Mary Beth Whitehead—is illegal and perhaps criminal." [45]

Consequent to the Supreme Court's ruling, and by mutual
agreement, William Stern now drives his daughter Melissa—
or Sassy, as she calls herself—every other Sunday morning to
visit her mother for the day. And every other Sunday evening,
Mary Beth drives her daughter back to the Sterns. [46]

Her Bond Was Better Than Her Word

Whitehead's lawyers had argued that surrogate motherhood
should be outlawed since no woman, prior to conceiving her
child, is in a position to make a binding decision about giving
it up once it is born. This line of reasoning naturally raises
issues concerning the effect pregnancy has on a woman's attitude toward the child she carries. Does pregnancy change a
woman so profoundly that her attitude to her child is not the
same as it was before she conceived? Is it possible for a woman
to view her procreative potential with such detachment that
the difference between a possible child and an actual child has
little or no impact on her? Is such detachment even desirable?

Those who endorse the employment of surrogates would
like to sunder pregnancy from motherhood. They would like
people to accept the idea that the transition from not being
pregnant to being pregnant does not of itself make a woman a
mother. If a woman is a surrogate mother, she is a mother for
someone else, but not a real mother or a mother in her own
right. According to one enthusiast for the new definition of
motherhood, the "mental conception" of the initiating couple
that desires to have a child is a more appropriate determinant
of motherhood than the mere biological conception of the

---

[45] Ibid., p. 2012.
[46] Joseph F. Sullivan, "Whiteheads Announce Separation", *The New York
Times,* Aug. 5, 1987, p. 81.

pregnant woman (the presence of the male member of the couple notwithstanding).[47]

Such ideological thinking, however, is grossly deceiving. A surrogate woman who becomes pregnant is a mother. Therefore, she has changed. The meaning of her motherhood is grounded in the fact that she has a motherly relationship with a real child, a circumstance that is radically distinguishable from her not being pregnant and having a possible relationship with a child that does not yet exist. The bond that exists between the woman and the child in her womb establishes her motherhood. The attempt to deny the existence of the bond and separate the woman from her pregnancy is necessary in order to deny her rightful motherhood. Such a denial is essentially Cartesian in that it separates mind from body in such a way as to create the impression that they are radically separable.

Many commentators have noted that courts are not likely to take a child from a natural mother who breaches a surrogate contract. George Annas, Associate Professor of Law and Medicine at Boston University states: "I can't see the court wresting the child out of its natural mother's arms."[48] Angela Holder, director of Yale University's program in law, science, and medicine adds: "There's not a court in the country that would uphold that [surrogate motherhood] contract if the surrogate decided she wanted to keep the baby."[49]

The basis for such assertions is the recognition of the fact that at the time of birth, the surrogate has not only been physically attached to the child for nine months, but has developed an emotional attachment to the child as well. Doctors Klaus and Kennel, in a study of women during pregnancy, report that a woman usually experiences feelings of attachment toward her unborn child.[50] In another study, these same re-

[47] Stumpf, p. 194–97.
[48] Cohen, 260.
[49] Angela Holder, *Tucson Citizen Weekender,* June 7, 1980.
[50] *Parent-Infant Bonding* (1982), p. 47.

searchers found that even when the child is originally unwanted, these feelings of attachment may develop in some women throughout the pregnancy, especially after quickening.[51] Concerning the deaths of newborns, Klaus and Kennel reported that even when the mother had no contact with her newborn, she grieved over his death.[52] Thus, they drew the conclusion: "If there had been no attachment, there would be no grief."[53]

Advocates of surrogate motherhood, particularly those who stand to profit from it, try to play down the attachment that transpires between mother and child. Nevertheless, despite being carefully instructed that the child she carries does not belong to her but to someone else, a surrogate commonly feels grief after relinquishing the child to the commissioning couple. The presence of this grief provides a most powerful and convincing testimony of the bond that develops between the surrogate and her child.

The pseudonymous Elizabeth Kane, the first successful surrogate whose story reached the press, stated that she loved her baby. She admitted being "naïve to think that . . . [she] could keep from being attached to the child".[54] Although she did relinquish the child, her attachment was rather strong. "I also went through depression", she told the news media, "on the third day in the hospital when my milk came in and the other woman was feeding the baby. And when I said good-bye to the baby, it broke my heart. I cried for weeks every Sunday because he was born on Sunday."[55] Another surrogate told a reporter that "turning away from the baby was the hardest thing I've ever done in my life. . . . It was the saddest good-

---

[51] *Maternal-Infant Bonding* (1976).

[52] Ibid., p. 46.

[53] Ibid., p. 45.

[54] "Surrogate Mother Elizabeth Kane Delivers the 'Gift of Love' Then Kisses Her Baby Good-bye", *People,* Dec. 8, 1980, p. 53.

[55] Betty J. Blair, "Surrogate Motherhood: Controversy and a Dilemma", *Detroit News,* Nov. 24, 1982.

bye I've ever known, even though I had told myself again and again during the pregnancy that it was really not my baby."[56]

A Toronto lawyer who has acted for couples who contracted with surrogates observes that few surrogate mothers emerge from the experience unscathed. "I've seen attempted suicide, depression, rejection by family and friends and a need for psychotherapy."[57] An associate professor of nursing of the University of Michigan who counselled 41 surrogate mothers, reports that many of these women suffered emotional trauma when they had to give up their babies. "They exhibited all kinds of grieving behavior," she went on to say, "the aching arms, the uncontrollable crying, the sense that their baby was gone. They couldn't interact with other babies, they couldn't go out and look at other newborns."[58]

Personal experience, public policy, and scientific opinion have coalesced to form a strong tradition that a pregnant woman cultivates a special bond with her child as it develops within the womb; as a consequence, she is prone to grief as a result of relinquishing her child. This tradition has identified such a woman as a mother. Thus, it is not difficult to understand why a powerful and pervasive force exists that opposes the legislation of surrogate motherhood. Courts faced with litigation on surrogate motherhood have taken the position that such arrangements are contrary to public policy, and the courts have refused to compel specific performance of these

[56] "A Surrogate's Story of Loving and Losing", U.S. News and World Report, June 6, 1983, p. 77. See also Robertson, "Surrogate Mothers: Not So Novel After All", 19 Hastings Center Report, Oct. 1983, p. 30. "Relinquishing the baby after birth may be considerably more disheartening and disappointing than [the surrogate] anticipated. Even if informed of this possibility in advance, she may be distressed for several weeks with feelings of loss, depression, and sleep disturbance."

[57] Sheryl Ubelacker, "$urrogates: Ethical and Legal Questions Persist When Women Bear Children for Pay", Kitchener-Waterloo Record, April 27, 1987: D1.

[58] Ibid., p. 30.

contracts.[59] Writing for the *American Journal of Law and Medicine,* Barbara Cohen argues that all surrogate contracts should be treated as "revocable prebirth agreements".[60] In England, the Warnock Committee recommended that all surrogacy agreements should be declared unenforceable and that those engaged in surrogacy, commercially or otherwise, should be subject to criminal prosecution. It also recommended that the bearing mother should have full parental rights over the child irrespective of genetic realities.[61]

In the United States, a National Coalition against Surrogacy has been formed, which includes 17 surrogate mothers who now oppose the practice. The testimony of one of its members, Laurie Yates, a Michigan surrogate, exemplifies the pain and misfortune that many surrogates experience. Mrs. Yates testifies that she suffered a miscarriage and was forced to take fertility drugs to have another child. She gave birth to twins and then proceeded to seek custody. She eventually settled out of court for visitation rights and other undisclosed provisions. According to Mrs. Yates, the surrogacy episode broke her family's finances, strained her marriage, and, she fears, adversely affected her own daughter. "Surrogacy was the biggest mistake of my life", she says.[62]

The Coalition cites other problems of surrogacy, such as diseased or defective children rejected by both parents, a baby born with AIDS, and a surrogate mother who died during pregnancy. Members of the Coalition charge that brokers play on the strained emotions, finances, and family relations of typically poor surrogates.

Nonetheless, a counterforce currently exists that challenges

---

[59] Holder, 1985, p. 3.

[60] Cohen, 243–85.

[61] Wright, 109.

[62] Andrew Malcolm, "Steps to Control Surrogate Births Stir New Debate", *The New York Times,* June 26, 1988.

society's traditional wisdom concerning the meaning of motherhood and the rights a mother has to the children of her own flesh. This counterforce has been made possible through the alliance of modern reproductive technologies and commercial interest. Surrogate motherhood is a product of this alliance. Inevitably, it must devalue biological motherhood[63] in order to endorse psychological motherhood.[64] Consequently, the congruence of the biological and psychological aspects of motherhood in the same woman is no longer viewed as normative.[65] Rather, divergence becomes the norm in which diverse aspects of motherhood are assigned to different people.

Harriet Blankfeld, who has arranged 57 surrogate births through her Infertility Associates International in Chevy Chase, Maryland, strenuously opposes banning surrogate arrangements. "It won't stop the practice", she remarks. "It'll just create an even more secret and dangerous one as we did with abortions. You know, every month a woman flushes an egg from her body. If she chooses in her own freedom to have that egg fertilized and carry that baby for an infertile couple that desperately wants a child, what sin has she committed?"[66]

The pressure to limit one's motherhood in accordance with this paradigm of divergence can produce great tension and anxiety in a woman who wants to be a mother in the full sense. The body-spirit unity of the person rebels when it is divided against itself. Mary Beth Whitehead could promise to

---

[63] Stumpf, 197. "Western society's historical tendency has been to squeeze the woman's role of mother into a biological pigeonhole."

[64] Ibid., 194. "The psychological dimension of procreation precedes and transcends the biology of procreation."

[65] Adoption, as it is traditionally understood, is not a norm (or an ideal). It is not what people intend from the beginning, that is, prior to conception. Adoption is a moral, humane, and practical way of providing the proper care for children when something goes wrong such as the death or incapacity of the natural parents.

[66] Malcolm.

give up her child as long as she was not thinking, acting, and feeling as a whole person—mind and body.[67] It is to her credit as a woman in whom body did not remain divorced from mind that her bond proved better than her word.

What Constitutes a Good Mother?

One of the central ironies concerning Mary Beth Whitehead was that one reason she was chosen among 300 candidates was because she convinced the Sterns that she would make a good mother. Indeed, she proved them right by being so good a mother that she was unwilling to give up her baby.

The reluctance or unwillingess to surrender the child that a woman has conceived, carried, and given birth to, is perhaps a minimal condition for qualifying as a "good mother". As one judge declared: the "Court will assume that no good mother will very readily and willingly give up permanently her baby."[68] In another case, a New York court held that a natural mother's prebirth agreement to part with her child "was contrary to the natural maternal instinct and against public policy".[69]

The commissioning couple finds itself in a "Catch-22" situation when selecting a surrogate mother. If she is a good mother, she may decide to keep the child; if she is not a good mother, the couple may not want her. After the Sterns found every reason to believe Mary Beth Whitehead would be a good surrogate mother, they found 35 reasons that she should not have custody. A Los Angeles attorney, prominent in the field of arranging surrogate contracts, thinks he has found a way around this dilemma. William Handel believes that women motivated primarily by monetary compensation are

[67] It is noteworthy that it is not the exchange of vows that consummates marriage, but the bodily union of husband and wife through sexual intercourse.

[68] *Watson v. Watson,* 134 S.C. 147, 159; 132 S.E. 39, 43 (1926).

[69] *Kingsbury v. Kingsbury,* 75, N.Y.S. 2d 699 (1947).

less likely to breach the surrogate contract.[70] Therefore, he will not let a woman into his program unless her sole motivation is money.[71] At the same time, Handel is well aware of the potential impact maternal bonding may have on a surrogate. With this in mind, he tells each surrogate, "If you decide to keep the child, we'll sue you for intentional infliction of emotional distress. You'll have ruined this couple's life. And we'll make it awfully expensive for you to hold on to the child."[72]

One couple who had employed a surrogate told their daughter when she was two years old that she had a "real" mother and a "biological" mother. They told her that her "biological" mother had carried her for nine months and must have cared for her very much. The natural father remarked that he wanted her "to respect her biological mother and realize that she did it for more than just the money".[73] Presumably the average two-year-old understands with intuitive clarity what a number of surrogate lawyers and radical feminists find unconvincing and highly conjectural, namely, that bonding takes place between a mother and her child-in-the-womb. However, what does a couple tell a child whose mother bore her for purely mercenary reasons?

Selecting surrogates who are motivated solely by monetary considerations also generates a nest of legal problems. A Michigan court, for example, prevented an infertile married couple from paying a fee to a surrogate for bearing a child. The court did so, in the interest of "[preventing] commercialism from affecting a mother's decision to execute a consent to the adoption of her child".[74]

In England, an unmarried couple hired a prostitute to have

---

[70] Sherwyn and Handel, *Surrogate Parenting, General Information* 1 (leaflet), May 1983.

[71] Lewis, "Surrogate Mothers Pose Issues for Lawyers, Courts", *Los Angeles Daily Journal,* April 20, 1981, p. 1, col. 6.

[72] Quoted in Gallagher, 30. See also Cohen, 246, f.n. 23.

[73] Katz, 23, f.n. 113.

[74] *Doe v. Kelley,* 307 N.W. 2d. 438 (1981).

a child for them in return for 500 pounds. The biological mother, however, refused to relinquish the child. The couple brought suit against her. The judge refused to enforce the surrogate agreement and awarded custody to the biological mother. He was thoroughly convinced that because of her devotion to the baby, she had abandoned her old occupation, would never revert to it, and had completely reformed.[75] The judge described the agreement as a "pernicious contract for the sale and purchase of the child".[76]

A good mother does not readily give up her child. Furthermore, a good mother is not easily duped or intimidated into believing that the child she carried for nine months and went into labor for and delivered is not her own child but someone else's. As one journalist comments: "[F]or a woman to let a child grow within her body, and all the while pretend it is not *her* child—that must be called a form of temporary insanity."[77]

Mary Beth Whitehead was a good mother in a very fundamental sense. She acknowledged her child as hers and was unwilling to part with it. In other words, she accepted her own motherhood. A psychiatric social worker who testified at the trial stated that having to give up Baby M constituted an "assault on her [Mary Beth Whitehead's] identity".[78] The new norms that the business of surrogate motherhood call for, however, demand the dissociation of pregnancy from motherhood. They also demand the dissociation of carrying a child from establishing emotional ties with it. The special institutions that society is trying to erect to validate surrogate motherhood must redefine an essentially unhealthy, unnatural, and perhaps even schizophrenic condition as a norm worthy of

[75] *Parade Magazine,* Feb. 11, 1979, p. 14.

[76] Cusine, "'Womb Leasing': Some Legal Implications", 128 *New Law Journal* 824 (1978).

[77] Gallagher, 30.

[78] "Surrogate Mother 'Grieving'", *Kitchener-Waterloo Record,* Feb. 26, 1987: A-11.

emulation. This will inevitably exact a high cost in personal identity and self-esteem, and an increase in tension and anxiety.

Why Surrogate Motherhood Must Be Disallowed

The moral issue at the heart of the debate is whether a surrogate mother is selling a baby or a service. It would seem purely a matter of convenient rationalization to fail to recognize the obvious. The preadoptive couple (or individual) does not want the service, it wants the child. In the typical surrogate motherhood arrangement, it is manifestly not the case that an infertile couple has an embryo it would like to incubate in a surrogate's womb. The couple wants more than the service, it wants a "product". An advertising surrogate makes this point rather graphically when she offers "to produce a beautiful child especially for you".[79] Or, as philosopher Patrick Derr points out, "If it is *not* a contract to buy a child, why does the mother receive $10,000 for a live-birth, but only $1,000 for a miscarriage?"[80]

No one confuses getting a car serviced with buying a new car. When a person wants a new car, he does not have another person's car serviced. Moreover, the facile separation of service from product that is commonly made in the business world does not apply to motherhood. The nature of motherhood is such that her service and her child are inseparable. This is exactly what it means to be a mother, to be symbiotically related to the child-in-the-womb, giving it life and continuing to nourish and sustain that life until birth. To deny the intimate relationship between the child and its mother is to deny the reality of motherhood. The mother's life-sustaining powers can no more be separated from the child she sustains

[79] George Annas, "Making Babies without Sex: The Law and the Profits", 74 *American Journal of Public Health,* 1984: 1416.

[80] "The Ethics of Surrogate Motherhood", *The Human Life Review,* Summer 1987, p. 93.

than Mozart's services as a composer can be separated from the compositions he composed.[81] The intellect can distinguish the pregnant woman from the child she carries, but the two are bound together in reality. And it is precisely this bound reality that is motherhood.

New York State Senator Mary Goodhue has introduced legislation that would legalize surrogate motherhood. Her bill would provide a father who makes a contract with a surrogate a guarantee that he obtain custody of the child he sires. When asked if her bill might create a market in babies, she replied: "How can a father buy his own child? What he's bought is the use of the surrogate's womb."[82] The fact that the surrogate is forced to relinquish her own child is apparently of no concern to Mrs. Goodhue. Nor does she regard the transaction in which a man pays for the use of a woman's womb—an act that has much in common with prostitution—at all objectionable. Yet, according to America's first celebrated surrogate, Elizabeth Kane, "Surrogate parenthood is nothing more than reproductive prostitution."[83]

Because surrogate motherhood is built on contradictions, those who approve it are obliged to conform their minds to its fluctuating contours. This is particularly evident in the matter of bonding between mother and child. One advocate of surrogate motherhood, writing in the *Harvard Law Review,* speculates that "mothers become more attached to their children than fathers, not for any biological reason but because

[81] Consider the following lines from "The Man with the Blue Guitar" by the American poet Wallace Stevens: "They said, 'You have a blue guitar, / You do not play things as they are.' // The man replied, 'Things as they are / Are changed upon the blue guitar.'" Oscar Williams (ed.), *A Little Treasury of American Poetry* (New York: Charles Scribner's Sons, 1952), p. 339. Stevens himself was a practicing lawyer, having studied at Harvard and New York Law School. The poem cited pays honor to Picasso's painting *Old Man with a Guitar.* Music is not separate from the instrument on which it is played.

[82] Gallagher, 30.

[83] Malcolm.

they are socialized to relate to children differently."[84] In order to confirm the commissioning father's claim to the child, it is necessary to downplay the bonding that takes place during pregnancy between mother and child. At the same time, surrogate advocates are fearful of the bonding that might take place if the mother is allowed to nurse her child. During the Stern–Whitehead trial, Judge Sorkow refused to hear evidence on mother-infant bonding. He also refused to allow testimony on changes in the mother's body during pregnancy that might have led her to change her mind. Nor did he allow an expert witness, Dr. Steven Nickman, to testify on the typical reaction of a child separated from its mother by the State.[85]

Another important issue is the kind of bond that develops between the surrogate father and his unborn child. Are there not occasions when the father's role can truly be described as minimal? The lawyer for Denise Bhimani, a California surrogate who breached her agreement by keeping her child, contended that the natural father made a negligible contribution to the child, since he had his frozen sperm flown to the West Coast from his home in New York. By contrast, Ms. Bhimani suffered through a difficult pregnancy.[86] According to the provisions of Mrs. Goodhue's bill, the New York father (and his transsexual partner) would be guaranteed custody of the child.

The identification of the child as a "product" and the mother's womb as a mere "servicing instrument" is a recurring theme in the literature on surrogate motherhood. Andrea Stumpf, writing in the *Yale Law Journal*, remarks that "the initiating parents must contend with 'reverse' product liability. They, as consumers, must bear the major risk, rather than the

[84] "Rumpelstiltskin Revisited: The Inalienable Rights of Surrogate Mothers", 99 *Harvard Law Review*, June 1986: 1984, f.n. 65.

[85] Richard A. Kruse, "The Strange Case of 'Baby M'", *The Human Life Review*, Fall 1987, p. 29.

[86] Lewis, 7, col. 2.

surrogate mother, as producer."[87] The commissioning parents do not want a damaged child. In the Malahoff–Stiver case, Alexander Malahoff sued surrogate Judy Stiver for "not producing the child he ordered"[88] when her child was born with microcephaly and a strep infection. A Tennessee woman who served as a surrogate for a Michigan couple was an alcoholic and gave birth to a child with fetal alcohol syndrome who needed medical treatment.[89] Concerning the surrogate's womb as a "servicing instrument", consideration has been given to its tax status as a "depreciable asset".[90]

Attempting to classify a surrogate transaction as a "'service' and not a sale", writes one lawyer, "is a distortion of the facts".[91] The primary intention of the initiating parties is that the natural mother provide them with a baby. And "it is a fundamental principle", as a Michigan Court ruled, "that children should not and cannot be bought and sold."[92]

The payment to a surrogate for the child she produces is so obviously suggestive of child selling, which is a form of slavery, that mention of this point is sometimes specified in surrogate agreements. Surrogate lawyer William Handel, for example, advises his clients that surrogate motherhood may violate the California anti-slavery law.[93] The Attorney General of the state of Kentucky stated in an advisory opinion in 1981 that contracts by which artificially inseminated surrogate mothers bear children on behalf of childless couples should be illegal and unenforceable. He found that the typical surrogate

[87] Stumpf, 204, f.n. 66.

[88] Lori Andrews, "The Stork Market: The Law of the New Reproduction Technologies", *American Bar Association Journal*, Aug. 1984, p. 56.

[89] Ibid.

[90] John Whitehead, "Surrogate Motherhood: Dehumanization of Mother and Child", *The Rutherford Institute*, Jan.–Mar., 1987, p. 12.

[91] Cohen, p. 250.

[92] *Doe v. Kelley* at II–B–15, II–B–19 (Mich. Cir. Ct. Jan. 28, 1980).

[93] Andrews, 1984, p. 52.

mother arrangement violated three separate statutes of Kentucky law. "The strongest legal prohibition against surrogate parenting in Kentucky", he wrote, "is found in the strong public policy against buying and selling of children."[94]

A number of lawyers have found the Thirteenth Amendment of the United States Constitution, which prohibits slavery, highly relevant to surrogate motherhood transactions. Angela Holder is one such lawyer. She views the surrogate contract as implying "the payment of money in exchange for a human being".[95] With the Thirteenth Amendment in mind, she opposes all surrogate motherhood arrangements. "Creation of children for money", she writes, "in the legal vacuum that exists today is a disservice to the children and to the legal system."[96]

Surrogate motherhood should be disallowed primarily because it involves baby-selling, and thereby treats the child unjustly, as a commercial product. But there are other reasons for proscribing this practice. It is, as has been amply demonstrated, exploitive of the surrogate woman. In addition, it violates the unity and sacredness of marriage, and tears at the integrity of the family, often dividing wife from husband and separating siblings from one another. It encourages exploitation and bears a disturbing similarity to prostitution and indentured servitude. Moreover, it raises to the level of a norm, a form of behavior in a mother (dissociation from her own child-in-the-womb) that traditional wisdom has seen fit to describe as aberrant. It negates the norm of unified motherhood, introducing in its place a bifurcated version which assigns gestation and child-rearing to different women. And it proposes to settle custody disputes between these two women by evaluating the "mental conception" of the initiating parties

[94] 7 *Family Law Report* (BNA) 2246, 2247.
[95] Holder, 1985, p. 9.
[96] Ibid.

as superior to the "biological conception" of the surrogate. Thus, it seeks to de-bodify motherhood, an operation that contains a dangerous element of Manichaeanism.

Finally, surrogacy contravenes public policy. Apart from the individual parties who stand to profit from surrogate motherhood, society in general is opposed to it. A good indication of this is the reaction to a surrogate motherhood bill that was defeated in the California Senate in 1986. The bill would have required surrogates to be 21 years old and to have already borne a child. In addition, it would have required medical evaluation and psychological counselling for the father, his wife, and the surrogate they hire. In an effort to quell the charges of baby-selling, the bill would have "declared" money given to a surrogate mother as compensation for her services and not as payment for the child. The bill was opposed by an unlikely alliance consisting of feminist groups, the California Catholic Conference, and the American Civil Liberties Union.[97] There are few issues that would unite such disparate groups as these.

No amount of sympathy for the plight of a childless couple can legitimize a method of redressing its problem that is unjust to the child, exploitive of the mother, and damaging to both marriage and the family. Surrogate motherhood is not a private affair. It has repercussions that affect the broad panorama of society. Therefore, it cannot be legalized without bringing about considerable harm to society in general. In the end, the good of the individual must be harmonious with the good of society. There is no other group than the traditional family unit that better provides this organic link with society. Thus, surrogate motherhood imperils not only particular individuals and their relationships, but society as a whole.

---

[97] Elizabeth Kolbert, "Baby M Adds Urgency to Search for Equitable Laws", *The New York Times,* Feb. 15, 1987: E22, col. 2.

Chapter Ten

The Conflict between Reason
and Will in the Legislation
of Surrogate Motherhood

In a 1986 article in the *Harvard Law Review,* the author comes
to the conclusion that courts should hold specific perfor-
mances of the promise not to abort unconstitutional, but
should uphold specific enforcement of the surrogate mother's
contractual promise to surrender the child she delivers to the
infertile couple that commissioned it.[1] This Note, which
bears the engaging title—"Rumpelstiltskin Revisited: The Inalienable Rights of Surrogate Mothers"—parallels neither the
historical course of jurisprudence in the West nor the well-
known Grimm Brothers' fairy tale. It does, however, accurately reflect a new social and legal attitude toward life and
motherhood that locates the basis for legal protection not in
the nature of things, which is subject to the analysis of reason,
but in the wills of the designated parties: in the above example, first with the surrogate; secondly, with the commissioning couple.[2]

The notion that a surrogate mother may abort her child but
should not be allowed to keep it may seem perplexing, if not
thoroughly contradictory. Nevertheless, it is the logical consequence of a radical shift from the objective perspective of
nature to the subjective perspective of will. *Roe v. Wade* gave

[1] 99 *Harvard Law Review* (June 1986), pp. 1936–55. In *Kingsbury v.
Kingsbury,* a New York court held that a natural mother's prebirth agreement
to part with her child "was contrary to the natural mother's instinct and
against public policy." See 75 N.Y.S. 2d 701 (1947).

[2] See also Phyllis Coleman, "Surrogate Motherhood: Analysis of the
Problems and Suggestions for Solutions", 50 *Tennessee Law Review* (Fall
1982), pp. 71–119.

women the right to abort not because it proved the fetus not to be human, but because it considered the fetus to belong to the sphere of a woman's privacy. Similarly, a sperm donor who fertilizes a surrogate wants to constrain her from aborting his child because he views her within the ambit of his private right to procreate. In both cases it is not *reason*—which would locate the individuality of the fetus and the autonomy of the woman—that holds sway, but *will*.

The press reports, almost on a daily basis, the tragic consequences associated with conceiving new life as an expression of will. A few examples: One couple announces its decisions to conceive a child for the purpose of using it as a bone marrow donor for its sibling.[3] A lesbian couple aborted two babies, conceived through artificial insemination, because they were of the "wrong" sex, before their third pregnancy achieved the desired female child.[4] The first "customer" at the Repository for Germinal Choice (also known as the "Nobel Sperm Bank") had lost custody of her two previous children because she had abused them in an attempt to "make them smart".[5]

Law severed from reason is willful. Only when law is properly allied with reason can it be said to be truly lawful. Justinian's statement that "whatsoever pleases the sovereign has the force of law"[6] and Thomas Hobbes's remark that "the law is made by the sovereign power, and all that is done by such power is warranted . . ."[7] are clear examples of expressions of will, rather than law. Inasmuch as they represent the will of

[3] *Los Angeles Times,* April 17, 1979, p. 12.

[4] Helen Hull, "A Questionable Deal", *National Catholic Register,* Feb. 27, 1983.

[5] "Two Children Taken from Sperm Bank Mother", *Los Angeles Times,* July 14, 1982, p. 13; "The Sperm-Bank Scandal", *Newsweek,* July 24, 1982.

[6] *Institutes,* bk. I, title II, 6.

[7] R. M. Hutchins (ed.), *Great Books of the Western World,* vol 23; Thomas Hobbes, "Leviathan", p. 157a.

the sovereign apart from any relationship with reason, they are essentially authoritarian. James Gibbon denounced this notion of law as it was practiced in the Roman Empire since "the will of a single man . . . was allowed to prevail over the wisdom of the ages . . . and the degenerate Greeks were proud to declare that in his hands alone the arbitrary exercise of legislation could be safely deposited".[8] What a lawmaker wills must be allied with reason, that is, it must be reasonable for his command to be lawful rather than lawless.[9] Law is not a *fiat* of the will.

Contemporary society judges authoritarianism harshly and is intolerant of any attempt to legislate from the point of view of willfulness. At the same time, however, it tends to be permissive of the citizen's willfulness, as if the *raison d'être* of law is to allow each citizen to do whatever he wills. Here law's dimension of *will* is accepted, but it is put in the wrong place. It is not uncommon today for people to express the belief that if a particular desire is sufficiently intense—such as the desire on the part of an infertile couple for a child—it is a right.

Law based on the willfulness of the people is anarchy; based on the arbitrary pleasure of the sovereign, it is authoritarianism. Reason is the essential factor that allows a law to be lawful and prevents it from degenerating into either anarchy or authoritarianism. And it is precisely the function of reason to ensure that the law conform to what is right, that is, what is good for those who are subject to the law.

Aristotle alluded to the fact that reason and will are elementary components of law when he stated that "law has a compulsive power, while it is at the same time a rule proceeding from a sort of practical wisdom and reason".[10] He also put

---

[8] Hutchins (ed.), vol 41; James Gibbon, "Decline and Fall of the Roman Empire", p. 74d.

[9] Mortimer Adler and Peter Wolff, *Philosophy of Law and Jurisprudence* (Chicago: Encyclopaedia Brittanica, Inc., 1961), p. 85.

[10] Hutchins (ed.), vol. 9: Aristotle, "Nicomachean Ethics", p. 435a.

will in the right place and understood the practical utility of reason in anchoring law in what is good for man. Aquinas developed and clarified this notion further when he defined law as "an ordinance of reason for the common good, made by him who has care of the community, and promulgated".[11] *Will* is properly placed in the vicegerent authorized to direct people to what is right, and *reason* is recognized as the faculty for locating that good. For Aquinas, reason is able to discover the dictates of the natural law and therefore ground law in the objective realm that relates to the nature of things. Not only did Aquinas put reason and will in the right place, but he also put them in the right order. He understood that reason must come first in order to discover what is good, and will should follow in order to ensure that law protects that good.

In the traditional approach to balancing reason and will, reason has always enjoyed a position of primacy. First, *reason* determines the good that needs to be protected and then *will* directs the application of the law to protect that good. In the new approach that advocates of surrogate motherhood endorse, there is an initial attempt to gratify the *will* of the infertile couple and then an attempt to employ reason in order to construct legislation. Thus, psychiatrist Philip Parker approves a concept of legal parenthood that is established solely on a "consent-intent" basis,[12] while David Rosettenstein, writing for the *New Law Journal,* accepts a similar "consent-based" approach where specialized reproductive technologies are used: "In such cases those who had manifested their consent to act as parents would be the people to whom the rights and duties of parenthood attached".[13]

---

[11] *Summa Theologica* I–II, Q. 90, A. 4.

[12] "Surrogate Motherhood: The Interaction of Litigation, Legislation and Psychiatry", 5 *Journal of Law and Psychiatry* (1982), p. 354.

[13] "Defining a Parent: The New Biology and the Rebirth of the *Filius Nullius*", *New Law Journal* (Oct. 22, 1981), p. 1096.

The new approach, however, invites no end of conflicts and contradictions. When will is left without the guidance and discipline of reason, it is highly susceptible to three rather unsettling possibilities: (1) that it does not conform to what is right; (2) that it will be in conflict with other people's rights; (3) that it will change from one moment to another. Because will is closely associated with desire and egoism, it is less objective than reason. Also, because will is more closely related to the emotions than is reason, it is more unstable and therefore more likely to change. Given these realities, the attempt to design legislation for an expression of will that may be indistinguishable from human desire—with all its volatility and capriciousness—invites no end of conflict between reason and will.

Proponents of surrogate motherhood believe that it can be judiciously regulated through carefully drafted legislation. These proponents are so intent on gratifying the will of infertile couples that they unavoidably lose sight of the nature of motherhood itself. By making the basis of motherhood the will of an infertile couple, rather than the womb of a pregnant woman, an unreasonable negation of motherhood ensues. This ultimately throws reason and will into an irresolvable conflict.

Denying the Nature of Motherhood

The legal definition of "mother" has traditionally carried an unshakeable presumption, namely, that she is the person from whose womb the child came.[14] Though not articulated as such

---

[14] Andrea E. Stumpf, "Redefining Mother: A Legal Matrix for New Reproductive Technologies", 96 *Yale Law Journal* (Nov. 1986), p. 188. According to the British House of Lords, maternity is in law "based on a fact, being proved demonstrably by parturition". See Ampthill Peerage Case (1977). A. C. 547, 577 *per* Lord Simon of Glaisdale.

in the legal field, this presumption has been so absolute that, until recently, it has generated no controversy. Traditionally, this "presumption of biology", which has formed the definition of motherhood, has been the unquestioned and pervasive rule for determining the placement of maternal rights and obligations.

A recent Michigan case in which a surrogate delivered a child who was conceived through in vitro fertilization has occasioned a reassessment of this traditional definition of "mother". Said the judge: "We really have no definition of 'mother' in our lawbooks . . . 'Mother' was believed to have been so basic that no definition was deemed necessary." [15]

In this case (*Smith v. Jones*), a New York couple's embryo was implanted, after in vitro fertilization, into a surrogate mother. The procedure, carried out by Dr. Wulf Utian at Mount Sinai Hospital in Cleveland, was a medical milestone. It marked the first time a surrogate mother gave birth to a child who was originally conceived with the egg and sperm of a couple otherwise unable to have a child. [16]

Because this bifurcation of biological maternity into genetic and gestational phases is novel, existing law provided no guidance in determining which of these two mothers should be regarded as the legal mother. Since the traditional presumption is that the birthing mother is also the genetic mother, it is her name that routinely appears on the birth certificate. If the genetic mother (who did not gestate the child) is to be recognized as the legal biological mother, she must first adopt the child.

In an apparently unprecedented ruling, however, the Michigan Circuit Court judge declared the legal biological

---

[15] "Surrogate Has Baby Conceived in Laboratory", *The New York Times,* April 17, 1986, p. A26, col. 4. See also Goodman, "High Technology Redefines Motherhood", *Toledo Blade,* April 25, 1986, p. 9, col. 3.

[16] Nancy Blodgett, "Who Is Mother? Genetic Donor, Not Surrogate", *American Bar Assoc. J.,* June 1, 1986, p. 18.

mother was not the woman who bore the child, but the one who provided the egg that was fertilized in vitro.[17] The law in Michigan and in most other states specified that even if she does not contribute genetically to the child, the woman who gives birth is nevertheless the mother.

The ovum donor (the genetic mother), pseudonymous Mary Smith, sought to establish her maternity, curiously enough, under Michigan's Paternity Act. Traditionally, this statute had served two purposes. It provided a mechanism by which a putative father who wanted to acknowledge his non-marital child could seek an order of filiation. It also served as a vehicle to establish paternity for the purpose of enforcing child support obligations against a man disavowing fatherhood. The Paternity Act is grounded in the biological fact that there can be only one biological father for a particular child; as such, it does not provide criteria by which an equitable judgment could be reached in determining which of two biological mothers (genetic and gestational) should be adjudged the legal biological mother.[18] Judge Marianne Battani determined that egg and sperm donors occupy equal positions. Thus, once blood tests verified the genetic mother, the gestational, "traditional", or "birthing mother" was relegated to the position of a "human incubator".[19] Mary Smith alone was declared the biological mother.

There are two revolutionary features about motherhood this case underscores. The first is that "the person from whose womb the child came" can be judged not to be the legal biological mother. The second is a notion of the "surrogate mother" that ascribes to a woman the depersonalized role of an "incubator". There is more than a hint of arbitrariness

[17] *Smith v. Jones,* no. 85-53201402 (Mich. Cir. Ct., Wayne County), March 14, 1986.

[18] Shari O'Brien, "The Itinerant Embryo and the Neo-Nativity Scene: Bifurcating Biological Maternity", 1987 *Utah Law Review* (1987), p. 15.

[19] No. 85-532014 DZ, slip op. at 9.

and willfulness about denying the gestational mother her maternity or resorting to mechanistic metaphors in describing her function of carrying a child. Nonetheless, this is an inevitable consequence of using technological modes of reproduction to transfer the basis of motherhood from the physically intimate realm of conjugal lovers to the mental world and abstract intentions of infertile couples.

Lori Andrews, a research attorney for the American Bar Foundation, speaks hopefully of courts taking into consideration an infertile couple's "preconception" intent.[20] Representative Richard Fitzpatrick has proposed a bill to be introduced to the Michigan legislature entitled the "alternative reproduction act". This act calls for "a societal father and a societal mother" who will have all parental rights and responsibilities for a child conceived through a reproductive technology such as IVF, embryo transfer, or artificial insemination. Such "societal parents" are defined as those who engage in a fertility technique to have a child and *intend* to have parental rights regardless of whether the child is biologically related to either one of them.[21]

Writing for the *Yale Law Journal,* Andrea Stumpf seeks to redefine motherhood by allowing "mental conception" to have primacy over "biological conception." She asserts, "The psychological dimension of procreation precedes and transcends the biology of procreation."[22] She further states, "Prior to physical conception of a child, the beginnings of a normal parent-child relationship can come from mental conception, the desire to create a child."[23] For Stumpf, the mental conception of the child on the part of the infertile couple who intend the child has a force and an existential power that can legitimate an infertile woman's claim to motherhood. "The

---

[20] Blodgett, p. 18.
[21] Ibid., p. 18.
[22] Stumpf, p. 194.
[23] Ibid., p. 195.

fact that the initiating parents mentally conceived of the child and afforded it existence prior to the surrogate mother's involvement must be acknowledged", she writes.[24] The surrogate mother herself, according to Stumpf, is merely a "third party".

Marcia Angell, a doctor of medicine, is less confident about how society should redefine motherhood. In an article in the *New England Journal of Medicine,* she agrees that the new forms of reproductive technology will "compel redefinitions of parenthood", but notes that "there is also a general unease that something so natural has become so unnatural."[25]

The *Smith v. Jones* case cited above has occasioned Andrews, Fitzpatrick, Stumpf, and others to redefine motherhood by hood by giving new legal weight to "preconceiving" or "mentally conceiving" a child. It does not, however, represent as strong a threat to overhauling the traditional notion of motherhood as does society's conventional understanding of surrogate motherhood. The *Smith v. Jones* case represents an instance of "partial surrogacy",[26] inasmuch as the gestational mother has no genetic link to the child she carries. The popular understanding of surrogate motherhood in the contemporary world is that of "full surrogacy", wherein a woman is artificially inseminated and carries the child so conceived with the intention of delivering it to the sperm donor and his wife. In this instance the "surrogate mother" is genetically and gestationally the mother of the child; her maternity is not bifurcated and shared with another woman.

In "full surrogacy", the woman who ovulates, conceives,

[24] Ibid., p. 205. "Mental conception", needless to say, does not have within itself the power of conferring existence upon the thing it conceives. Only in God are conception and creation (or idea and act) perfectly unified. Stumpf debodifies and de-sexes man and then asks law to treat him as if he were God.

[25] Marcia Angell, M.D., "New Ways to Get Pregnant", *The New England Journal of Medicine,* Oct. 25, 1990, p. 1201.

[26] Moira Wright, "Surrogacy and Adoption: Problems and Possibilities", 16 *Family Law* (April 1986), pp. 109–10.

gestates, labors, and delivers, is not called a mother (as tradition always defined her). Rather, she is called a mere "surrogate" mother, the presumption being that the real mother is the wife partner of the infertile couple. This maneuver, a triumph of marketing strategies over common sense, has brought about not only a distortion of the notion of motherhood but widespread confusion about the very notion of surrogacy.

A woman whose surrogacy provoked hostile comments from members of her church congregation replied, "Mary was a surrogate for God."[27] This remark has the same validity as a wife saying that she is a "surrogate" for her own husband's child. Another surrogate hinted that giving away her child was an "ultimate" act of "charity" on a level with Mother Teresa's work. She said, "I'm not going to cure cancer or become Mother Teresa, but a baby is one thing I can sort of give back, something I can give to someone else who couldn't have it any other way."[28]

Some have found a precedent and justification for surrogate motherhood in Scripture.[29] The Hagar Institute in Topeka, Kansas, one of many surrogate parenting brokerages in the United States, takes its name from Sarah's handmaid (Gen 16:1-15). In the Old Testament story, Sarah gave her husband Abraham permission to sleep with Hagar, who, as a result, bore Ishmael. The relationship that developed between Hagar and Sarah was anything but cordial. Hagar, of course, was not a surrogate mother for Sarah and Abraham. The Bible makes it clear that Ishmael's mother was Hagar, not Sarah. Hagar was Abraham's second *wife*. If the proponents of surrogate mother arrangements wish to draw lessons from this

[27] B. Kantrowitz, et al., "Who Keeps 'Baby M'?", *Newsweek,* Jan. 19, 1987, p. 47.

[28] Ibid., p. 47.

[29] See, e.g. Margaret D. Townsend, "Surrogate Mother Arrangements: Contemporary Legal Aspects of a Biblical Notion", 16 *Univ. of Richmond Law Journal* (Winter 1982).

Genesis narrative, they might well look to the end of the story: how Hagar and Ishmael were driven out by Sarah after she (Sarah) gave birth to Isaac. As one authority has pointed out, "The family animosity of thousands of years ago is with us today as the sons of Ishmael (the Arabs) and the sons of Isaac (the Jews) still have some difficulties getting along.[30]

Today's conventional "surrogate mother" is really a surrogate wife; she is the "second wife", whom the husband fertilizes because his first wife is infertile. Barbara Rothman, author of *The Tentative Pregnancy,* has made the point quite forcefully by exclaiming: "A mother is a mother is a mother. . . . These are surrogate wives, not surrogate mothers. He is hiring himself an extra wife."[31]

To make matters even more confusing, the sperm donor is referred to as a "surrogate father",[32] and the child the surrogate mother carries is called a "surrogate child".[33] Surrogate motherhood demands a great deal of alienation: the pregnant woman from her child as well as from her own motherhood, the husband from his wife, and the surrogate from her own husband and children, and even her children from their surrogate sibling. Such alienation on so many fronts weakens personal identities as well as the family unity. The inevitable result is to leave people unprotected, vulnerable, and highly susceptible to commercial exploitation.

In order to sell "surrogacy" to the public, it is necessary to convince people that surrogate motherhood is simply a beautiful and loving way of providing infertile couples with the babies they cannot have in any other way. It is just as necessary to suppress the dangers, both physical and moral, that

[30] H. T. Krimmel, "When Children Are Conceived for Others: The Case Against Surrogate Parenting", *The Hastings Center,* Oct. 1983, p. 36.

[31] Kantrowitz, p. 46.

[32] Angela Holder, "Surrogate Motherhood: Babies for Fun and Profit", 90 *Case and Comment* (March–April 1985), p. 4.

[33] Gwen Yount Carden, "The Baby Maker", *Woman's World,* July 28, 1987, p. 10.

surrogate motherhood presents, not only to the contractual parties, but to the family and society as a whole. Roger Scruton, writing for the *Times* of London, expresses with remarkable moral acumen why the inherent dangers of surrogate motherhood far outweigh its potential benefits:

> Surrogate motherhood should be seen in its wider context—not as an answer to the problem of sterility but as the outcome of a revision in moral perceptions, comparable to that foretold in *Brave New World*. In surrogacy, the relation between mother and child ceases to issue from the body of the mother and is severed from the experience of incarnation. The bond between mother and child is demystified, made clear, intelligible, scientific—and also provisional, revocable and of no more than contractual force.[34]

Contradictions Inherent in the Legislation of Surrogate Motherhood

Employing reason in an attempt to contain the unbridled movements of will is like trying to catch the wind with a butterfly net. When will is initially independent of reason, it shifts from one concern to another. Therefore, when reason tries to capture its fluctuations and describe them according to a coherent pattern, it inevitably contradicts itself.

Pro-abortionists advanced their cause by insisting that the fetus was merely a part of the woman's body. The same fetus, however, underwent a metamorphosis when it came time to endorse surrogate motherhood. Then, the fetus was regarded as a "tenant" or a "resident" in a rented womb.[35] At the same time, the pregnant woman's motherhood evaporated, leaving her as a mere "babysitter", "incubator", or "nest-watcher."[36]

[34] "Ignore the Body, Lose Your Soul", *The Times,* Feb. 5, 1985, p. 10.

[35] L. E. Karp and R. P. Donahue, "Preimplantation Ectogenesis", *The Western Journal of Medicine,* 1976, 124 (4).

[36] Philip J. Parker, "Motivation of Surrogate Mothers: Initial Findings", *American Journal of Psychiatry,* 140 (1).

The nature of the fetus did not change. What did change was the way people willed to see it and the rhetoric constructed on that new vision.

Advocates for surrogate motherhood are adamant that the "real" mother is the infertile woman who wants the child. However, when embryo transfer is used to relocate the unborn child from the genetic to the gestational mother, motherhood is once again conferred upon the woman who carries the child. According to Dr. John Buster, a leading pioneer in embryo transfer technology, the real mother is "the woman who nurtures and shapes a child for nine months. If that isn't a mother, what is?"[37]

In one particular surrogate motherhood episode, the husband and wife who contracted for the child divorced before the pregnancy came to term. Given their new outlook on each other and "their" child, they successfully pressed the surrogate mother to abort.[38] It would be left to the courts to decide the extent of the father's obligations to support the child where the surrogate refused to abort, or the extent to which he could be sued for damages if the abortion rendered the woman permanently sterile.

Noel Keane, the most prominent surrogate motherhood broker in the United States, has said: "If you asked me to give you a profile of a perfect surrogate, I would give you Mary Beth Whitehead".[39] Yet, as noted earlier, when Mary Beth changed her mind and the case went to court, the lawyer for the infertile couple found 35 reasons why she was unsuited for motherhood.[40] As pointed out, Mary Beth was selected over 300 other applicants because she seemed to be the ideal mother. But the ideal mother does not surrender her child. As one judge declared: the "Court will assume that no good

[37] *The Phil Donahue Show,* no. 08223.

[38] Richard Lacayo, "In the Best Interests of the Child", *Time,* April 13, 1987, p. 50.

[39] Kantrowitz, p. 47.

[40] See infra, text accompanying f.n. 69.

mother will very readily and willingly give up permanently her baby."[41] In another case, a New York court held that a natural mother's prebirth agreement to part with her child "was contrary to the natural maternal instinct".[42]

The "ideal" surrogate mother is a contradiction. She is motherly enough to coneive a child and carry it to term, but she is also willing to distance herself from her child-in-the-womb so that she can easily give it up. Can a mother regulate the closeness she has with her unborn child according to whether she is going to keep or not keep it? Given the fact that our society is already suffering from alienation within marriage and between parents and children, do we want to encourage and even to help pregnant women become more alienated from the children they carry?[43] Can we make alienation in such areas of natural human intimacy an ideal without bringing additional trauma upon ourselves?

The status of the sperm donor is also subject to contradictions. Twenty-eight states have laws that assert that if a married woman becomes pregnant, her husband is the legal father of the child.[44] This presumption is said to be one of the strongest known to law. In some states the presumption is said to be conclusive.[45] According to a California appellate court, it exists to protect "the integrity of the family unit and to protect the child from the social stigma of illegitimacy".[46] The Wyoming Supreme Court held that the presumption served two important state objectives: protecting and preserv-

[41] *Watson v. Watson*, 134 S.C. 147, 159: 132 S.E. 39, 43 (1926).

[42] *Kingsbury v. Kingsbury*, 75, N.Y.S. 3d 699 (1947).

[43] See Sidney Callahan, "Lovemaking and Babyselling: Ethic and the New Reproductive Technology", *Commonweal*, April 24, 1987, p. 238.

[44] "Guidelines Issued on Surrogate Motherhood", *Am. Med. News*, June 10, 1983.

[45] Barbara Cohen, "Surrogate Mothers: Whose Baby Is It?" 10 *American Journal of Law and Medicine* (Fall 1984), p. 266.

[46] *Vincent B. v. Joan R.*, 126 Cal. App. 3d 624, 179 Cal. Rptr. 11 (1981).

ing family integrity and protecting the child's interest in remaining legitimate.[47]

In addition, a man who donates sperm to be used in artificial insemination forfeits his rights, in many states, to any
child who may be conceived. According to the Supreme
Court's *Planned Parenthood v. Danforth* ruling (1976), the father cannot veto his wife's decision to abort, nor does he have
a right to notification or consultation in the matter. Given this
erosion of biological fatherhood, it would seem that the
courts are ill prepared to award paternity to a sperm donor
who has artificially fertilized a married woman who wants to
keep the child. Yet this is precisely what is demanded in surrogate motherhood contracts, although outside the arena of
surrogacy, nowhere does the law state that the child-in-the-
womb belongs to the father more than to the mother.[48]

It is interesting to note that surrogate entrepreneurs prefer
to use women who have already borne children. The contradiction involved in a mother keeping one child and giving
away (or selling) another must have its impact on those she is
raising. Angela Holder, president of the American Society of
Law and Medicine, expresses her concern that granting a
mother the freedom to give away some of her children could
very well make those remaining at home feel insecure. "I
think we have to consider", she says, "how those children feel
when their mamas sell a little brother or sister, and they start
wondering if they're going to be sold."[49] On the other hand, a
sibling might find the prospect of giving away a brother or
sister much to his liking. According to one newspaper account, when a surrogate mother informed her nine-year-old
daughter that she planned to give away her new baby, the girl

---

[47] *A v. X, Y, and Z,* 641 P 2d. ad 1222.
[48] Hadley Arkes, "Judge Sorkow May Have Overstepped His Bounds",
Wall Street Journal, April 9, 1987.
[49] Kay Longcope, "Surrogacy . . ." *The Boston Globe,* March 23, 1987.

replied: "Oh, good. If it's a girl we can keep it and give Jeffrey [her two-year-old half-brother] away." [50]

A number of lawyers who endorse the legislative regulation of surrogate motherhood believe that it is constitutionally protected in the interest of privacy. They cite a long line of cases, going back to *Skinner v. Oklahoma*,[51] which state that procreation is a fundamental interest and private right. They also contend that these decisions that have brought a number of personal activities relating to the bearing and begetting of children under the Constitution's implied protection can be extended to the practice of surrogate motherhood.[52] There are, however, two salient points these advocates overlook. The first is that reducing the surrogate to the status of "incubator" and denying her the right to rear the child she conceived, carried, and delivered constitutes a *violation* of her privacy (as well as a violation of her identity). Secondly, the involvement of a sperm donor, a host of nonmedical professionals, and technological interventions that often demand much time and travel, give surrogate motherhood a quasi-public character. "When the initiation, continuation, and consummation of the pregnancy necessitate the acute involvement of third parties," as one lawyer has commented, "the right of privacy acquires a bloated, oddly communal silhouette." The word "'privacy' wanes as the individual or couple moves away from the intimacy of a bedroom into the

---

[50] *Los Angeles Herald Examiner,* Sept. 21, 1981, p. A3.

[51] Also including the following Supreme Court cases: *Griswold v. Conn.,* 381 U.S. 479 (1965); *Eisenstadt v. Baird,* 405 U.S. 438 (1972); *Roe v. Wade,* 410 U.S. 113 (1973); *Carey v. Population Sevs. Int'l,* 431 U.S. 678 (1977). *Skinner v. Oklahoma,* 316 U.S. 535 (1942).

[52] See Karen Marie Sly, "Babysitting Considerations: Surrogate Mother's Right to 'Rent Her Womb' for a Fee", 18 *Gonzaga Law Review* (1982–83); Matthew R. Eccles, "The Use of In Vitro Fertilization: Is There a Right to Bear or Beget a Child by Any Available Means?" 12 *Pepperdine L. Rev.* (1985).

concourse of a clinic." [53] One might very well use the right to privacy as an argument to justify proscribing surrogate motherhood rather than promoting it. The very reason so many people stand to be hurt by surrogate arrangements lies in the fact that once their privacy, identity, and integrity have been assaulted, they have little protection left to resist forces of exploitation.

To demonstrate that regulating surrogate motherhood through legislation will meet with invincible contradictions, a review of several prominent surrogacy cases is provided. There is nothing "surrogate" about the pain that the victims of surrogate motherhood experience. The pain that results when identity and reality intersect is far beyond the reach of surrogacy's promotional rhetoric.

The Ohio Surrogate and the Divorced Couple

Beverly Seymour and Richard Reams, a married couple, enlisted the services of a surrogate, Norma Lee Stotsky, to provide them with a child. They agreed to pay $10,000 plus expenses. It was originally believed that the infertility problem lay solely with Ms. Seymour. Therefore, a contract was prepared through the Association for Surrogate Parenting Services on the assumption that Richard Reams would be the biological father. When Mr. Reams proved infertile, the couple turned to a sperm donor. [54]

Three times a month, for six months, Norma Stotsky had unsuccessfully undergone artificial insemination with Reams' sperm. Later, after 18 months of trying, she finally became pregnant using the donor's sperm. [55]

[53] O'Brien, 1987, p. 20.

[54] Tamar Lewin, "A Custody Case with Extra Tangles", *The New York Times,* Jan. 26, 1989.

[55] David Grogan and Beth Austin, "Little Girl, Big Trouble", *People,* Feb. 20, 1989, p. 39. Some news reports spell the surrogate's last name, "Stotski".

Mrs. Stotsky, who lives with her husband and their three children, gave birth to a baby girl, Tessa, on January 21, 1985.[56] One day later, she handed the child over to the commissioning couple. The following year, however, the Reams' marriage broke up. The question of who had the right to raise Tessa, now six years old, then developed into one of the most tragic and convoluted cases to date among those involving surrogate motherhood.

Tessa's case has been in and out of the judicial system for more than four years, with more than a dozen lawyers involved. Richard Reams, Beverly Seymour, and Norma Stotsky had each sought to adopt the child. In addition, a couple on the East Coast, reported to have a six-figure annual income, expressed interest in adopting Tessa.

Ms. Seymour ran out of money for lawyers. Mr. Reams' business failed and he lost his home following bankruptcy proceedings. Mrs. Stotsky had discontinued her attempt to gain custody of the child because of financial considerations and the fact that "it was taking too much of a toll on her family."[57] In the meantime, Tessa travelled 100 miles every three and a half days between Sunbury, Ohio, where Mr. Reams lived, and Ashville, Ohio, where Ms. Seymour resided.[58]

Tessa's birth certificate, which initially named Mrs. Stotsky's husband as the father, later was changed to list Mr. Reams as the father. Four years later it was discovered, after an investigation, that the biological father was the sperm donor, 62-year-old Leslie Miner. Thus, Tessa is not biologically related to either of the two parties who had custody of her.

The attorney appointed by the courts to represent Tessa had remarked: "We find ourselves tongue-tied just trying to decide the players."[59] The probate judge regarded the continued

[56] Ibid., p. 37.
[57] Quoting Patricia Grimm, Mrs. Stotsky's lawyer, in Lewin, A12.
[58] Ibid., A12.
[59] Ibid., A12.

acrimony between Reams and Seymour to be the overriding issue in the case.[60] In June 1986, Reams was able to obtain a court order giving him custody of Tessa, and sheriff's deputies arrived on Seymour's doorstep to take the child from her. In an attempt to get Tessa back, Seymour begged Stotsky to intercede on her behalf. Stotsky then petitioned the courts to void Reams' paternity.

In May of 1987, Stotsky decided that Tessa's life with Seymour and Reams was too chaotic and filed for custody herself. But Seymour was adamant that the child is her own: "This child was originally conceived for me. From the time Mrs. Stotsky got pregnant, I've felt this is my baby. I'm Mommy here."[61]

Mrs. Stotsky's decision to allow Reams and Seymour to raise the child could be construed as child abandonment. Joint custody between Reams and Seymour appeared unlikely because of the strong animosity they continued to have for each other. Says Norma Stotsky: "No one else should ever have to go through this."[62]

This convoluted episode culminated in tragedy on August 27, 1990. After learning that day that he was granted permanent custody of the child, Mr. Reams drove to Ms. Seymour's apartment where he allegedly began assaulting his ex-wife. At that point she took out a gun and shot and killed her former husband.

Beverly Seymour has been sentenced to 11 years in prison, a jury having found her guilty of manslaughter. She intends to appeal the conviction. A *New York Times* report (Dec. 8, 1990) quotes her as saying: "I'm guilty of being a woman not wanting to be hit by that man's fists again." On the other hand, prosecutors argue that she killed Reams in anger because he had won custody of Tessa.

[60] Grogan, p. 38.
[61] Ibid., p. 41.
[62] Ibid., p. 38.

Mother-Daughter Surrogacy in Italy

In Rome, a 20-year-old woman served as a surrogate for her own mother. Turin's daily newspaper, *La Stampa,* reported that the young woman's 35-year-old stepfather wanted to have a child that was biologically his.[63] Doctors had advised his wife, 48, and already the natural mother of three, against having further pregnancies.

According to newspaper reports, the daughter gave birth to a boy in a Rome hospital after carrying to term the artificially fertilized egg of her mother.[64] In effect, her son is also her half-brother. Moreover, her mother is at the same time mother and grandmother to the baby. The stepfather is the natural father to his wife's grandchild.[65]

L'Osservatore Romano criticized the procedure in the strongest terms, stating, "If separation of procreation from the conjugal act is permitted, conception becomes a question of mere technical reproduction. And terms such as conjugal love, maternity and procreation become meaningless."[66]

Mother-Daughter Surrogacy in South Africa

Karen Ferreira-Jorge had her uterus removed after the birth of her first child because of complications at delivery. She and her husband passionately wanted more children.[67] Her natural mother volunteered to be a surrogate gestator for her daughter. As part of her preparation for this demanding role, Pat Anthony gave up her three-pack-a-day cigarette habit.[68]

[63] "Mother-Daughter Surrogacy Report Stirs Controversy", *The Boston Sunday Globe,* Oct. 30, 1988, p. 16.

[64] Ibid., p. 16.

[65] See also "When Baby's Mother Is Also Grandma—and Sister", *Hastings Center Report,* vol. 15, no. 5, Oct. 1985, pp. 29–31.

[66] "Mother-Daughter Surrogacy. . . ."

[67] "Woman Bearing Daughter's Triplets Viewed as Heroine in South Africa", *Toronto Globe and Mail,* April 8, 1987, A5.

[68] Eric Levin, "Motherly Love Works a Miracle", *People,* October 19, 1987, p. 41.

After giving Karen drugs to stimulate her ovaries, infertility specialists at Johannesburg's Park Lane Clinic removed 11 of her eggs and placed them in vitro with her husband's sperm. After 48 hours, four fertilized eggs were surgically implanted in Pat Anthony's uterus. Three developed. Triplets were delivered by caesarian section, two weeks premature. The boys weighed 5 pounds, 1 ounce and 4 pounds, 10 ounces, and the girl, delivered last, weighed 2 pounds, 13 ounces.[69]

Karen, who for nine months had been taking hormones to stimulate lactation, was able to breast-feed the neonates within hours of their birth. According to South African law, however, the triplets would be considered the children of Mrs. Anthony and her husband until Karen and her spouse formally adopted them. The Johannesburg *Star* ran a front-page cartoon in which one tiny triplet quipped to another, "Legally, I could be your uncle."[70]

Mrs. Anthony is the first woman to give birth to her own grandchildren as well as the first surrogate mother to produce in vitro triplets. Twenty-three years ago, giving birth to her son had been so agonizing that she vowed to her husband that she would never willingly endure anything like it again. She was not willing to have any more of her husband's children when she was young, but was more than eager to bear triplets for her son-in-law at age 48. As one journalist has remarked: "What she had not been willing to suffer for her own sake or her husband's, she determined to do for her daughter."[71]

Surrogate Twin Rejected by the Contracting Couple

Mrs. Patty Nowakowski agreed to be a surrogate for a contracting couple. After undergoing a fertility drug regimen and artificial insemination, she became pregnant with twins. Two

---

[69] "Granny Bears Triplets", *The Toronto Star,* October 2, 1987, p. 4.
[70] Quoted in Ibid., p. 4.
[71] Ibid., p. 40.

weeks before the twins—a boy and a girl—were born, the couple, who already had children, told Nowakowski that a doctor recommended against adding more children to their family because of the added stress.[72] The couple agreed to take one of the twins only if the baby was a girl.

The couple accepted the girl, and Patty and her husband placed the boy in a foster home.[73] Then, after feeling guilty about what they had done, the Nowakowskis, who have three other children, decided to raise the boy themselves. Later, after a custody battle, the Nowakowskis agreed to keep both children.[74]

The British Case Concerning the Prostitute-Surrogate

An unmarried British couple, living in the same household, wanted a child through a surrogate as a prelude to their future marriage.[75] The male is a 27-year-old professional man and his partner is a 32-year-old divorcée. She has two children from a previous marriage; her eight-year-old is living with her.[76] The man invited a prostitute to serve as a surrogate. She declined, but accepted a £500 fee to procure a woman who would. The couple then paid the second woman, also a prostitute, £500 to be artificially inseminated by the man's sperm and carry the pregnancy to term.[77] During her pregnancy, the prostitute was housed rent-free.

When the child was born, the prostitute refused to relinquish it. The couple tried to change the woman's mind by

[72] "Couple Shuns Boy", *The Kitchener-Waterloo Record,* April 25, 1988, A3.

[73] "Surrogate's Twins Must Live Apart", *USA Today,* April 21, 1988, 2A.

[74] "Mothers Denounce Surrogate Parenting at Hearing", *The New York Times,* Dec. 11, 1988.

[75] Louis Waller, "Borne for Another", 10 *Monash U. L. Rev.* (Sept. 1984), p. 119.

[76] 8 *Family Law* (1978), pp. 170–71.

[77] D. J. Cusine, "'Womb-Leasing': Some Legal Implications", 128 *New Law Journal* (Aug. 24, 1978), pp. 824–25.

offering her up to £3,000 (their life savings), their secondhand car (valued at £850), and finally their house.[78] The prostitute-mother, however, remained firm. The father then instituted wardship proceedings. The case was heard in Family Division Court.[79] The judge treated the father as the father of an illegitimate child. He awarded custody to the prostitute because he was convinced that because of her baby she had abandoned her old occupation, would never revert to it.[80] The court declared the surrogate motherhood contract void and described the agreement as a "pernicious contract for the sale and purchase of a child".[81] The child's Christian name was the mother's choice and the surname was hers. The father was granted access to the child one hour twice a week.

Noyes v. Thrane

Early in 1980, Denise Lucy Thrane, of Arcadia, California, contracted with Mr. and Mrs. James Noyes, of Rochester, New York, to be artificially inseminated by Mr. Noyes. After the first attempt failed, Mrs. Thrane, who is also known as Nisa Bhimani, had second thoughts about being a surrogate mother. According to her attorney, Stan Springer, she only "begrudgingly" agreed to try once again to become pregnant.[82] She became pregnant in the second attempt with sperm that had been frozen and flown to Los Angeles from New York.

Mrs. Thrane, a divorced mother of three in her early twenties, had not been paid for her role as a surrogate mother. When she learned that other surrogates were being paid be-

[78] Ibid. See also *The Daily Telegraph and The Times,* June 21, 1978.

[79] *A v. C,* Comyn J; June 20, 1978.

[80] *Parade Magazine,* Feb. 11, 1979, p. 14, col. 2.

[81] P. J. Vieth, "Surrogate Mothering: Medical Reality in a Legal Vacuum", 8 *Journal of Legislation* (Winter 1981), note 32, at 148 n. 58.

[82] "Surrogate Mother-to-Be Fights to Keep Unborn Child", *The New York Times,* March 25, 1981.

yond the pregnancy-related expenses, she gave notice that if she did not receive $7,500 she would either abort the child or keep it after it was born.[83] The Noyeses, in a hearing in Los Angeles Superior Court, asked that custody of the child be awarded to them as soon as it is born or that it be immediately placed in a foster home. Believing that no court would enforce the terms of the surrogate contract,[84] the couple's attorney sought a paternity ruling and custody of the child. Nonetheless, the attorney would still have to convince the court that the California artificial insemination statute, which treats the donor of semen as if he were not the natural father of the child conceived, should not apply to the case at hand.[85] At the same time, Springer asked that the suit be dismissed precisely because California law does not currently treat semen donors as natural fathers. He further argued that the natural father's contribution is negligible: "Look at the respective contributions. . . . He lives 3,500 miles away, some frozen sperm is flown out here [and] she suffers through a difficult pregnancy."[86]

The paternity custody suit was withdrawn, however, when, during the preliminary investigation before the trial, the reason the Noyeses could not have children of their own was discovered. The natural father's wife was a transsexual who had had a sex change operation some five years earlier.[87]

---

[83] J. J. Mandler, "Developing a Concept of the Modern 'Family': A Proposed Uniform Surrogate Parenthood Act", 73 Georgetown Law Journal (June 1985). See also Noel P. Keane with Dennis L. Breo, The Surrogate Mother (New York: Everest House, 1981), pp. 201–4.

[84] Lewis, "Surrogate Mothers Pose Issues for Lawyers, Courts", Los Angeles Daily Journal, April 21, 1981, p. 7, col. 2.

[85] See Cal. Civ. Code, 7005 (West. Supp. 1983). "Whose Baby Is It Anyway?" Newsweek, April 6, 1983, p. 83.

[86] Lewis, p. 7.

[87] Noyes v. Thrane, No. CF 7614 (Los Angeles County, California Sup. Ct., filed Feb. 20, 1981). See also The National Law Journal, April 6, 1981, p. 4, col. 4 and June 22, 1981, p. 9, col. 1.

The Lesbian Surrogate from Tennessee

A Michigan couple arranged to have a surrogate mother, a woman from Tennessee, artificially inseminated in October 1977.[88] The woman initially agreed to forego a fee because Tennessee law where she resided forbids monetary payment in connection with either the adoption of a child or the termination of parental rights. During her pregnancy, however, she extorted[89] more and more money from the couple in order to sustain her alcohol and drug addiction. Also, throughout her pregnancy, she lived with a series of lesbian lovers under circumstances that posed an additional threat to her physical health and mental stability.[90] Her child was born with fetal alcohol syndrome and was detoxified at birth. After the birth of the child, she continued to demand more money. When Tennessee authorities tried to take custody of another child of hers, she fled to Florida with the child.

The Malahoff-Stiver Case

Alexander Malahoff, of Middle Village, New York, signed a contract with Mrs. Judy Stiver of Lansing, Michigan, who agreed to act as a surrogate mother. Malahoff is an accountant. Mrs. Stiver is an inventory clerk; her husband, a part-time bus driver.[91] Malahoff selected Mrs. Stiver to bear his child from a photograph of her and her three-year-old daughter Mindy.[92] He and his wife Nadja agreed to pay Mrs. Stiver

[88] Lori Andrews, "The Stork Market: The Law of the New Reproduction Technologies", 70 *American Bar Association Journal* (Aug. 1984), p. 56.

[89] Shari O'Brien, "Commercial Conceptions: A Breeding Ground for Surrogacy", 65 *North Carolina L. R.* (Nov. 1986), p. 134.

[90] Mandler, pp. 1286–87.

[91] M. Abraham, "Case of the Surrogate Mother and Unwanted Baby", *The Boston Globe,* Jan. 31, 1983, p. 4.

[92] Iver Peterson, "Legal Snarl Developing Around Case of a Baby Born to Surrogate Mother", *The New York Times,* Feb. 7, 1983, pp. 1–2.

$10,000 to be artificially inseminated with his sperm, bear the ensuing child and give them custody of the baby. The Stivers reported that they agreed to the arrangement because they needed the money to "pay bills and take a vacation". [93] During Mrs. Stiver's pregnancy, the Malahoffs separated. Nonetheless, the husband hoped that the arrival of the child would provide what was needed to persuade his estranged wife to return and resume their marriage. [94]

On January 10, 1983, after a long labor, Mrs. Stiver, with Mr. Malahoff and her husband present, delivered a baby boy. The child was microcephalic, a condition marked by a smaller-than-normal head that often indicates mental retardation. The infant's umbilical cord had two knots in it and the child had a severe streptococcal infection. [95] When the hospital pediatrician approached Malahoff in order to obtain permission to begin the medical treatment needed to save the baby's life, the presumed natural father—according to the Stivers and court records—refused to authorize treatment. According to Mrs. Stiver, Malahoff had advised her to let this baby die and provide him with another one. [96] The hospital went to court and won permission to care for the child. [97] Mrs. Stiver said that she never developed a maternal feeling about the child. Her husband spoke for himself and his wife, saying, "We feel no maternal or paternal relationship." According to Michigan legislator Richard Fitzpatrick, "For weeks the baby was tossed back and forth like a football—with no one having

[93] "Deformed Surrogate Infant Is Left Unwanted", *The New York Times,* Jan. 23, 1983.

[94] A. E. Weiss, *Bioethics: Dilemma In Modern Medicine* (Hillsdale: Enslow, 1985), p. 46.

[95] Waller, p. 120. See also *The New York Times:* Jan. 23, Feb. 3, Feb. 7, 1983.

[96] Peterson, pp. 1–2.

[97] A. Press and F. Maier, "A Surrogate Mother's Story", *Newsweek,* Feb. 14, 1983, p. 76.

responsibility."[98] The child became a ward of the Michigan Department of Social Services and was looked after by a foster family.

Meanwhile, a Washington-based group called the American Life Lobby claimed that it sent telegrams to pertinent judicial authorities requesting an investigation of whether actions by Alexander Malahoff in ordering the withholding of treatment from Baby Doe constituted a "solicitation of homicide."[99]

Before they had time to cash their $10,000 check, the Stivers were informed that Malahoff, after seeing the baby's blood type listed on the birth certificate, asserted that he could not be the father. Malahoff and Stiver had blood tests to establish the child's paternity and then, in a move that Boston University health-law professor George Annas said makes soap operas appear pallid by comparison, went on the Phil Donahue Show to let the world know exactly who the real father was.[100] During a commercial break, a hospital informed Donahue—and soon thereafter, 8 million television viewers—that Ray Stiver was the biological father.

The Stivers accepted the child as theirs and named it Christopher Ray. Malahoff reacted by filing a $50 million lawsuit against the Stivers for not producing the child he ordered.[101] "Instead of a baby," he told the press, "I end up with a lawyer."[102] The Stivers also sued the doctor, lawyer, and psychiatrist of the surrogate program for not properly advising them about the timing of sex. Ray Stiver also claimed that the doctors "misdiagnosed" his wife's pregnant condition on the day

---

[98] Lori Andrews, *New Conceptions: A Consumer's Guide to the Newest Infertility Treatments, Including In Vitro Fertilization, Artificial Insemination, and Surrogate Motherhood* (New York: St. Martin's Press, 1984), p. 240.

[99] "Paternity Tests Set in Surrogate Case", *The Boston Globe,* Jan. 28, 1983.

[100] Phil Donahue television interviews, no. 02023, Feb. 2, 1983.

[101] "Paternity Test in Surrogate Suit", *The Boston Herald,* Feb. 1, 1983.

[102] Press and Maier, p. 76.

of the artificial insemination procedure.[103] In addition, the Stivers took Malahoff to court for violating their privacy by making the whole affair public.

Christopher Ray's prognosis is not encouraging. He has cytomegalovirus, a virus of undertermined origin he contracted before birth. At age two, he could not walk, crawl, sit without support, or hold up his head for more than a few seconds. Crying is the only sound he makes. Because of brain damage caused by the virus, he is believed to be almost totally deaf and blind. He is fed through a tube in his stomach. A monitor watches his tiny heart.[104]

In early January 1985, the Stivers filed suit in U.S. District Court at Detroit, seeking $100 million from Alexander Malahoff. The suit claims Malahoff's semen transmitted the cytomegalovirus to Mrs. Stiver, who then gave it to her son. This virus may have caused the unborn child to develop an infection that left him severely handicapped. The suit claims that Malahoff's sperm was not tested for diseases as required in the surrogate contract.[105]

The Venezuelan Gestational Surrogacy Case

A Venezuelan woman was not able to bear children since her uterus had been removed after complications from an illegal abortion. She and her husband hired two surrogate gestators to assist them in having their own children. In a hospital laboratory in Pasadena, California, doctors brought together eggs from the wife and sperm from the husband in a petri dish to

[103] Roger Martin, "'Surrogate' Mom, Husband Accept Baby Doe as Own", *The Detroit News,* Feb. 3, 1983, p. 8A.

[104] "'Rough Year,' 'Surrogate' Baby Turns 2, Faces Uncertain Future", *The Detroit News,* Jan. 7, 1985.

[105] "Surrogate Mother Asks $100 Million", *The Grand Rapids Press,* Jan. 13, 1985, p. A14.

produce eight embryos. Four were placed in each of two surrogate gestators.

One of the gestators, who spent the last six weeks of her pregnancy in the hospital, gave birth to triplets, two boys and a girl. Ten days later, the second surrogate presented the Venezuelan couple with one more baby boy. The first surrogate, a married woman with four children of her own, admitted to "feeling bonded" with her triplets and feeling sad when she left them.[106]

The Surrogate Who Lost Her Child to His Genetic Parents

Mrs. Crispina Calvert was unable to become pregnant because she had had a hysterectomy. She and her husband conceived an embryo by in vitro fertilization and hired another woman to carry it to term. However, Anna Johnson, the surrogate gestator, was unwilling to relinquish the child when it was born. Ms. Johnson, who had been on disability from her nursing job because of pregnancy complications, also sought child support and damages for emotional distress.[107]

California Superior Court judge Richard Parslow, Jr., in a modern version of King Solomon's approach, threatened to send the newborn to a foster home if the three parents could not agree. The genetic parents, but not the birthing mother, were willing to allow this to happen. Ms. Johnson, a single parent of a three-year-old, is the first surrogate mother to seek custody of a child not genetically related to her.[108]

The judge eventually ruled that the woman who carried the child to term had no parental rights under California law. Al-

[106] Carol Lawson, "New Birth Surrogates Carry Couples' Babies", *The New York Times*, August 12, 1990.

[107] "Surrogate Mother Sues for Baby's Custody", *The New York Times National*, August 15, 1990.

[108] Marcia Angell, M.D., "New Ways to Get Pregnant", *The New England Journal of Medicine*, Oct. 25, 1990, p. 1200.

though his ruling is the first of its kind, it will not establish a precedent unless confirmed by a higher court.[109] In essence, he ruled that Ms. Johnson was just a prenatal "foster parent."[110]

Concerning Legislation

According to the American Infertility Society, about 500 infertile couples—138 in the United States—have entered into surrogacy agreements.[111] This is a relatively small number in proportion to the number of contentious, painful, and even tragic cases that have been reported. There is universal consensus that the present relationship between surrogacy and the law is intolerable. Responses to the problem, however, differ greatly. Some legal writers predict that surrogate motherhood will become as well established as AID.[112] University of Texas law professor John Robertson judges the legal issues associated with surrogacy and AID as being basically the same.[113] Others believe that legislation is needed so that surrogacy is not driven underground.[114] Yet drawing up an acceptable form of legislation that does not violate personal rights and is not contrary to public policy has been a formidable task. There is currently no legislation that regulates surro-

[109] Susan Peterson and Susan Kelleher, "Surrogate Loses Child to His Genetic Parents in California", *The Boston Globe,* Oct. 23, 1990.

[110] Ellen Goodman, "Surrogacy and the Moral Limits of Commerce", *The Boston Globe,* Oct. 25, 1990, p. 21. In language according primacy to the will, Ms. Goodman, in expressing her support for the Calverts, states: "They willed the existence of this baby."

[111] Mark Rust, "Whose Baby Is It? Surrogate Motherhood after Baby M", 73 *Am. Bar Assoc. J.* (June 1987), p. 54.

[112] Robert C. Black, "Legal Problems of Surrogate Motherhood", 16 *New England Law Review* (1980–81), p. 395.

[113] John Robertson, "Surrogate Mothers: Not So Novel After All", *Hastings Center Report* (Oct. 1983), p. 28. See also Suzanne M. Patterson, "Parenthood by Proxy: Legal Implications of Surrogate Birth", 67 *Iowa L. R.* (Jan. 1982).

[114] Cynthia A. Rushevsky, "Legal Recognition of Surrogate Gestation", 7 *Women's Rights Law Reporter* (Winter 1982), p. 135.

gate motherhood. In fact, the worldwide trend seems to be in the direction of banning surrogacy altogether.

In the wake of Baby M, 22 of the bills introduced in 26 states and the District of Columbia call for the prohibition of surrogate motherhood.[115] A year before, there were bills opposing it in only four states. Attorney Generals in Ohio and Oklahoma have issued written opinions declaring surrogate agreements to be a violation of state law.[116] On July 9, 1987, Louisiana became the first state to outlaw surrogacy.[117] Nebraska, Indiana, and Kentucky soon followed in enacting legislation prohibiting the enforcement of surrogate contracts.[118] Since then, Florida and Michigan have banned commercial surrogacy.[119] The American Medical Association declared through its Judicial Council that surrogacy "does not represent a satisfactory alternative for people who wish to become parents."[120] The report expressed concern about "the potential legal and ethical jeopardy that physicians face. When all considerations are brought together, these arrangements do not appear to serve societal interests."

Two major national adoption organizations—The National Committee for Adoption (NCFA) and the American Adoption Congress (AAC)—have aserted that surrogate mother contracts are not in the public interest and do not safeguard the child's best interest.[121] William Pierce, president of the NCFA, which represents 130 adoption agencies, stated: "We

[115] Joseph F. Sullivan, "Brief by Feminists Opposes Parenthood", *The New York Times,* July 31, 1987.

[116] Rust, p. 55.

[117] Sullivan, July 31.

[118] Andrew Malcolm, "Steps to Control Surrogate Births Stir Debate Anew", *The New York Times,* June 26, 1988.

[119] Robert Hanley, "Limits on Unpaid Surrogacy Backed", *The New York Times,* March 12, 1989.

[120] "AMA Raps Surrogate Motherhood as Ethical and Legal Quagmire", *Medical World News,* Jan. 9, 1984, p. 24.

[121] "Groups: Give Baby Back to Birth Mom", *Am. Med. News,* Nov. 14, 1986.

cannot believe that society would sanction surrogate mothering contracts—whatever the circumstances—because they
not only exploit the women, but also the children."[122] He
went on to say, "The idea of treating a woman as a mere re-
ceptacle and then expecting her to sign an irrevocable contract
relinquishing all her rights, *prior* to the baby's birth, is un-
speakable and against public policy."[123] The AAC filed an *amicus curiae* brief with New Jersey's State Supreme Court
arguing that Mrs. Whitehead's ties to Baby M should not be
broken.[124] Even the American Fertility Society has expressed
its deep misgivings about surrogate motherhood. In an ethical
report released late in 1986, the AFS stated that the legal risks,
ethical concerns, and potential physical and psychological
effects of surrogate motherhood "render this method of
reproduction more problematic than most other technologies".[125] Finally, a group of well-known feminists filed an
amicus curiae brief in the Baby M Case, arguing that the commercialization of surrogate motherhood violates the United
States Constitution and the dignity of women.[126]

After observing the Baby M Case, Israel decided to outlaw surrogate motherhood. Health Ministry representative
Shmuel Algrabli said that his ministry would publish regula-
tions outlawing the practice. In a statement to the Associated
Press, Algrabli declared: "We have decided that, from an ethical point of view, surrogate motherhood cannot be permitted
in this country. It is just an unacceptable practice."[127] The
French health minister, who refers to surrogacy as "a form of
slavery", has effectively banned surrogate arrangements in

[122] Ibid.

[123] Carol O'Brien, "Surrogate Motherhood: An Emotional, Legal Quan-
dary", *Am. Med. News,* Jan. 2, 1987, p. 28.

[124] Sullivan, Aug. 5.

[125] O'Brien, p. 27.

[126] Sullivan, July 31.

[127] "Israel Outlaws Practice of Surrogate Motherhood", *Am. Med. News,*
June 12, 1987, p. 44.

France.[128] Spain has prohibited surrogacy both with and without payment.[129] The German Parliament has passed a law banning surrogate motherhood which some have described as the strictest in the world. The law bans women from being used to carry children for childless couples and allows IVF only when the egg used comes from the woman who is to have the baby.[130]

Australia has criminalized most surrogacy practices. Its Infertility Act makes it an offense to give or receive payment pursuant to a surrogacy agreement.[131] The Victorian Minister of Health has advised that surrogate motherhood could involve questions of slavery.[132]

In England, the Surrogacy Arrangements Act of 1985, which partially implemented the Warnock Commission's recommendations to prohibit surrogate motherhood, makes the operation of commercial surrogacy a criminal offense.[133] The Act "passed smoothly through the legislative process", according to one legal commentator, "with almost universal blessing".[134] It sets penalties of up to three months in jail or a fine of $2,300 for violators.

A storm of public protest to surrogate motherhood in England followed the "Baby Cotton Case" in which an infertile couple from the United States secured the services of a British surrogate who bore them a child which they adopted and

[128] Robin Herman, "French 'Baby M' Case Leads to Surrogacy Restrictions", *Washington Post Health*, 3(42) : 5, Oct. 20, 1987.

[129] "Biomedical Ethics: A Multinational View", Special Supplement, *Hastings Center Report*, vol. 17, no. 3, June 1987, pp. 6–7.

[130] "Ban on Surrogate Motherhood, Gene Changes Voted in Germany", *The Boston Globe*, Oct. 24, 1990.

[131] Thomas A. Eaton, "Comparative Responses to Surrogate Motherhood", 65 *Nebraska Law Review* (1986), p. 706.

[132] *The Age*, Jan. 5, 1985.

[133] Eaton, p. 688.

[134] Derek Morgan, "Making Motherhood Male: Surrogacy and the Moral Economy of Women", 12 *Journal of Law and Society* (Summer 1985), p. 226.

took back with them to America.[135] The natural mother, Kim Cotton, had openly admitted that she had no intention of caring for her baby.[136]

The Canadian response to surrogacy appears singularly atypical. The Ontario Law Reform Commission has taken the following position: "We have been persuaded that, on balance, the legislation should provide for immediate surrender of the child. Hence, where a surrogate mother refuses to transfer custody, she could be compelled to do so by court order."[137]

The Commission appears to be unaware that any bonding between mother and child takes place either during pregnancy or as a result of delivery. It assumes that the biological mother exists at a sufficiently remote psychic and emotional distance from her child as to allow the "social mother" to establish the earliest bonding with it. Hence, it believes that the "social mother", like the woman who "preconceives" or "mentally conceives" the child, is actually closer to the child than is the "biological mother" and therefore has a stronger claim to motherhood.

> [I]mmediate surrender to prevent bonding with the surrogate mother and to facilitate bonding with the person—the social mother—who, in the vast majority of cases, would be the ultimate recipient of the child and who, therefore would be the primary influence in its life during the neonatal period and infancy.[138]

The negative experiences of surrogate motherhood may not have been sufficient to bring about its universal prohibition,

---

[135] Avi Katz, "Surrogate Motherhood and the Baby-Selling Laws", 20 *Columbia Journal of Law and Social Problems* (1986), p. 42.

[136] Steven Erlanger, "Baby Given to Couple Who Paid Surrogate", *The Boston Globe*, Jan. 15, 1985.

[137] *Ontario Law Reform Commission, Report on Human Artificial Reproduction and Related Matters* iv (a) (1985).

[138] Ibid.

although they provide a strong argument in that direction. There is still a fairly widespread belief that surrogacy is inevitable and the best way to protect people from being victimized is to introduce carefully thought-out legislation.

Contemporary society, given its reluctance to ban anything and its disproportionate commitment to practicality, technological remedies, and helping people to fulfill their desires, should take a long, hard look at the fundamental reasons that make surrogate motherhood unacceptable. These reasons have to do with safeguarding the integrity of marriage and the family, of honoring and preserving the dignity and the very meaning of motherhood and fatherhood, of protecting women from exploitation and babies from commodification. These reasons, in effect, embrace the whole of civilization, for the family is still the basic and indispensable unit of society, the one inviolable human community for which there can be no surrogate.

Thus, in the framing of law, reason must come first, discovering and elucidating those real human goods that are worthy of protection. Will comes second, because what is worthy of protection must indeed be protected. This is the only way in which law can be both lawful and salutary, that is, capable of helping human beings to protect as well as cultivate the good that is in them. The attempt to legislate surrogate motherhood starting from a basis in will glorifies will but makes an invalid of reason. Born of such distorted and disharmonious parents, law is not law at all, and the problems that continue to plague society remain unredressed.

Chapter Eleven

New Reproductive Technologies and Church Teaching

The Vatican *Instruction on Respect for Human Life in Its Origin and on the Dignity of Procreation* is a highly reasoned document. As such, it reflects the mind of the Church, rather than her heart. It is, as Instructions inevitably must be, *doctrinal* rather than *pastoral*. The Church's pastoral dimension is best carried out by its people in a face-to-face context. Nonetheless, the mind and heart of the Church are one. It is only in their mode of expression that they differ.

It is expected, then, that many Catholic couples whose infertility is a source of indescribable disappointment and hardship will find neither consolation nor enlightenment in the *Instruction*, for it addresses them in an essentially logical and impersonal manner. Reason is a poor transmitter of love, and seldom soothes the afflicted.

Not surprisingly, therefore, many infertile couples and fertility experts found the *Instruction* disappointing. After all, it rejected all forms of artificial insemination as well as in vitro fertilization and embryo transfer, surrogate motherhood, and embryo freezing. At the same time, many saw hope for infertile couples, since the *Instruction* made no judgment about a number of new reproductive technologies that were already in use.

Cardinal Ratzinger, prefect of the Congregation for the Doctrine of the Faith, stated that in the absence of a Church decision, individual Catholic doctors should rely on their "informed conscience" in deciding whether to utilize these reproductive techniques. On the day the *Instruction* was released, he spoke to reporters at a press conference in Rome. He said, "When the discussion is still open and there is not yet a decision by the Magisterium, the doctor is required to stay informed, according to classic theological principles and concrete circumstances", and "make a decision based on his informed conscience."[1]

Specifically, two well-publicized techniques were omitted from the *Instruction:* Gamete Intrafallopian Transfer (GIFT) and Low Tubal Ovum Transfer (LTOT). Jesuit Father Bartholomew Kiely, a moral theologian who helped prepare the document, said: "The instruction does not pronounce a judgment on GIFT. It leaves it open to research by biologists and to further discussion by theologians."[2] Concerning LTOT, he said that it "seems to fall within the GIFT area that is not yet defined by the document, but is left open to further research." Another important technique known as TOT (Tubal Ovum Transfer), which is a modification of GIFT, was also omitted. The main element in judging these methods, Kiely explained, is whether they *assist* marital intercourse in attaining procreation or *replace* it with a laboratory technique. Monsignor Elio Sgreccia, an Italian ethicist who also helped prepare the document, corroborated Kiely's distinction. Methods that help marital intercourse attain fertility, he stated, should be considered "within the range of licitness".[3] Sgreccia expressed the hope that science could make available fertility techniques that would assist the conjugal act to reach its full effect in a way that allowed the conjugal act to be truly the source of life.[4]

The distinction between assisting and replacing marital intercourse—which Kiely and Sgreccia mention and which the *Instruction* details—was first brought into the discussion by Pope Pius XII. Between the years 1949 and 1958, Pius XII de-

[1] *Origins,* March 19, 1987, marginal notes, p. 699.
[2] Ibid., pp. 699–700.
[3] Ibid., p. 700.
[4] Ibid., p. 700.

livered four important scholarly addresses on the subject of artificial insemination to a variety of medical personnel.[5] It was in his presentation to Catholic doctors, in 1949, that the Pope first made reference to the distinction between *assisted* and *artificial* insemination. This critical distinction opened the way for the possible moral acceptability of certain bio-technical interventions that did not violate the integrity of the conjugal act. The Pontiff states:

> Although one cannot *a priori* exclude new methods because they are new, yet, as far as artificial insemination is concerned, not only does it call for an extreme reserve, but it is absolutely to be rejected. To say this is not necessarily to proscribe the use of certain artificial means designed only to facilitate the natural act or to assist that act, done in the normal way, to attain its end.[6]

This statement was destined to play a significant role in helping to distinguish those reproductive technologies that are morally acceptable from those that are not. After referring to the guidelines proposed by Pius XII, the Vatican *Instruction* made the following comment: "If the technical means facilitates the conjugal act or helps it reach its natural objectives, it can be morally acceptable. If, on the other hand, the procedure were to replace the conjugal act, it is morally illicit."[7]

It should be noted here that the two conditions specified— assisting either the conjugal act or the attainment of its natural objective—represent *necessary* but not *sufficient* conditions for moral acceptability. In order to qualify as morally acceptable, a technical procedure must not contradict either of these two conditions; at the same time, its mere consonance with them

---

[5] *Doctors* (Sept. 19, 1949); *Midwives* (Oct. 29, 1951); *Fertility Experts* (May 19, 1956); *Hematologists* (Sept. 12, 1958).

[6] Pope Pius XII, "Fourth International Congress of Catholic Doctors", in *Canon Law Digest*, II (Milwaukee: Bruce, 1954), p. 433. This passage is cited in the *Instruction*, II B. 6 and given its reference in f.n. 53.

[7] *Instruction*, II B. 6.

is not sufficient. Moral acceptability demands that other conditions be met, namely, that intercourse take place within the context of marriage, that the integrity of the sex act not be compromised, that the reproductive procedure be neither hazardous nor exploitive, and so on. The *Instruction* does not say that a technique is morally acceptable if it facilitates the conjugal act or helps it to reach its natural objectives, but that it *can* be acceptable. The implication is that it *is* acceptable only when it fulfills all the relevant moral criteria.

In his work, *Medical Ethics,* Father Edwin Healy argues that a physician may use a syringe to project the semen toward the uterus. He regards this procedure as exemplifying Pius XII's notion of "assisted insemination". He writes:

> It is permissible for a physician, however, after husband and wife have rightly performed the marital act, artificially to propel the semen deposited in the vagina into the uterus and Fallopian tubes, for the physician's act in this case would consist merely in aiding nature . . . This process is rightly called, not artificial, but assistant, insemination.[8]

Gerald Kelly, in his classic study, *Medico-Moral Problems,* draws upon the distinction between assisted and artificial insemination to illuminate the moral difference between the use of the cervical spoon and the cervical cap. The function of the spoon is to aid sperm in their migration through the cervical os. Kelly judges, "Obviously, this procedure is not artificial insemination. . . .; it is merely a technique for aiding marital intercourse to be fertile by overcoming certain physiological obstacles. Some might call it 'assisted insemination'."[9] In the cervical cap technique, semen, which may be obtained

---

[8] Chicago: Loyola University Press, 1956, p. 154.

[9] St. Louis: The Catholic Hospital Association, 1957, pp. 239–40. The cervical spoon was invented by Joseph B. Doyle, M.D. See J. B. Doyle, "The Cervical Spoon: A Preliminary Report", *Journal of Urology,* Dec. 1948, pp. 986–89.

through masturbation or collected after intercourse, is placed in a cuplike container (the cap), and then fitted over the cervix. Kelly judges this to be an instance of artificial insemination and therefore "a substitute for intercourse".[10] The purpose of the spoon and the cap is the same, to bring about fertilization. But their moral difference, as Kelly concluded, is that the former assists intercourse in achieving its end, whereas the latter replaces it with an artificial technique.

The use of a device (such as a spoon, or syringe, or dilator) to enable sperm to move more readily toward the egg, was approved by moralists and canonists such as DeSmet, Merkelbach, Payen, and Ubach. They were careful to note, however, that the seminal deposit could not be exteriorized, that is, withdrawn from the vagina.[11]

The distinction between assisted and artificial insemination may be further clarified by a number of analogies. An athlete who is injured during the course of a game may be helped or "assisted" from the playing field, or he may be carried off on a stretcher. In the former case, he is able to walk off the field under his own power. In the latter instance, the stretcher provides a substitute for his natural manner of movement. It is artificial, not natural. Similarly, a teacher can help a student to work out a math problem. This is help or assistance. On the other hand, the teacher can simply tell the student the answer. This is a substitute or replacement for thinking, not assistance. This same distinction separates an athlete's legitimate use of training as a natural way of assisting him to prepare for an event, and the use of illegal substances such as steroids, which are artificial and seem to be a substitute for natural means of physical development.

[10] Ibid., p. 240. See James Whitelaw, M.D., "Use of the Cervical Cap to Increase Fertility in Cases of Oligospermia", *Fertility and Sterility,* Jan. 1950, pp. 33–39.

[11] See John Wakefield, *Artful Child Making* (St. Louis: Pope John XXIII Medical-Moral Research and Education Center, 1978), p. 44, f.n. 81.

In each of these examples, the distinction between "assisted" and "artificial" is crucial in determining the degree of autonomy of the subject. Is the player ambulatory? Did the student solve the problem? Did the athlete accomplish his feats on his own? The question for the married couple is whether the husband and wife performed the act that resulted in new life and made them parents. The distinction between "assisted" and "artificial" is widely employed in teaching, sports, and in law. It is not in any way peculiar to the Catholic Church. The moral significance underlying this distinction involves self-identity. Concerning reproductive technologies, the Church wants to make the link between parents and children as clear as possible. It wants husband and wife to know that *they* (and not an external technique) are the generators of new life and to know what set of circumstances establishes their identity as parents.

In "assisted" forms of insemination, the sperm retains its own capacity for movement and travels through its naturally appointed course. Insemination is artificial when the sperm is entirely passive with regard to its manner of relocation, and travels through a route that nature did not provide. In conventional, unambiguous forms of artificial insemination (either AIH or AID), the sperm is transported outside of the woman's body along a path not established by nature, and directed into her body by mechanical means. Thus, the motive force and the route are artificial and not natural. In this perspective, insemination is not achieved as a result of sexual intercourse but by an artificial method.

The morality of new reproductive technologies such as LTOT, TOT, and GIFT hinges largely on whether they represent assisted or artificial forms of insemination. Before moral assessment can be made, however, it is necessary to have a clear idea of exactly what these procedures are and how they operate. This is a fairly complicated issue in itself, but it is further complicated by the influence of historical circumstances and promotional interests. A careful historical and medical review of these three techniques is therefore demanded before a reliable or meaningful moral assessment can be made.

LTOT

The St. Elizabeth Medical Center in Dayton, Ohio, issued a news release on September 1, 1983, announcing the inauguration of a new fertility procedure. This procedure would provide a medical alternative to the morally controversial in vitro fertilization.[12] The procedure was designed for women whose infertility was caused by blocked, damaged, diseased, or absent fallopian tubes. In essence, it relocates the egg, bypassing or circumventing the area of tubal pathology, in order to situate it in an environment where fertilization might possibly occur. Specifically, it reinserts the egg (or eggs) in the mid or lower portion of the tube or in the uterus itself. Consequently, the technique is called Low Tubal Ovum Transfer.[13] In May 1982, the British medical journal, *Lancet* had reported the first successful pregnancy using a technique similar to LTOT. In this instance, 2 of 14 women became pregnant when oöcytes and sperm were inserted transcervically into the uterus.[14]

Experimental research on LTOT was undertaken a few years earlier at the National Institutes of Health. Working with monkeys, a team of scientists devised a procedure whereby an egg is removed immediately prior to ovulation and inserted into the lower end of one of the fallopian tubes.

[12] " 'In Vitro' Alternative: Catholic Hospital Begins 'In Vivo' Ovum Transfer", *The Catholic Standard and Times* (Philadelphia), Thursday, Sept. 22, 1983, p. 14.

[13] See Pope John XXIII Medical-Moral Center, "Should Catholic Hospitals Encourage Low Tubal Ovum Transfer?" *Hospital Progress,* March 1984, pp. 55–56.

[14] Ian Craft, et al, "Human Pregnancy Following Oöcyte and Sperm Transfer to the Uterus", *Lancet,* May 8, 1982, pp. 1031–33.

Following normal mating, 5 out of 31 monkeys so treated after their fallopian tubes had been surgically ligated conceived and had a normal pregnancy and birth.[15] Dr. Gary Hodgen, who pioneered the LTOT procedure and conducted the initial animal studies, pointed out an important moral advantage that LTOT has over IVF: "The need for someone to decide whether a given embryo is fit for transfer to the uterus or should be discarded is not encountered with low tubal ovum transfer."[16]

The treatment offered to infertile women at St. Elizabeth's Medical Center begins when ovulatory drugs are used to stimulate the maturation of multiple eggs. The couple engages in intercourse just prior to the predicted time of ovulation. Immediately thereafter, the doctors perform a laparoscopy on the wife in order to retrieve her eggs. After the eggs are repositioned in the mid, or lower portion of the fallopian tube or in the uterus, the couple repeats the sex act with the hope that fertilization and implantation will take place.[17] The time between the removal of the eggs from the ovary to their reinsertion is less than two hours.

The LTOT procedure appears to be consonant with Church teaching and an exemplification of Directive #21 of the *Ethical and Religious Directives for Catholic Health Facilities,* which states, "Help may be given to a normally performed conjugal act to attain its purpose."[18] With LTOT, conception is in vivo, the embryo is not manipulated, and the integrity of marital intercourse is fully respected. Some have questioned whether the repositioning of the egg is a truly therapeutic

[15] "'In Vitro' Alternative", p. 14.

[16] O. Kreitman and G. Hodgen, "Low Tubal Transfer: An Alternative to In Vitro Fertilization", *Fertility and Sterility,* October 1980, pp. 375–78.

[17] Donald G. McCarthy, "Infertility Bypass: A Possible Treatment of Blocked Fallopian Tubes", *Ethics and Medics,* 8, 10 (1983), p. 1.

[18] See Orville N. Griese, *Catholic Identity in Health Care: Principles and Practice* (Braintree, Mass.: The Pope John Center, 1987), pp. 480–81.

procedure since it does not correct the tubal pathology and offers, at best, a momentary opportunity for achieving pregnancy.[19] Most people who have commented on LTOT, however, viewed it as genuinely therapeutic inasmuch as it is "a remedial treatment of a bodily disorder".[20] Although LTOT does not offer a permanent remedy, it appears to be analogous to the treating of a diabetic person on a day-to-day basis by supplying insulin and bypassing the defective Islets cells of the pancreas.

In contrasting LTOT with IVF, Donald McCarthy, Director of Education for the Pope John Center, stated, "LTOT offers a therapeutic intervention to assist conception through an act of conjugal love, while IVF produces a child through the laboratory process of fertilization."[21] Other moralists have endorsed LTOT, including William May of Catholic University, who commented, "This procedure, should it prove workable, is in my judgment morally permissible, and offers great hope for those married couples for whom the laboratory generation of life is now proposed."[22] Finally, the Archbishop of Cincinnati, Daniel E. Pilarczyk, affirmed the technique when he said that "the LTOT procedure is in accord with the Church's teaching."[23]

[19] "New Conception Technology", *Ethics and Medics,* 6, 1 (1981), p. 3, reprinted from *Bionews—An Ethical Focus.*

[20] McCarthy, p. 1. See also David Q. Liptak, "New 'Infertility Bypass (LTOT)' Assessed", *The Catholic Transcript* (Hartford), Jan. 6, 1984.

[21] "Should Catholic Hospitals", p. 56.

[22] William May, "'Begotten Not Made': Reflections on Laboratory Production of Human Life", *Pope John Paul II Lecture Series in Bioethics,* vol. I, Francis J. Lescoe and David Q. Liptak (eds.), (New Britain, Connecticut: Mariel Publications, 1983), p. 55.

[23] "'In Vitro' Alternative". See also "New Hospital Infertility Program Seen as a Blessing", by Peter Feuerherd, in *The Catholic Telegraph,* Cincinnati, Ohio, Sept. 9, 1983, p. 124; here the Archbishop is quoted as follows: "It is my opinion that the procedure as described is not contrary to Catholic moral teaching." See also *Hospital Progress,* March 1984, pp. 55–56 where the Archbishop remarks that LTOT is "not contrary to Catholic teaching".

TOT

Despite the hope that LTOT offered infertile women with tubal pathologies, the medical team led by Dr. David S. McLaughlin did not succeed in helping to bring about a single pregnancy in 65 cycles with approximately 40 women.[24] After 23 months of failure, Dr. McLaughlin and his associates decided to try a different procedure. They named this procedure "TOT". Because of its acronymic similarity with LTOT and the fact that it came close on the heels of that failed procedure, it is easy to understand how many people either confused the two or believed them to be either the same or virtually the same. Hence, Monsignor Orville Griese, for example, the senior research director of the Pope John Center, refers to TOT as a "modified" form of LTOT.[25] A procedure that would have been the logical corollary to LTOT was never tried because funding was not available.[26] This procedure might have aptly been named HTOT (High Tubal Ovum Transfer) in which the egg would have been relocated high in the fallopian tubes, the site where conception ordinarily takes place.

Most doctors believe that human conception takes place in the upper or distal region of the fallopian tubes. Moreover, it has been suggested that the embryo's two- or three-day jour-

[24] David McLaughlin, "A Scientific Introduction to Reproductive Technologies", Donald G. McCarthy (ed.), *Reproductive Technologies, Marriage and the Church* (Braintree, Mass: The Pope John Center, 1988), p. 63. Hereafter referred to as McCarthy, 1988. Although conception can occur in the lower region of the fallopian tubes in monkeys, apparently such may not be the case with humans (telephone conversation with David McLaughlin, Jan. 20, 1988). Moreover, the surgically produced conditions in the tubes of the monkeys did not mimic those in women with tubal disease arising from tubal infection, endometriosis, or ectopic pregnancy. See *Media Briefing*, "An Alternative to In Vitro Fertilization", Oct. 9, 1980, sponsored by the National Institute of Child Health and Human Development—National Institutes of Health, p. 6.

[25] Griese, p. 44.

[26] Personal communication with Dr. McLaughlin, Feb. 2, 1988, at the Pope John Center's Bishops' Workshop for 1988 in Dallas, Texas.

ney to the uterus is significant. If the journey is cut short, as would happen if fertilization took place in the lower region of the fallopian tube, a spontaneous abortion might ensue.[27]

TOT differs radically from LTOT in several important ways. The environment in which prospective fertilization is to take place is as *high* in the fallopian tube as possible. Hence the elimination of the "L" in the acronym LTOT. TOT, therefore, would not offer any hope of achieving pregnancy for women with damaged fallopian tubes. TOT requires exteriorizing the egg rather than directly relocating it within the woman's body. Altogether, the procedure is longer, lasting an estimated three hours.[28] Also unlike LTOT, TOT demands the exteriorization and processing of the sperm. Masturbation, however, is avoided. This is made possible when the husband engages in intercourse using a perforated silicone sheath that self-seals after the initial propulsion of seminal fluid is deposited in the vaginal tract. The remainder of the sperm is collected from the sheath, washed, treated, and inserted by catheter into the distal region of the tube using air spaces between the semen and the eggs to prevent fertilization outside the body.[29]

Of six patients who underwent TOT at the St. Elizabeth Medical Center in the late summer of 1985, two became pregnant. The two expectant mothers had experienced infertility for nine and five years, respectively. One mother miscarried at 18 weeks, and the second gave birth to a baby boy at 34 weeks' gestation.[30] A second child, and first to Catholic parents, was born on August 5, 1987.[31]

---

[27] Ken Platt, "Artificial Assistance in the Achievement of Pregnancy", *"Splintered Image" Conference,* Edinburgh, August 1988, p. 4 of transcript.

[28] Ibid., p. 5.

[29] Hanna Klaus, "The Laboratory Generation of Life", *Fellowship of Catholic Scholars Newsletter,* June 1986, p. 9.

[30] Donald G. McCarthy, "Infertility Bypassed", *Ethics and Medics,* 11, 3 (1986), pp. 3–4.

[31] McCarthy, 1988, p. 63.

The Pope John Center evaluated as morally acceptable the TOT procedure where masturbation is avoided and fertilization takes place in vivo. The experts at the Center concluded that the use of the husband's sperm in TOT was "a legitimate form of assistance to the natural marital act, allowing the act to attain its end".[32] They reasoned that TOT was in accord with Pius XII's notion of "assisted insemination". Nonetheless, Archbishop Pilarczyk, who had endorsed LTOT, did not give his approval to TOT. In a letter to the chairman of a natural family planning organization in England, the Archbishop wrote:

> I really do not believe that it is appropriate for me to comment on the TOT procedure since I have not been provided with the technical information which would render such comment responsible. I stand by my evaluation of LTOT.[33]

To his credit, the Archbishop was aware that there might have been technical as well as moral differences between TOT and LTOT. Monsignor Orville Griese, on the other hand, neglected them. As a result, he assumed that the moral evaluation Archbishop Pilarczyk gave LTOT would also apply to the TOT procedure.[34] This same assumption is reflected in a letter appearing in *Lancet* entitled "Tubal Ovum Transfer: A Catholic-Approved Alternative to In-Vitro Fertilisation".[35] In the letter, cosigned by Donald McCarthy, the authors state, "We felt that the TOT protocol met Vatican approved guidelines and accorded with official Catholic views on sex within marriage, on masturbation, and on contraception."[36] The let-

---

[32] Ibid., p. 4.

[33] Letter to Ken Platt, chairman of a national family planning group in England, N.A.O.M.I., an affiliate of W.O.O.M.B. (dated June 3, 1987).

[34] Griese, p. 44.

[35] David McLaughlin, et al. *Lancet,* Jan. 24, 1987, p. 214.

[36] Ibid., p. 214.

ter was seriously misleading. The assumption that TOT was morally equivalent to LTOT had now passed to the presumption that the Church had approved it.

Acronymic similarity and chronological sequence do not imply either technical or moral equivalence. But describing the procedure as TOT was a contrived attempt to create this implication. Some people in the field have rejected this contrivance as simply "dishonest".[37] Moral theologian William May has complained that he was originally misled by the acronym TOT into thinking (quite logically) that it referred to removing the egg and placing it in the fallopian tube prior to the marital act.[38]

Dr. McLaughlin himself has seen fit to amend his acronym and now calls it TOTS, the last initial referring to the sperm.[39] In truth, TOTS' sister procedure is not LTOT at all but GIFT. Therefore, an understanding of TOT(S) is not complete without an appreciation of GIFT.

GIFT

Between the time David McLaughlin inaugurated LTOT and the time he introduced TOT, Ricardo Asch and his associates at the University of Texas in San Antonio successfully employed a technique virtually identical with TOT. They identified it as GIFT, the acronym for gamete intrafallopian transfer.

Asch detailed the GIFT technique in a 1984 issue of *Lancet*.[40] Semen was obtained from the 35-year-old patient's 37-year-old husband 2½ hours before laparoscopy. Four oöcytes

---

[37] Platt, p. 6.

[38] McCarthy, 1988, p. 165.

[39] Ibid., p. 84.

[40] Ricardo Asch, et al., "Pregnancy after Translaparoscopic Intrafallopian Transfer", *Lancet*, Nov. 3, 1984, pp. 1034–35.

were obtained by translaparoscopic follicular aspiration; two were classified as preovulatory. All four oöcytes were maintained in an incubator with 5% CO_2 and air at 37°C until the time of transfer. The semen and oöcytes were placed in a catheter separated by air spaces. The catheter tip was inserted about 1.5 cm into the fimbriated end of the fallopian tube and the contents gently injected. This procedure was repeated for the contralateral fallopian tube. Twins resulted. The mother was in the twentieth week of her pregnancy at the time of the report.

In a subsequent report, Asch documented the successful completion of the first pregnancy and disclosed that of 10 patients undergoing the GIFT procedure, 4 conceived, though 2 experienced abortions.[41] Employing Asch's method, an Australian team achieved a clinical pregnancy rate of 27% in a series of 71 treatment cycles involving 70 patients (19 pregnancies, 4 clinical abortions, 3 sets of twins among the 16 continuing pregnancies). Husbands were requested to produce sperm samples through masturbation. In one case, a husband's sperm was frozen and in two instances frozen donor sperm was used. In all, 558 ova were retrieved, a median of 7 ova per patient, with 4 ova transferred in 63 of the cycles.[42]

In another early experience with the GIFT procedure, the technique was performed in 19 cycles on 15 couples. The result was 4 conceptions, with one of these ending in an early

[41] Asch, et al., "Birth Following Gamete Intrafallopian Transfer", *Lancet,* 2:163, 1985. See also Asch, et al., "Preliminary Experience with Gamete Intrafallopian Transfer (GIFT)", *Fertility and Sterility,* vol. 45, 1986, p. 366; Asch, et al., "Gamete Intrafallopian Transfer (GIFT): A New Treatment for Infertility", *International Journal of Fertility,* 30:41, 1985.

[42] David Molloy, et al., "A Laparoscopic Approach to a Program of Gamete Intra-Fallopian Transfer", *Fertility and Sterility,* vol. 47, no. 2, Feb. 1987, pp. 289–94; Molloy, et al., "The Establishment of a Successful Programme of Gamete Intra-Fallopian Transfer (GIFT): Preliminary Results", *Aust NZ J Obstet Gynaec* 26: 206, 1986.

pregnancy loss.[43] Three of the men involved were sperm donors and 11 had their sperm tested with the hamster egg penetration assay (SPA—a test used on spermatozoa to determine their egg-penetrating capacities).

More recently, a nonsurgical form of GIFT has been developed in which eggs are retrieved with the aid of ultrasound guidance. More experience, however, is needed in order to assess its success rates when compared with laparoscopic techniques.[44] In addition, another offspring of GIFT known as "Laser GIFT" has been developed where laser surgery is combined with GIFT to provide "one-stop" medical repair and impregnation.[45]

GIFT/IVF

One of the physiological drawbacks of the GIFT procedure is the inability to determine if fertilization has occurred in the absence of pregnancy. This problem which has important diagnostic implications for couples with unexplained infertility, is avoided in a more recent technique known as Pronuclear Stage Tubal Transfer (PROST). In this procedure, fertilization of oöcytes occurs in vitro; the very young embryo is then transferred into the fallopian tube.[46] In a similar procedure, the pronucleate stage embryo, 16 hours after fertilization, is inserted into the uterus.[47] These modifications of GIFT are

[43] Stephen L. Corson, et al., "Early Experience with the GIFT Procedure", *The Journal of Reproductive Medicine,* vol. 31, no. 4, April 1986, pp. 219–23.

[44] Mark Bustillo, et al., "Pregnancy after Microsurgical Ultrasound-Guided Gamete Intrafallopian Transfer", *New England Journal of Medicine,* Aug. 4, 1988, p. 313.

[45] Rick McGuire, "'One-Stop' Approach to Infertility: Laser Surgery and Gamete Transfer", *Medical Tribune,* Jan. 28, 1988, pp. 3, 11.

[46] Phillip Matson, et al., "The Role of Gamete Intrafallopian Transfer (GIFT) in the Treatment of Oligospermic Infertility", *Fertility and Sterility,* vol. 48, no. 4, Oct. 1987, pp. 608–12.

[47] Ian Craft, et al., *Fertility and Sterility,* vol. 44, 1985, p. 181.

also designed to offset the difficulties encountered during conventional IVF in culturing, fertilizing, and maintaining embryos in the dish.[48]

GIFT represents another disadvantage when compared with IVF in that the surgical insertion of the eggs into the fallopian tube is less desirable than the nonsurgical ultrasonographic retrieval of eggs in the IVF-embryo transfer method. Some of the advantages and disadvantages of GIFT and IVF are complementary. For example, IVF, like LTOT, is designed for women who have tubal pathologies, whereas GIFT requires at least one healthy tube. For such reasons, Ricardo Asch, who has initiated a program in which IVF is used with the extra oöcytes (along with embryo freezing for future use), emphasizes the complementarity of IVF and GIFT.[49]

A number of fertility teams routinely involve IVF along with GIFT.[50] Some have reported no significant difference in the pregnancy rates associated with each of these methods.[51]

Confusion and Misunderstanding

LTOT, TOT(S), and GIFT are commonly confused with each other. Part of the reason for this lies in the relative newness of

[48] "Gamete Intrafallopian Transfer for Infertility", *Intelligence Reports in Ob-Gyn,* March 1986, vol. 4, no. 3, p. 9.

[49] Asch, 1986, p. 370.

[50] Martin Quigley, et al., "Simultaneous In Vitro Fertilization and Gamete Intrafallopian Transfer (GIFT)", *Fertility and Sterility,* vol. 47, no. 5, May 1987, pp. 797–801. See also Paul F. Serhal, et al., "Ovum Donation—A Simplified Approach," *Fertility and Sterility,* vol. 48, no. 2, Aug. 1987, pp. 265–69.

[51] John Leeton, et al. See also J. C. Jarrett, et al., "In Vitro Fertilization-Embryo Transfer and Gamete Intrafallopian Transfer: Pregnancy Initiation Center, Indianapolis, Indiana", *Journal of In Vitro Fertilization and Embryo Transfer* (Letter to the Editor), vol. 4, no. 6, 1987, pp. 356–57 where the Center reports an IVF ongoing pregnancy rate with 418 women of 17.1% and a GIFT ongoing pregnancy rate with 143 women of 29%. The Center's 1987 pregnancy rate is 23% for IVF and 35% for GIFT.

these procedures and their technical differences, which are not well known to either the public or the journalistic world. In addition, they are often misrepresented to appear more conformable with Catholic teaching than they actually are. The medical, public, and media sympathies are solidly on the side of the infertile couple. By contrast, Catholic teaching is made to appear umsympathetic and abstract.

Examples are legion. On the medical frontier, a 1986 issue of the *Journal of Reproductive Medicine* suggests that the Catholic Church will accept GIFT because it does not require the exteriorization of the embryo.[52] *Fertility and Sterility* states in a 1987 issue that GIFT has an advantage over IVF because of "its acceptance by the Roman Catholic Church".[53] Ricardo Asch maintains that the Vatican "approves" of GIFT.[54]

When the NC wire service carried the story of the first baby born as a result of the TOTS procedure, it described it as though it were LTOT and reported that Archbishop Pilarczyk had approved it.[55] Similarly, the *National Catholic Reporter* described TOT with clinical precision in terms of LTOT, announced the arrival of an LTOT baby which that method never produced, and expressed the belief that TOT had been approved by Archbishop Pilarczyk.[56]

In Springfield, Massachusetts, twins were born on January 15, 1989. They were the first reported births resulting from GIFT performed at a Catholic hospital. The local Catholic newspaper described the procedure as "the only fertility procedure

[52] Corson, p. 223.

[53] John Leeton, et al., "A Controlled Study Between the Use of Gamete Intrafallopian Transfer (GIFT) and In Vitro Fertilization and Embryo Transfer in the Management of Idiopathic and Male Infertility", *Fertility and Sterility,* vol. 48, no. 4, Oct. 1987, p. 607.

[54] Dawn Di Martino, "Doctor Says Vatican Approves In Vitro Method", *National Catholic Reporter,* Nov. 6, 1987, p. 6. See also Asch, 1986, p. 370.

[55] Deborah McCarty, "First Baby Born from Ovum Transfer; Church Approved", *The Globe* (Sioux City, Iowa), May 22, 1986.

[56] Jim McManus and Susan Hansen, "Rome Document Sparks Firestorm of U.S. Reactions", *National Catholic Register,* March 18, 1987, p. 8.

currently approved by the Catholic Church".[57] Reporting this event in America's oldest Catholic newspaper, *The Pilot*, the writer remarked that "because the Holy See has not pronounced on it [GIFT], it is a probable opinion that it will be approved."[58] In Canada, Toronto's *Catholic New Times* reported the event as being "approved by the Catholic Church".[59] Another Canadian Catholic periodical, *Challenge*, told its readers that the GIFT protocol is "allowed by the Church".[60] Even the Italian Press was eager to baptize GIFT.[61]

John Carlson, in a careful, scholarly analysis of GIFT and IVF in the context of Catholic teaching, comes to the conclusion that there is no essential moral difference between them. He also concludes that in neither the cases of IVF or GIFT "can it plausibly be said that fertilization arises simply from an act of conjugal union."[62]

One of the more bizarre distortions of the new reproductive techniques and their relationship to Catholic teaching belongs to Peter Hebblethwaite. In commenting on a passage in the Vatican *Instruction*, he makes the gratuitous inference that John Paul (who did not write the document) appears to be recommending the use of a perforated condom. He then ridicules the Pontiff for not using the word (which is really a

[57] Sharon Stefanik, "The 'GIFT' of Life", *The Catholic Observer*, Feb. 24, 1989, p. 6.

[58] "New Procedure Seen as Major Step toward Fertility", *The Pilot*, Boston, Mass., Feb. 17, 1989, p. 9.

[59] *The Catholic New Times* (Toronto), April 16, 1989, p. 2.

[60] *Challenge* (Winnipeg, Manitoba), May 1989, p. 11.

[61] Vito Cioce, *Il Tempo* (Roma), "Nuova tecnica di fecondazione: giudizio positivo della Chiesa? Il teologo moralista mons. Caffarra spiega i motivi inducono ad accettare il GIFT: non è dell'atto coniugale concepimento avviene nel corpo della donna", Friday, Oct. 11, 1985, p. 24; Vito Cioce, *Il Tempo* (Roma), "Con il 'GIFT' forma speciale di 'procreazione assistita", Wednesday, Oct. 10, 1985, p. 27; Pier Giorgio Leverani, *Italia* (Roma), "Fecondazione/Convegno", Saturday, Sept. 21, 1985, p. 5.

[62] John Carlson, "*Donum Vitae* on Homologous Interventions: Is IVF-ET a Less Acceptable Gift Than 'GIFT'?" *The Journal of Medicine and Philosophy*, 14:536, 1989.

sheath rather than a "condom"), chastizes him for employing "sexist" language (though *Donum Vitae* was written in Latin), and proclaims that TOT, which he inaccurately represents, "conforms to the Vatican instruction". Then, confusing TOT with other reproductive technologies, he claims that 23 women had become pregnant at the hospital where Dr. McLaughlin works.[63] In fact, at the time of Hebblethwaite's writing, only 2 TOT-conceived pregnancies had been reported.[64] Indeed, McLaughlin himself has stated that on a scale from "A" to "Z", he would place TOT (which his clients often find incomprehensible) squarely at "Z".[65]

The Pope John Center's Defense of TOTS

The Pope John Center recognizes that LTOT does not work and that GIFT relies on masturbation. But it has gone on record in support of TOTS.[66] The weakness of its position lies in the fact that it uses the wrong model for comparison. It views TOTS favorably because this technique compares well with IVF and GIFT. In contrast with IVF, TOTS allows conception to take place in vivo and respects the moral significance of conjugal union. In contrast with GIFT, TOTS avoids masturbation and presents the possibility (though it is highly unlikely) that conception will occur as a direct result of sexual intercourse. This methodology, however, is radically defective. One cannot demonstrate the moral permissibility of an act by showing that it does not share the conspicuous defects of certain other acts. It must be shown to be good in itself. Rather than explain how TOTS is different from IVF and GIFT, the Center would have been wiser to show how much

[63] Peter Hebblethwaite, "Vatican Instruction Seen as Warning Signal to Doctors and Scientists", *National Catholic Register,* March 18, 1987, p. 23.

[64] *Lancet,* Jan. 1987.

[65] McLaughlin, Pope John Center Bishops' Workshop for 1988, Feb. 2.

[66] McCarthy, 1988, p. 140. Lloyd W. Hess, "Assisting the Infertile Couple", *Ethics and Medics,* 11, 2 (1985). Griese, p. 44.

it has in common with AI (artificial insemination), a procedure which the Church has flatly rejected.

The Center's position does not pay sufficient attention to
the integrity of the sexual act and how TOTS compromises
that integrity. TOTS is antagonistic to the reposefulness,
intimacy, spontaneity, and fullness of sexual union. As a
spokesman for the Center, Albert Moraczewski admits that
TOTS "pushes the principle (of the Vatican instruction) to its
limit".[67] Nonetheless, Donald McCarthy steadfastly maintains that with TOTS "we are not in *any* sense undermining
the essential significance of the conjugal act" (emphasis added).[68] By overstating his case, he is clearly weakening it.
Moreover, his understanding of AI is incorrect and misleading. He asserts, "Truly artificial insemination is the insemination that takes place in the doctor's office with no regard for
the marital act and with no effort to collect the male sperm
from the marital act."[69] The "doctor's office" is wholly extra-
neous to the moral issue. But more importantly, AI does not
disregard sexual intercourse. Fertility experts, realizing that
intercourse produces a greater supply of semen than masturbation does, are now advocating coitus with a silastic
sheath as a preferred method of obtaining semen in the AI
procedure.[70]

Neither are McCarthy's arguments from authority very
convincing. For example, he cites Father Thomas O'Donnell's opinion that there is a "solid probable opinion" that
TOTS is morally acceptable.[71] But he does not represent
O'Donnell's contention that TOTS is "much more than a
minor modification of LTOT", and that it is "essentially iden-

---

[67] Di Martino, p. 6.
[68] McCarthy, 1988, p. 142.
[69] Ibid., p. 142.
[70] See f.n. 87.
[71] McCarthy, 1988, p. 142.

tical" with GIFT.[72] As for McCarthy's claim that O'Donnell considers TOTS an instance of assisted insemination,[73] O'Donnell makes it categorically clear that he does not.[74]

If TOTS is antagonistic to the integrity of the marital act, this will be borne out by a series of discordances. The critical question here is whether TOTS is a single, continuous moral act in which technology truly assists insemination, or whether there are two distinct, discontinuous, and discordant acts in which TOTS is a disharmonious hybrid of a limited act of intercourse followed by a limited enactment of artificial insemination.

Moral Assessment of TOTS

For successful implantation, there must be the right synchrony between the particular stage of embryo development and the hormonal climate of the uterine environment. Premature entry into the uterus can result in expulsion of the embryo or egg.[75] Some specialists have suggested freezing embryos and implanting them during subsequent cycles when the uterine environment is more receptive. Freezing, however, poses unknown hazards for the embryo.

Cryoprotectants are introduced to safeguard the embryo during the freezing process. Hormones are injected to help regulate the woman's cycle. And so on. This multiplication of medical techniques well illustrates a fundamental problem in trying to assist a couple to achieve pregnancy. Science can attempt only in a piecemeal fashion what nature ordinarily accomplishes as a unified whole. A basic conflict exists, there-

---

[72] Thomas J. O'Donnell, *The Medical-Moral Newsletter,* vol. 24, no. 1, Jan. 1987, p. 2.

[73] McCarthy, 1988, p. 142.

[74] See f.n. 100.

[75] Craft, 1982, p. 1033.

fore, between a method that is directed toward one event at a time and a natural process in which they are all in synchrony. The separation of specific operations from their web of natural unity inevitably invites discordance between one operation and another. Concerning human fertility, this is a problem of considerable significance because the marital act and its invocation to new life should be a physical and moral unity.

The TOTS procedure brings to light several instances of this discordance. These instances of discordance demonstrate that TOTS is not in continuity with the sexual act. In addition, they represent a series of antagonisms that are potentially injurious to the sperm and egg, and the prospective child, as well as to the bond between husband and wife, and the chances of their achieving pregnancy.

1. The Exteriorization of the Gametes

After normal intercourse, prostaglandins contained in semen are ordinarily neutralized by the cervical mucus.[76] If semen is to be delivered through the TOTS procedure directly into the upper tract, it must first be washed in order to neutralize the prostaglandins artificially. This is done in order to prevent peristalsis, leading to more rapid propulsion of the ovum, possibly causing it to arrive in the uterine cavity before the endometrium is fully prepared for imbedding, or simply speeding it out of the uterus. This same effect is also produced by prostaglandin F2 alpha, which acts as an abortifacient. But the treatment of the sperm also requires storage for a brief period in CO_2 and the effect of that gas on sperm is still under investigation.[77]

The exteriorization of the egg is also potentially hazardous. Some fertility specialists require the laboratory lights to be turned off while the egg is temporarily outside of the woman's

---

[76] Klaus, p. 10.

[77] Corson, p. 223. The effect of CO_2 on ova is also subject to further investigation.

body. They consider the structure of the egg (which is the largest of all body cells) sufficiently delicate that it could be damaged when exposed to light.[78] In addition, exteriorizing the gametes deprives nature of screening out inferior sperm and eggs so that the child has a better chance of being formed with the best sex cells available.

2. The Introduction of a Contraceptive Element

TOTS avoids conception outside the woman's body by interposing an air bubble between egg and sperm while they are in the catheter. The aim of achieving conception in vivo is unassailable. But the fact that a contraceptive is employed, though only temporarily, is not without moral significance. William May has alluded to the irony of using an air bubble as a "contra-ceptive".[79] The presence of a contraceptive manifests the discordance between a natural process, sexual union, where conception is desired, and a technical procedure, TOTS, where it is undesired as long as the gametes are in the catheter. It is witness to the fact that the patterns of nature and technique are not in accord.

The air bubble also presents the possibility of contraceptive failure, in which case TOTS would be equivalent to IVF since conception would take place in vitro. Here it can be seen how tenuous the line is that separates TOTS from IVF.

The exteriorized gametes also create the possibility that they could be transferred to another woman. Conception would be in vivo, though maternity would be bifurcated into gestational and genetic motherhood. Then again, owing to certain unforeseen problems, the contents of the catheter could be discarded.

---

[78] See a British-made film entitled *Agony and the Ecstasy* which deals with IVF, AID, and GIFT procedures, and has some excellent footage on retrieving eggs and other aspects of artificial insemination.

[79] McCarthy, 1988, p. 167.

3. The Bifurcation of the Insemination Route

TOTS divides the avenues through which sperm approach the site where conception is to occur. The sperm deposited in the woman take one route while those transported in the catheter take another. These two routes illustrate dividedness as well as disunity. They also exemplify discordance inasmuch as conception that results from sperm arriving from one direction renders useless sperm travelling from the other. TOTS makes nature appear to be at odds with itself. It is something like having two digestive systems where the function of one is to prevent the operation of the other.

4. The Deprivation of Full Intercourse

It has been well established that the exchange of hormones, which takes place during sexual intercourse, contributes significantly to physical and emotional processes which contribute to a harmonious married life.[80] As a result of full, natural intercourse, male and female hormones are exchanged and assimilated through permeable mucous membranes. Husband and wife contribute something of their physical selves to each other, which assists in the bonding process and confers mutual benefits. Intercourse with a perforated sheath reduces these mutually conferred benefits, perhaps more emphatically in the direction of female to male since the husband is well insulated against the hormonal contribution of his wife. This point should not be taken too lightly.

The male's seminal secretions contain a variety of hormones including at least 13 prostaglandins. These hormones have a beneficial effect on his partner. Psychiatrist Philip Ney has found clinical evidence that as a result of diminishing levels of prostaglandins, when marital intercourse is avoided or condomistic intercourse is practiced, a woman can experience

---

[80] See F. X. Arnold, *Woman and Man: Their Nature and Mission* (Freiburg, West Germany: Herder, 1963), p. 133.

a mild depression. He contends that such a mood could advance to irritability and then to aggressive behavior, which takes on added importance if the woman has small children. "The decline in the prostaglandins available for absorption from the woman's vagina", he writes, "would produce a continuing decline in the mother's mood, thus cutting her off from a woman's usual source of exogenous prostaglandins."[81]

Intercourse with a perforated sheath may signify the marital act. But that consideration—apart from the chemical, hormonal, physical, and psychological bonding of a full, natural union—suggests a dualistic mindset. One should not depreciate or underestimate the physical benefits that husband and wife confer upon each other as a consequence of their sexual union.

5. The Impairment of the Artificial Insemination Attempt

The TOTS procedure requires the husband to use a perforated sheath. This is done in the interest of respecting the integrity of the marital act.[82] Nonetheless, this practice may be contraindicated from the viewpoint of maximizing the chances of achieving conception. The first of a series of ejaculations contains the most motile, viable, and highly concentrated sperm.[83] If this portion of the semen is deposited in a woman who most likely cannot conceive without the assistance that TOTS provides, it is not used in the interest of effecting conception. This could mean the difference between failing or not failing to achieve pregnancy. Ricardo Asch uses a sperm concentration of 100,000 spermatozoa per 25μ (about

[81] P. G. Ney, "The Intravaginal Absorption of Male Generated Hormones and Their Possible Effect on Female Behaviour", *Medical Hypotheses* 20: 221–31, 1986, p. 227.

[82] Jeremiah McCarthy, *Health Progress,* March 1987, p. 48. The author sees the great challenge of morally acceptable modes of reproductive technology in terms of ensuring that "the integrity of the marital union be maintained"

[83] Richard D. Amelar, *Male Infertility,* Saunders, 1977, p. 193.

4/10 of a drop) of fluid. McLaughlin attests that this is a satisfactory quantity.[84] Nonetheless, this concentration may not be adequate when the cause of infertility is oligospermia. Phillip Matson, therefore, introduced a modified form of GIFT in which a much higher concentration of sperm is utilized. He uses a minimum concentration of 325,000 that has resulted in a 29% pregnancy rate with 21 couples. Husbands produce the semen samples through masturbation. This makes sense from a strictly practical point of view because the oligospermic male may not be able to afford sacrificing the first spurt of his ejaculate if he wants to inseminate his wife. Matson concludes that this modified form of GIFT is an effective treatment of oligospermic infertility.[85] There is also a qualitative consideration. Since the superior sperm are in the first spurt, one might want the child to be formed with what is best. Matson's modified GIFT procedure, by employing masturbation, has at its disposal all of the male ejaculate, including the most potent sperm. Here the moral question concerning the unity of the marital act in its relation to TOTS is brought into sharper focus. It is a plausible hypothesis that by adhering to the TOTS stricture of avoiding masturbation, a couple's chances of achieving pregnancy is reduced, especially with oligospermia. Since it is natural for conception to follow intercourse, it would seem that modified GIFT, which obtains sperm by masturbation, is more natural than TOTS, which employs a

[84] McCarthy, 1988, p. 144.

[85] Phillip L. Matson, et al., "The role of gamete intrafallopian transfer (GIFT) in the treatment of oligospermic infertility", *Fertility and Sterility,* vol. 48, no. 4, Oct. 1984, pp. 608–12. At the same time, Yovich does not find this method encouraging for treating oligospermic infertility. See J. L. Yovich, "Limitation of Gamete Intrafallopian Transfer in the Treatment of Male Infertility", *Medical Journal Australia,* 144:444, 1986. Even Matson is cautious and states that "it would be premature to conclude that this constitutes a demonstrated benefit of the higher sperm concentration." See McLaughlin, et al., p. 214, where a sperm concentration of 200,000 was used in TOT.

perforated sheath. But it is only "natural" inasmuch as it enhances the chance of achieving conception. It is not more natural on another level, the level of the unity between husband and wife. The mentality that affirms GIFT is a dualistic one that can separate the spiritual from the physical and not believe it has lost something of moral significance. Nonetheless, TOTS can be less natural than GIFT on a purely biological reproductive level. The discordance between the personal and the biological that both GIFT and TOTS introduce inevitably invites dualistic thinking.

The GIFT procedure violates a primary unity—between husband and wife—for the sake of achieving a secondary unity—a unity of gametes. TOTS attempts to achieve conception and honor marital unity at the same time. But it does it in such a way that both are compromised. From a purely technical point of view, GIFT makes more sense; from a purely personal viewpoint, natural intercourse makes more sense. The Vatican *Instruction,* in reiterating the words of Pius XII, states that "in its natural structure, the conjugal act is a personal union, a simultaneous and immediate cooperation on the part of the husband and wife, which by the very nature of the agents and the proper nature of the act is the expression of the mutual gift which, according to the words of Scripture, brings about union 'in one flesh.'"[86] In the hierarchy of unities, the marital unity of two persons in one flesh is primary and cannot be compromised for the sake of another unity. The Church wants to keep the procreative process personal.

TOTS presents two major defects: *deprived intercourse* and *impaired artificial insemination.* Intercourse is best performed when it is done completely and naturally. The perforated condom and other aspects of the TOTS procedure compromises

---

[86] II B. 6. See also Pius XII, *Fourth International Congress of Catholic Doctors,* Sept. 29, 1949: AAS 41 (1949) 560.

sexual union. The best way to perform AI, scientists now say, is to use a nonperforated silastic sheath.[87]

Recent studies have shown that the silastic sheath is the best device for collecting seminal fluid.[88] It is superior to a glass jar, the polyethylene Milex sheath, and the latex condom. Semen collected after intercourse in the silastic sheath contain spermatozoa that are more plentiful, motile, and healthy than those found in other collection devices. The reason for this is twofold: first, the chemical neutrality of the silastic material interferes either slightly or negligibly with the sperm; second, the sexual stimulation of the male by the female partner plays a positive role in ejaculation improvement. Scientists predict that the silastic sheath used during intercourse will become a more frequently employed method of obtaining sperm for use in AID as well as IVF and GIFT. In this regard, one specialist advises that "the collected specimen should as closely as possible resemble the ejaculate delivered during intercourse."[89]

Natural, complete intercourse and the most efficient technique for achieving fertilization are both possible. But they are not *compossible*. This indicates that TOTS is not a unified act, but two separate and distinct acts: one of compromised intercourse and the other of compromised artificial insemination. Since the Church has already judged artificial insemination to be morally unacceptable, it is difficult to understand how it could endorse TOTS, which includes artificial insemination.

---

[87] The sheath is made of silicone material (dimethylpolysiloxane elastomer) and registered under the trade name Silastic. See Lloyd Hess, "Assisting The Infertile Couple, Part I", *Ethics and Medics,* 10, 8 (1985), pp. 1–2.

[88] Cy Schoenfeld, et al., "Evaluation of a New Silastic Seminal Fluid Collection Device", *Fertility and Sterility,* vol. 30, no. 3, September 1978, pp. 319–21; Panayiotis M. Zavos, "Characteristics of Human Ejaculates Collected Via Masturbation and a New Silastic Seminal Collection Device", *Fertility and Sterility,* vol. 43, no. 3, March 1985, pp. 491–92.

[89] Zavos, p. 492.

The *Instruction* states that reproductive technologies must not be judged "from the conjugal acts which may precede or follow it".[90] Having intercourse shortly before or soon after conventional AI hardly justifies the practice, even if intercourse is performed with a perforated sheath as part of the AIH protocol. Thus, it does nothing to justify TOTS. The *Instruction* also states that fertilization should be the *"expression and fruit of a specific act of the conjugal union"*.[91] Given the number of clearly discordant features that TOTS exhibits, it strains credibility to interpret it as one specific act.

Critics of TOTS

In the early seventies, Bernard Häring spoke of the perforated condom as a virtual moral anachronism:

> In the past some moralists suggested the use of a slightly perforated condom, so that by depositing a portion of the seed in the vagina, the biological nature would be respected; today, this method is considered abusive and immoral.[92]

Today, the moral intuition of many academics on the matter is that the perforated sheath is an embarrassing legalism. Bishop Conti has remarked that "talk of a perforated condom is a nonsense—legalistic casuistry that would bring the Church, if it was ever thought to be an official view, into ridicule".[93] Australian bioethicist Raymond Campbell states, "Talk of the use of a perforated condom appears to be a return to the sort of physicalism which I thought we were happily leaving behind."[94] Richard McCormick is perhaps most vehe-

---

[90] B. 5, para. 2.

[91] B. 5, para. 5.

[92] *Medical Ethics* (Notre Dame: Fides, 1973), p. 92.

[93] Platt, p. 5.

[94] "An Ethical Appraisal of G.I.F.T.", *St. Vincent's Bioethics Centre Conference,* May 14, 1987, p. 4 of transcript.

ment in his rejection of TOTS and the perforated sheath it requires:

> Frankly, I find such casuistry debasing and repugnant. If the congregation wants to insist on a procreation worthy of human beings, it should give no support to such moralistic nitpicking. If it does, it is contributing to a casuistry unworthy of human beings and reducing a healthy morality to an embarrassing moralism.[95]

A number of moralists, William May,[96] John Haas,[97] and Raymond Campbell[98] among them, view TOTS and its requirement to use a perforated sheath as a surreptitious or roundabout way of obtaining sperm. Bartholomew Kiely regards TOTS as a form of artificial insemination that is explicitly rejected by *Donum Vitae*.[99] So does Bishop Augustine Harris.[100] Thomas O'Donnell also sees TOTS as an instance of artificial insemination:

> A less interrupted continuity between marital intercourse and conception would seem to be required for the whole procedure to qualify as an 'artificial aid to natural insemination' rather than an 'artificial insemination'.[101]

Finally, Ken Platt remarks that anyone who can believe that TOTS is a moral unity can believe anything.[102]

Mr. Platt's point is well taken. If one were to duplicate the loose thinking that has been employed in trying to make certain reproductive technologies appear Catholic, he could defend the most outrageous procedures imaginable. For the sake

---

[95] "New Vatican Instruction on Human Life and Procreation", *America*, March 18, 1987, p. 248.
[96] McCarthy, 1988, p. 166.
[97] Ibid., p. 166.
[98] Campbell, p. 4.
[99] Platt, p. 6.
[100] Ibid., p. 6.
[101] O'Donnell, p. 3.
[102] Platt, p. 5.

of illustrating this penchant for attempting to validate a procedure by affirming its good points while ignoring its shortcomings, consider THEFT (The Hijacking of the Embryo
from the Fallopian Tube). This technique would be permitted
only under certain highly restricted conditions: (1) the embryo is removed only from women who have decided to have
an abortion (it is then transferred to the fallopian tube of the
infertile wife); (2) only a childless, infertile couple can benefit
from THEFT; (3) the procedure does not subject either the
embryo or the women to any dangers; (4) the infertile couple
cannot have a child in any other way. THEFT appears morally acceptable because it assists an infertile couple in attaining pregnancy, conception occurs in vivo, masturbation is
avoided, the integrity of the sex act is fully respected, life is
valued over the death of the embryo through abortion, and
the infertile couple has the child they so ardently desired.
Since the Holy See has not pronounced on this new reproductive technology, it is a solidly probable opinion that it will approve THEFT (along with TOTS, PROST, GIFT, SIFT,[103]
ZIFT,[104] POST,[105] and VISPER).[106]

One final reproductive technology, Intravaginal Culture
(IVC) should be discussed since it is currently under examination in certain Catholic circles and hailed in the medical literature as a technique that may very well be in harmony with
Church teaching. IVC has similarities with TOTS and IVF.
According to the procedure, ovulation induction and oöcyte
retrieval are employed. Up to 10 identified oöcytes are placed
in a 3-ml tube which is completely filled with culture me-

---

[103] Sperm Intrafallopian Transfer.

[104] Zygote Intrafallopian Transfer.

[105] Peritoneal Oöcyte and Sperm Transfer. See Pamela F. Sims, "Test Tube
Babies in Debate", *Ethics and Medicine: A Christian Perspective*, 4:3 (1988),
p. 41. In this technique, a mixture of egg and sperm is placed near the end of
the fallopian tube in the peritoneal cavity.

[106] Vaginal Intra-peritoneal SPERm transfer. See ibid. In this procedure the
sperm is placed directly in the peritoneal cavity.

dium. Spermatozoa (which can be obtained from the post-intercourse supply of sperm left in a perforated silastic sheath) are added to the tube. The tube is then hermetically sealed, wrapped tightly in a cryoflex envelope to prevent vaginal contamination, inserted in the woman's vagina, and held in place with a diaphragm. Approximately 44–50 hours later, the tube is removed and its contents poured into a petri dish and examined for the presence of embryos. Up to four embryos are immediately transferred into the uterus. Excess embryos are cryopreserved.[107]

Ranoux and Seibel state that the IVC technique may "prove to be particularly suited for Catholic patients [because] the Catholic Church does not approve IVF, in large part because fertilization occurs outside of the body".[108] In the *Hastings Center Report,* they argue that couples with religious objections to IVF and other similar techniques might find IVC acceptable because conception takes place in vivo.[109]

IVC, apart from being incongruent with the unity of the sexual act, does *not* take place in vivo. The contention that IVC allows for in vivo conception is erroneous. Fertilization occurs not in the woman's body, but in the hermetically sealed tube.

The issue here is one of place; i.e., where does fertilization take place. If we refer to a neutral and philosophical notion of place, we find, citing Aristotle, that place is "the innermost immobile surface of a surrounding body."[110] Consequently,

---

[107] Claude Ranoux and Machelle M. Seibel, "New Techniques in Fertilization: Intravaginal Culture and Microvolume Straw", *Journal of In Vitro Fertilization and Embryo Transfer*", vol. 7, no. 1, 1990, p. 6.

[108] Ibid.

[109] Ranoux and Seibel, "Taking In Vitro out of Fertilization", *Hastings Center Report,* Sept./Oct. 1989, p. 4. See also Machelle Seibel, *Infertility: A Comprehensive Text* (East Norwalk, CT: Appleton and Lange, 1990), p. 584.

[110] *Physics,* IV, 5, 212a, 220–21.

as far as IVC is concerned, it is the tube that is the site of fertilization. Similarly, an airplane passenger is in the plane and not in the air; it is the plane that is in the air. A bird is not "in the air" if it is in the plane; neither is a diver in the water if he is in a bathyscaphe (nor must he wear scuba equipment).

Moreover, the contents of the tube do not interact with the mother's body. The mother does not undergo any hormonal changes as a result of fertilization. The hermetically sealed tube might as well be placed in an incubator.[111] There is no symbiotic relationship between the zygotes and the mother. The woman is a host more than a mother and could, since her embryos are extracted, easily be a surrogate for another woman.

The modern world, conditioned as it is by the mindset of the media, is attuned to information that is singular, new, and sensationalistic. It is not particularly receptive to a message that is universal, old, and abstract. Louise Brown is the media's notion of a "miracle". The Sermon on the Mount is no longer a hot item.

The articulation of moral norms, of course, must be expressed in a language that embraces everyone regardless of place or time, and in a manner that can be comprehended intellectually. This simply means that it must be pertinent, timeless, and meaningful. These values are exactly what the world is searching for, whether it realizes it or not. Moral norms remind man of his nature, his origin, and his destiny. The media conjures up a world that is exciting, eventful, and entertaining. But this world of momentary intoxication is constantly in danger of relapsing into boredom. It is not a world that can sustain life on a day-to-day basis and inspire human beings to live their lives with dignity and grace. It is a

---

[111] Ranoux, et al., "A New In Vitro Fertilization Technique: Intravaginal Culture", *Fertility and Sterility,* vol. 49, no. 4, April 1988, p. 656.

distraction from the real business of life. The Vatican *Instruction* is about reality. It addresses real people in the context of real values. That may not be news, but it is what is needed. And though it finds its formulation in language that is universal and impersonal, it does get to the heart of the matter.

Chapter Twelve

Biotechnology and Feminist Ideology

"Ideology" and "philosophy" are opposite terms. An ideology is born in passion and treats a limited area of moral concern as if it were all that mattered. Its essential shortcoming is its myopia. Philosophy, that is, in the best sense of the term—love of wisdom—has its genesis in a dispassionate regard for everything that is. It recognizes the organic structure of reality and does not occupy itself with certain areas of concern to the exclusion of others. Its essential virtue is its comprehensiveness.

Ideologies, because of their one-sidedness, are easy to grasp; because of their appeal to emotions, they are difficult to give up. Philosophy, on the other hand, demands discipline and balance, as well as the capacity to resist the fashionable ideology that conforms to one's self-interest.

The modern era is a stage upon which a wide assortment of one-sided ideologies compete against each other for supremacy. In the continuing struggle, which no particular ideology can hope to win, philosophy becomes ignored or discredited. Ideology is inherently antagonistic to the philosophical enterprise. Individualism, hedonism, materialism, Marxism, Freudianism, and Social Darwinism are but a few examples of current ideologies. To this list we add Feminism.

Feminism, like all other ideologies, suffers from a lack of coherence and consistency. The specific application of Feminism to the area of reproductive technology makes this readily apparent. Because of its narrow ideological focus, Feminism is unable to reconcile its two most cherished values—freedom and equality. The freedom of choice it enthusiastically advances often invites particular choices that are incompatible with equality. To cite one example, in the interest of pursuing "reproductive freedom", many surrogate

239

mothers have found themselves in a position of subordination to both the prenatal child and the contracting couple. As feminists themselves have noted, surrogacy provides men with new and effective opportunities for exploiting women. Moreover, Feminism's notion of equality conflicts with freedom. This is evident where granting the father an equal relationship with their unborn child interferes with the mother's freedom to abort or not to abort.

In addition to its inability to reconcile freedom with equality, Feminism fails to provide a consistent image of either freedom or equality when these values are taken singly. On both counts, it oscillates between absolutism and ambivalence. Often, its unqualified enthusiasm for freedom is really a mask to cover a deeper interest in power. And its interest in equality often disguises a greater enthusiasm for a belief in gender superiority.

In Canada, the National Action Committee, which represents 600 different women's groups, has submitted a brief to the Royal Commission on New Reproductive Technologies. The brief calls for an immediate moratorium on opening new IVF clinics. Spokeswoman Varda Burstyn states: "Our experience with medical and other technologies has shown us that there are always unforeseen negative consequences. We are not just talking about putting this generation at risk, but future generations as well."[1]

Undergirding the brief is a strong commitment to the equality between the sexes. Its authors see IVF as another invasion of the womb by a male-dominated medical profession where women are used as guinea pigs.[2] At the same time, many members of the NAC take strong exception to the brief. The commitment of these dissenters is not to protecting women's equality from male exploitation but to freedom of

[1] Paul Taylor, "The Technology of Reproduction", *The Toronto Globe and Mail,* Nov. 10, 1990, D2.

[2] Ibid., D2. See also Varda Burstyn, "Group Warns against Fertility Methods", *The Toronto Globe and Mail,* Oct. 29, 1990.

choice. According to a representative of this group, opposition to such technologies as IVF is a violation of private choice: "I don't think it is anyone's business except the people involved. It's my own choice. A lot of the people who are opposed to IVF have children of their own. They don't know what it's like to be infertile. It really makes me mad."[3]

Another illustration of this same conflict between equality and freedom can be found in a recently developed procedure that allows post-menopausal women to bear children. This new procedure achieves in vitro fertilization with eggs donated by younger women and sperm from the older women's husbands. The resulting embryos are then implanted in the wombs of these older women.[4]

Marcia Angell, executive editor of the *New England Journal of Medicine,* states, "The limits of child-bearing years are now anyone's guess."[5] Dr. Arthur Caplan, director of the Center for Bioethics at the University of Minnesota, remarks, "It does not make sense to say that there is some natural point beyond which it is too late or immoral to become a parent. Men have become parents in their 70's and no one has blinked an eye at that. I see no ethical reason for taking a different attitude."[6]

Not everyone, however, is so beguiled by the ideology of equality that he is blinded to the difference between the momentary act by which a 70-year-old man provides sperm and the 9-month period of gestation required for a post-menopausal woman to carry a child to term. Some regard the pro-

[3] Taylor, D2. See also Judy Rebick, "Fertility Clinics Defended", *The Toronto Globe and Mail,* Oct. 30; Susan Rappolt, "NAC Contradictory on Women's Rights", *The Toronto Globe and Mail,* Nov. 10, 1990, D7.

[4] Mark V. Sauer et al., "A Preliminary Report on Oöcyte Donation Extending Reproductive Potential to Women over 40", *New England Journal of Medicine,* Oct. 25, 1990, pp. 1157–60.

[5] "Post-menopausal Pregnancy Now Possible", *The Boston Herald,* Oct. 25, 1990, p. 36.

[6] Gina Kolata, "Giving Older Women a Shot at Motherhood", *The New York Times,* Oct. 28, 1990.

cedure as "technology run amok".[7] Others regard it as potentially exploitive since older women would be more likely to have medical problems that might interfere with their ability to carry a pregnancy to term.[8] The plain fact of the matter is that from the standpoint of human physiology, young women and old men are not equal to women who are postmenopausal. Ideological libertarianism and ideological egalitarianism are simply incompatible with each other.

Feminist interest in reproductive technology is very strong, and rightly so since reproductive interventions have their direct and immediate impact on women. The feminist discussion of reproductive technology's moral implications is most extensive and is usually articulated with great passion. When the Feminist International Network on the New Reproductive Technologies (FINRET) changed its acronym to FINRRAGE (Feminist International Network of Resistance to Reproductive Technologies), it provided a symbol that accurately describes the passion animating the feminist discussion. Nonetheless, as much as one may sympathize with the righteousness of another's rage, he should not forget that this volcanic emotion does not serve the interest of philosophical coherence, consistency, or clarity.

An essential part of every ideology is its idealism. And it is precisely this idealism that gives an ideology its attractiveness. However, ideologies are notoriously deficient in distinguishing between how things are in their intellectual purity and how they are used in concrete situations. Feminists hailed contraception, sterilization, and abortion because they offered women "reproductive freedom", the opportunity to control their own bodies. It was logical and inevitable, then, that they would greet the more recent reproductive technologies with similar enthusiasm. The ideology of freedom made freedom absolute. The "right to choose" became an end in itself, di-

---

[7] Diane White, "Babes in Old Arms", *The Boston Globe,* Oct. 27, 1990.

[8] Richard Strauss, "When the Biological Clock Pauses", *The Boston Globe,* Oct. 30, 1990, p. 1.

vorced from any concern to choose well. The popular phrase "choose choice" exemplified the ideological belief that choice is a terminal value. The feminist ideology of reproductive freedom directed all enthusiasm toward choice and none toward the wisdom to choose what is good.

When it became clear that many women were making unwise uses of reproductive technologies, feminist intellectuals reasoned that it was because women are not truly free. As one feminist explains:

> The "right to choose" means very little when women are powerless . . . women make their own reproductive choices, but they do not make them just as they please; they do not make them under conditions which they themselves create but under conditions and constraints which they, as mere individuals, are powerless to change.[9]

Defining freedom in such idealistic terms makes it appear unattainable. If women are powerless to change the conditions prerequisite to their freedom, it is not likely that they could ever be free. This tactic allows feminists to maintain their ideological view of freedom and avoid entering into a world of political realism. It does not occur to them that it is their ideology—which absolutizes freedom and ignores everything else—that needs to be changed. This strategy is self-defeating because it discourages women from entering into political activities on a realistic basis that would be potentially beneficial to them.

This same ideology also idealizes women while focusing blame for depriving them of their full freedom exclusively on men. Thus men become the enemy, even though women welcomed the reproductive technologies that men had devised. The move "to value positively women's roles in reproduction", writes one representative feminist, "has given tech-

---

[9] Rosalyn P. Petchesky, "Reproductive Freedom: Beyond a Woman's Right to Choose", *Signs: Journal of Women in Culture and Society*, vol. 5, 1980, pp. 667–85.

nopatriarchs within medical research a justification for their continuing control of and experimentation with women's bodies, in the name of the power of mothering."[10]

Yet other feminists blame men not for urging women to become mothers but for depriving them of the right to the unrestricted selling of their reproductive services. Carmel Shalev, a liberal feminist lawyer, believes that women have the moral and constitutional right to sell their reproductive services. In her book, *Birth Power*,[11] she welcomes the buying and selling of these services as a way of empowering women, of allowing them to "reclaim the procreative power that has been subsumed under patriarchy".[12]

Femicide

One issue within the broad range of reproductive technology that well illustrates the need to combine freedom with its proper use, is abortion based on gender. Feminists had assumed that once women secured the "right" to abortion, they would exercise that freedom in ways consistent with feminist thinking. Nonetheless, the gap between ideology and practice can be considerable. It is hard to imagine anything more at odds with feminist principles than a woman aborting her female child simply because it is female.

In her book, *Gendercide*, Mary Anne Warren demonstrates how unbending feminist ideology can be. She acknowledges that the fear of genocidal uses of contraception and abortion is sometimes fully justified. But, she argues, it is not the freedom to choose as much as poverty and racism that are at the root of the genocidal impulse. Analogously, the tendency to-

[10] Robyn Rowland, "Technology and Motherhood: Reproductive Choice Reconsidered", *Journal of Women in Culture,* vol. 12, no. 3, 1987, p. 527.

[11] Carmel Shalev, *Birth Power* (New Haven: Yale University Press, 1989).

[12] Quoted by Mary Ellen Gale, "The Right to Pregnancy by Contract", *The New York Times Book Review,* Dec. 17, 1989, p. 12.

ward gendercide does not originate with freedom, but with sexism.[13]

Warren assumes that there is no conflict between the acquisition of freedom and its proper use, or between freedom and equality. If women are choosing to abort their female unborn, it is only because they are not fully free. The fault lies not with women but with men who establish conditions that deny women the fullness of their freedom to choose. "As long as economic and political institutions are dominated by men," she writes, "both overt and subtle forms of gendercide will continue to occur."[14]

Presumably, men are free to obstruct women's freedom, but women are not free to resist the pressure to abort. "Injustices such as the greater earning power of males may virtually force parents to prefer sons, and thus may be covertly gendercidal." Unintentionally, Ms. Warren introduces a radical inequality between the sexes that depicts men as free from the influence of external circumstances and women as bound by them. The depiction is an unrealistic one, but is created in order to preserve the notion that women would never use their freedom wrongly.

It would be impossible to refute Warren's contention that under ideal conditions women would use their freedom wisely, since the ideal conditions her ideology demands would never be realized. In this way, ideology is a barrier to political realism. The freedom that Warren talks about is an ideological freedom. The political realist discusses the limited, real freedom that people actually have as well as the need to change social conditions in the direction of enhancing that freedom.

The feminist premise that abortion is a right which women will not use wrongly is an unrealistic assumption that does

---

[13] Mary Anne Warren, *Gendercide* (Totowa, New Jersey: Rowman & Allenheld, 1985), p. 197.

[14] Ibid., p. 197.

not serve the interest of women. It leads to a deeper rift between the sexes while failing to encourage women to make choices that are truly moral. It also interferes with true social progress.

Then, too, using all men as a homogeneous category for social analysis does not reflect their real diversity. The difference, let us say, between a community of Franciscan friars and members of a Hell's Angels gang, or between men who are Quaker pacifists and those who are inveterate warmongers, defies the kind of simplistic categorization that feminists want to employ. Such wanton disregard for the real diversity of men epitomizes the very *sexism* that feminists purport to abhor.

Reproductive freedom should not be separated from its proper use. Neither should political power be separated from its proper use. When Mary Anne Warren advises that "we must not seek to counteract gendercide through the erosion of reproductive freedom",[15] she seems unaware that reproductive freedom itself—cut off as it is from moral responsibility—may be a factor that contributes to personal as well as social injustices.

Social conditions do influence personal choices. But this does not imply that the only way to counteract wrong choices is to attack the conditions that may provoke them. In the face of assault, one must deal with the assailant rather than go directly and immediately to the possible root causes of his aberrant behavior. To fail to confront genocidal and gendercidal activities directly is to deny their iniquity and the great harm they bring to society. In this regard, maintaining an ideological stance while significant moral transgressions are taking place is very much like the ostrich burying its head in the sand. Mother Teresa is universally admired because she responds directly and immediately to the concrete problems at

[15] Ibid., p. 197.

hand. She does not preoccupy herself exclusively with speculating about whatever social conditions there might be that contribute to these problems.

The charge that men are not cooperating in the advancement of female freedom simply ignores the facts. Recent surveys indicate a growing willingness on the part of male geneticists to approve abortion on the basis of sex. One such survey reports that the percentage of geneticists who approve of prenatal diagnosis for sex selection has risen from 1 percent in 1973 to nearly 20 percent in 1988.[16] Geneticists say that one of the reasons for their change in attitude is a growing disinclination of doctors to be paternalistic, deciding for the patients what is best, and an increasing tendency for female patients to ask for the tests.[17] As one doctor who does prenatal diagnosis for sex selection remarks, "It is very hard to make a moral argument about terminations for sex when you can have abortions for any reason."[18]

The conflict over gender-based abortions among pro-abortion libertarians is a direct consequence of the fact that feminist ideology itself is in conflict with reality. One can think ideologically, but one cannot live that way for very long. Alan Dershowitz speaks of "the conflict between the right of a woman to terminate her pregnancy and the wrong inherent in terminating it on sexist grounds".[19] But this conflict is not a logical one since abortion for all reasons logically includes abortion for the particular reason of gender rejection. It is a conflict between ideology and reality. Freedom without restraint welcomes its unrestrained expression.

Dershowitz finds himself in the dilemma of trying to affirm

---

[16] Gina Kolata, "Fetal Sex Test Used as Step to Abortion", *The New York Times,* Dec. 25, 1988.

[17] Ibid.

[18] Ibid.

[19] "Abortion Leads to 'Femicide'", *The Human Life Review* Fall, 1988, p. 111.

women's right to abort while opposing abortions for sexist reasons and refraining from criticizing women for choosing abortions for such reasons. He suggests that a way out of the dilemma is for the government to make it illegal to disclose to a pregnant woman the sex of her fetus. This may prove to be a practical move, but it ignores the weakness inherent in feminist ideology, namely, that the fact of freedom does not guarantee its proper use. It also creates the impression that the central evil is in knowing the gender of one's child and not in the misuse of that knowledge. In the interest of preserving ideological freedom, libertarians find themselves in the embarrassing position of urging the government to deny women the real freedom of knowing the sex of their own unborn children.

George Annas, another abortion libertarian, also strongly objects to the practice of sex-based abortions. His solution is curious, if not contradictory. "If you're worried about a woman's right to an abortion," he writes, "the easiest way to lose it is not to set any limits on this technology."[20] Here he puts the motivation in the wrong place. The reason sex-selected abortion is morally wrong is not because it endangers the right to abortion. Rather, one should argue that one of the reasons that the unqualified right to abortion is wrong in the first place is that it inevitably leads to immoralities such as sex-selected abortions. It is far more realistic to begin with principles that take moral considerations into account than to begin with an ideology and then try to limit it. What other limitations to abortion might Annas envision? And what moral principles would he appeal to in order to justify them? At any rate, it is not fashionable to oppose feminist liberationists these days, even when they endorse a position that invites such self-defeating possibilities as femicide.

---

[20] Kolata, op. cit.

Surrogacy

Mary Beth Whitehead received a great deal of emotional support from sympathetic feminists. It appeared to be a classic example of how patriarchal society victimizes powerless women. Nonetheless, her predicament as a mother who lost the custody battle for her own child could be construed as having been engineered by feminists themselves. In fact, one widely respected journalist perceived the Baby M ruling precisely as a "Triumph of Feminist Ideology".[21]

Despite the feminist protest against Judge Sorkow's decision to validate the surrogacy contract and award sole custody of Baby M to William Stern, his verdict was a faithful enactment of feminist principles. If women have the right to control their own bodies, which includes the right to terminate an unwanted pregnancy, should they not also have the right to gestate a child for a fee? Is surrogacy not a choice that a liberated woman can freely make? Is this choice not as personal and private as the decision to abort? Sorkow's validation of the surrogacy contract reflected his conviction that a woman is fully capable of entering into such an agreement. In upholding the contract, he was respecting her freedom, a freedom to choose that is fully in accord with feminist thinking.

Perhaps nothing is more anathema to feminist ideology than the proposition that "biology is destiny". At one time, mothers used to win custody disputes routinely on the basis of "maternal instinct". It was readily assumed that because of her biology, the mother was a better nurturer of children than the father. But, as one observer has pointed out, "Take away the biological superiority of the mother and the class supremacy of the father will win 9 out of 10 times."[22] It should not be

[21] Charles Krauthammer, "The Baby M Verdict: A Triumph of Feminist Ideology", *The Washington Post*, April 3, 1987, A27.
[22] Ibid., A27.

surprising, therefore, that William Stern, the biochemist, would win custody of Baby M over Richard Whitehead, the garbage collector.

Even in defeat, Mrs. Whitehead's supporters had difficulty seeing the discrepancy between theory and practice. "I don't want the primacy of biology to triumph", said a *Ms.* magazine editor who signed her name in support of Mary Beth Whitehead. "I'm suspicious of anything that uses the 'maternal instinct'."[23] Another signatory, ironically enough, was Meryl Streep, who starred in *Kramer vs. Kramer* as the liberated career woman and estranged wife who lost her child-custody battle to her husband.

Feminist ideology advocates a reproductive freedom without restraint. Unfortunately, such an irresponsible view of freedom alienates the woman from her moral selfhood. It also rejects the importance of the woman's biology. Such a rejection alienates the woman from her natural selfhood. This twofold alienation of women from their moral and natural selfhood can hardly be a prescription for fulfillment. Indeed, it is a formula designed to liberate women from their very own being.

Motherhood

The feminist understanding of reproductive freedom is so intensely individualistic that motherhood itself—with its bonding and relationships with others—is regarded with great suspicion. By contrast, many of the more radical feminists prefer "sisterhood" to "motherhood". In an ideological context, "sisterhood" connotes political factors such as power and solidarity that serve to strengthen female individuality. Motherhood compromises individuality by sharing itself with others.

At a feminist conference on the subject of reproductive

[23] Ibid., A27.

technology, one feminist proposed that we strike the word "mother" from our vocabulary since it is "an emotionally loaded word" that prevents people from objectively assessing the importance of other roles women have.[24] Ideally, motherhood should be a neutral category. In this way, it does not threaten to compromise the purity of a woman's reproductive freedom.

The real experience of motherhood, however, does not cooperate with such ideological demands. A mother is rarely indifferent to the bonding she experiences between herself and her developing child-in-the-womb. Nature inclines women to enjoy their motherhood. Thus, nature itself becomes an enemy to reproductive freedom. Mary O'Brien, for example, writes about "nature's traditional and bitter trap for the suppression of women".[25]

Feminists have spoken about the "particularly distressing side effect" of ultrasound diagnosis in prenatal care: the "bonding effect between mother and fetus".[26] Such bonding, they fear, may lead to greater stress in the decision to abort a "defective fetus". At the same time, other feminists have objected to the pressures placed on women to abort when the "quality" of their unborn child is less than desirable. Robin Rowland remarks that "in gaining the choice to control the quality of our children, we may lose the choice *not* to control the quality, i.e., the choice of simply accepting them as they are."[27]

Delivery is another occasion for bonding. This can be troublesome in the case of surrogacy. In order to prevent

[24] E. Virginia Sheppard Lapham, "Living with an Impaired Neonate and Child", *The Custom-Made Child?* Helen Holmes and Betty Hoskins (eds.), (Clifton, New Jersey: Humana Press, 1981).

[25] Mary O'Brien, *The Politics of Reproduction* (London: Routledge and Kegan Paul, 1981).

[26] Regina Kenen, quoted in Jean Bethke Elshtain, "A Feminist Agenda on Reproductive Technology", *The Hastings Center Report,* vol. 12, no. 1, February 1982, p. 42.

[27] Rowland, p. 42.

bonding between the surrogate mother and her baby, according to one physician, "sedate her while in labor and by the time she comes to, the child has been delivered, removed, and transferred to new parents."[28] Such an arrangement, the good doctor advises, could be made part of the surrogate contract.

If every form of bonding could be prevented, in the interest of producing a freedom that rises above all influence, no woman would ever want to become a mother. Ironically, the main function of the new reproductive technologies is to help infertile women become mothers. In the rarefied atmosphere of ideological freedom, choice becomes divorced from every influence and objective. Thus alienated from the world of real goods, choice becomes its own end. One chooses choice, so to speak. But choice has real value only when it is directed to something good. If the good is withheld so that freedom of choice will not be impaired, then no choice is possible. It is a case of defining something so idealistically that one defines it right out of reality. Like the mythological Anteus, we cannot retain our real strength unless we touch the earth with our feet at regular intervals. We are free not because we can fly but because our feet touch the ground.

Certain thinkers of antiquity speculated that a vacuum would allow birds to fly at maximum speed. The truth, of course, is that without air resistance to push their wings against, birds could not fly at all. Similarly, there is no freedom of movement for a person who has no place to stand. One contemporary critic of Feminism has remarked, "It is as foolish to think that we are most free when we are uninfluenced by desire as to think that tennis is at its best when played without a net."[29]

Reality is a world of forces and resistances, limitations and

---

[28] Dr. H. Lehnhoff, "Letter to the Editor", *The New York Times,* February 19, 1987.

[29] Michael Levin, "Male/Female Differences Are Obvious", *Feminism: Opposing Viewpoints,* Andrea Hinding (ed.), (St. Paul, Minnesota: Greenhave Press, 1986), p. 174.

imperfections. Natural inclinations direct us to what is good, what is worthy of our capacity to choose. If we distrust these very natural inclinations, we soon find ourselves withdrawing from reality. Under such circumstances, the only notion of freedom we could construct would be the unrealistic, ideological notion of freedom, one so isolated from real objects of choice that it could do nothing more than hold people in a state of perpetual catatonia.

Feminists buttress their ideological notion of equality between the sexes by denying the significance of the male and female anatomy. This also serves to reinforce their concept of freedom as one that is removed from concrete reality. Writing in the *New England Law Review,* Marie Ashe takes strong exception to this common practice of denying the importance of bodily existence. She deplores "the 'egalitarian' error involved in denials of the singularities of female bodily experience. . . . That error," she states, "holding nature in contempt, would destroy the best work of female bodies as well as that of female minds."[30] We are, indeed, incarnate beings. We are not indistinguishable wraiths. Nor are we neutral monads. Human reality is personalized. It is always contextualized by gender, individuality, time, place, and destiny. Take away our being and there is no basis for any moral impulse, for equality or for freedom or for anything else. Man is not a ghost that haunts the cosmos; he is a person, a being-in-the-world, a moral agent who is bound by all he knows and loves.

Science Fiction

Elizabeth Badinter, the wife of France's ex-minister of Justice (under Mitterand), has remarked that full equality between the sexes will be achieved only when technology allows the transfer of the embryo to the male body and then its retransfer

---

[30] "Law-Language of Maternity: Discourse Holding Nature in Contempt", 22 (4) *New England Law Review* (March 1988), p. 559.

to the mother who gives it birth.[31] Such a suggestion, which is both fantastical as well as fanatical, has an unmistakable science-fiction ring to it. Indeed, feminist ideology is more suited to this literary form than it is to real life. No doubt this explains why so many feminists have turned to this idiom to express their ideology. It also offers them the opportunity to express their views in a completely uninhibited manner. A thumbnail sketch of some of the more popular works in this genre offers additional insight into the mind of the feminist idealogue.

Marge Piercy's book, *Woman on the Edge of Time,* has been regarded as a kind of bible for many feminists.[32] Its central message is that only by women giving up their power of reproduction can equality between the sexes be achieved. Children are incubated in a prenatal nursery called a "brooder", a giant aquarium where they joggle happily together. Each child has three parents. Men are able to suckle the young. Under these conditions, no child can ever suffer the stigma of being owned or being illegitimate.[33]

Ursula LeGuin's *The Left Hand of Darkness* depicts humans as belonging to neither one sex nor the other. During a period of sexual desire, known as "kemmer", individuals blossom into sexual beings, mate, and produce offspring. Until "kemmer", one never knows which sex one will become. After this period, each individual returns to the neither/nor state. Throughout a lifetime, a particular individual could be a mother of several children and a father of several others.[34]

In Sally Gearhart's *Wanderground,* women are able to reproduce without any assistance from men. In Charlotte

[31] Thomas Molnar, "The Assault on the Family", *The Human Life Review,* Summer 1987, p. 63.

[32] Elaine Baruch, "A Womb of His Own", Baruch et al., (eds.), *Women and Health,* vol. 13, no. 1/2, 1987, p. 135.

[33] See also Ruby Rohrlich and Elaine Baruch (eds.), *Women in Search of Utopia* (New York: Schocken Books, 1984).

[34] New York: Walker and Co., 1969.

Gilman's *Herland,* the author has her women reproduce by a sheer act of the will.[35] Both novels portray men as alien to women, as creatures who are in some fundamental way inhuman.

The *Female Man* is about an all-female society where reproduction is achieved by merging ova. The members of this society are lesbian and sexually self-sufficient.[36] In *Motherlines,* genetically altered women are able to mate with their genetically altered stallions.[37]

All these works, in one way or another, describe a self-sufficient community of fulfilled women who live and breed independently of men. Women are free from male influence and all members of their community enjoy perfect sexual equality. In these science-fiction narratives, freedom and equality are happily reconciled.

Women are not alone in creating literary sexual utopias that reflect the bias of their own gender. In John Norman's best-selling novels, for example, the author describes life on a planet called Gor where men have reduced women to slavery.[38] Norman's "Virism", a mirror image of "Feminism", depicts the same sexual one-sidedness that characterizes the writings of the feminist science-fiction writers. Then there is the cinematic portrayal of Virism in popular motion pictures starring the likes of Sylvester Stallone, Charles Bronson, Arnold Schwarzenegger, Chuck Norris, and Clint Eastwood. Nonetheless, Virism, while retaining its degree of force and popularity, is unfashionable in today's culture and is not seriously proposed as a desirable way of life. It has no legal or political value whatsoever. If it has any philosophical value at all, it is only negative in that it offers a lifestyle that is clearly deficient and unworthy of adoption.

[35] New York: Pantheon, 1979.

[36] Joanna Russ, *The Female Man* (New York: Ballantine, 1975).

[37] Suzy McKee Charnas, *Motherlines* (New York: Berkley Putnam, 1978).

[38] See Nicholas Davidson, *The Failure of Feminism* (Buffalo: Prometheus Books, 1988), p. 275.

The one-sidedness of contemporary culture, particularly the way it is manifested in Feminism and Virism, is symptomatic of the immense rift that exists between the sexes. Issues involving human generation, which on a fundamental level require the physical cooperation of the sexes, also require their cooperation on a spiritual, philosophical, and moral level. Feminist ideology may be to some extent a reaction to Virism, but it is clearly not a remedy for it. Men and women must learn how to speak to each other from a basis that unites them in their humanity and respects them in their diversity.

The ethics of reproductive technology demands approaches that are unifying rather than alienating, complementary rather than one-sided, realistic rather than ideological. Political scientist Jean Bethke Elshtain is correct when she states that the "core of *human* ethics" requires "men and women to join together in opposing a headlong race toward social engineering". "Otherwise," she warns, "we will face more insidious political domination than we have yet known." [39]

Men and women must find ways to combine freedom *with* responsibility, equality *with* distinctiveness, knowledge *with* emotion, and authority *with* love. It is vain to look to an ideology to find the key to this kind of endeavor. We must first recover the universal good that binds all human beings together as one family. By placing this good above self-interest, we will begin to discover a way that embraces the best interest of all.

[39] Elshtain, p. 43.

INDEX